Easy dBASE for Windows™ Object-Oriented Programming

Richard A. Biegel
Technical Documentation Specialist
Borland International

Sumant S. Pendharkar
Product Group Manager in dBASE Technical Support
Borland International

Prentice Hall PTR
Englewood Cliffs, New Jersey 07632

Library of Congress Cataloging-in-Publication Data

Easy dBASE for Windows object-oriented programming / Richard A. Biegel, Sumant S. Pendharkar
   p. cm.
Includes index.
ISBN 0-13-184540-3
1, Object-oriented programming (Computer science).   2. dBASE for Windows.
I. Pendharkar, Sumant S.   II. Title.
QA76.B54   1994   94-34548
005.75'65--dc20   CIP

Editorial/Production Supervision: Lisa Iarkowski
Acquisitions Editor: Mark Taub
Manufacturing Manager: Alexis R. Heydt
Cover Design: Design W

Editorial/Production Supervision: Lisa Iarkowski
Acquisitions Editor: Mark Taubs
Manufacturing Manager: Alexis R. Heydt
Cover Design: Design W

© 1995 Prentice Hall PTR
Prentice-Hall, Inc.
A Simon & Schuster Company
Englewood Cliffs, NJ 07632

All rights reserved. No part of this book may be
reproduced, in any form or by any means, without
permission in writing from the publisher.

Quoted material on the dedication page courtesy
of Encyclopedia Brittanica, 15th Ed., pp. 186-87.

The publisher offers discounts on this book when ordered in bulk quantities.
For more information, contact:

   Corporate Sales Department
   PTR Prentice Hall
   113 Sylvan Avenue
   Englewood Cliffs, NJ 07632
   Phone: 800-382-3419
   FAX: 201-592-2249
   E-mail: dan_rush@prenhall.com

Printed in the United States of America
10 9 8 7 6 5 4 3 2 1

ISBN 0-13-184540-3

Prentice-Hall International (UK) Limited, London
Prentice-Hall of Australia Pty. Limited, Sydney
Prentice-Hall of Canada, Inc., Toronto
Prentice-Hall Hispanoamericana S.A., Mexico
Prentice-Hall of India Private Limited, New Delhi
Prentice-Hall of Japan, Inc., Tokyo
Simon & Schuster Asia Pte. Ltd., Singapore
Editora Prentice-Hall do Brasil, Ltda., Rio de Janeiro

With profound reverence, we dedicate this book to the memory of Bhaskaracharya (Bhaskara II, b. 1114 - d. 1185), who

- In his mathematical works (Lilavati and Bijaganita), showed for the first time understanding of division by zero, used decimal systems, worked on quadratic equations, polygons up to 384 sides and obtained value of PI to 6th decimal places.
- In his astronomical treatises Siddhantasiromani ("Head Jewel of Accuracy") and Karanakutuhala ("Calculation of Astronomical Wonders") dealt with planetary positions, eclipses, conjunctions, cosmography, etc., and thus proved himself to be a worthy lineal successor of the noted Indian mathematician Brahmagupta (b. 598 - d. 665) as head of the observatory and mathematical center in the city of Ujjain, India.

To all the programmers in the world who must make the leap from DOS to Windows.

Richard and Sumant

Contents

PREFACE   ix

ACKNOWLEDGMENTS   x

CHAPTER 1   LANGUAGE ELEMENTS   1

The Object-Oriented Approach   1

Data Types and Control Objects   1
    Basic Data Types   2
    Character Type   4
    Numeric and Float Types   5
    Date Type   7
    Logical Type   7
    Memo, Binary, and OLE Types   8
    Memo Type   8
    Binary Type   9
    OLE Type   9

Object Management Data Types   11
    Object Reference Type   12
    Codeblock Type   13
    Function Pointer Type   14

Expressions   15
    Variables   15
    Literals   16
    Field Names   17
    Array Objects   18
    Functions   18

Operators   19
    Logical Operators   19
    Mathematical Operators   20
    Relational Operators   20
    String Operators   22
    Function Call Operators   22

Object Operators   23
    The NEW Operator   23
    The Dot Operator   24
    The Index Operator   24

Two Syntax Styles   25

What Next?   26

CHAPTER 2 TABLES, INDEXES, AND QUERIES TABLES 27

Using dBASE Terminology 27
Creating and Using Table Files 28
Indexes 43
    Basic Index Types 46
    Simple Indexes 46
    Modified Indexes 48
    Compound Indexes 50
    Creating indexes with the Expression Builder 53
QBE 57
What Next? 63

CHAPTER 3 INTRODUCTION TO OOP 64

What is OOP? 64
    Introducing Objects 64
    Properties 64
    Object Classes 65
    Creating Objects and Using Properties 66
    Using the Object Inspector 69
    Programming With Objects and Properties 72
    Creating Event Handlers 73
    Creating Custom Properties 84
    Using the DEFINE Command 90
What Next? 95

CHAPTER 4 CUSTOM CLASSES 96

Creating Custom Classes 96
    Inheritance 96
    Custom Methods 99
    Containership 102
    Custom Classes for Control Objects 119
What Next? 131

CHAPTER 5 THE FORM DESIGNER 132

Using the Form Designer 132
Two-Way Tools 137
Reacting To Mouse Events 143
Object Refreshing 149
Object Grouping 154
What Next? 167

CHAPTER 6 WORKING WITH MENUS 168

The Menu Object Class 168
Using the Menu Designer 182
What Next? 198

CHAPTER 7 DDE and OLE 199

Dynamic DATA Exchange 199
 Establishing a DDE Link 200
 Sending Data To a Server Document 205
 Extracting Data From a Server Document 208
 Sending Instructions To a Server Application 211
Region Walking 213
 Moving From Field To Field, Cell to Cell 213
 Moving From Record To Record, Row To Row 217
Object Linking and Embedding 225
 Linking To OLE Document Files 226
 Embedding OLE Documents 230
 OLE Objects 233
 Using the DoVerb Property 237
What Now? 238

Index 241

Preface

Getting started with the language of dBASE for Windows can seem daunting and frustrating. The new keywords, symbols, and syntax often appear counterintuitive at first. This problem is compounded by the fact that Windows programming differs significantly from DOS programming; it requires that you change the way you view programming and problem solving.

This book was written to get you past these difficulties as quickly as possible. It was also written to dispel any misgivings you might have; contrary to what many believe, there is nothing particularly bizarre or difficult about Object-Oriented Programming (OOP). Programming in the OOP language of dBASE for Windows is a rational and straightforward process that anyone can learn with a little patience and effort. This book shows you how to view OOP as easy, not difficult.

More important, this book shows you how to think like an OOP programmer. We introduce OOP programming with step-by-step exercises in which you create programs and learn concepts simultaneously. These exercises are designed to give you a solid understanding of OOP principles, and to help you gain confidence in your ability to master the technology.

For many experienced programmers, the biggest challenge in learning OOP is discarding old concepts learned from programming the old way. To help you avoid this pitfall, we discuss each OOP concept in a meaningful context. We not only show how to use OOP techniques, but demonstrate why they are preferable to the old techniques. In fact, many of OOP's advantages speak for themselves. As you progress through the exercises, you'll discover how efficient and convenient OOP really is.

OOP will change the way you think about programming. It's an entirely different approach that frees you from many of the tedious, labor-intensive tasks that programmers had to face in the past.

We hope you enjoy using the book as much as we enjoyed writing it.

Acknowledgments

We'd also like to thank members of the dBASE for Windows Technical Publications, Technical Support, Quality Assurance and other teams at Borland, who were invaluable sources of technical information and support: Anneke, Barbie Bissinger, Nan Borreson, Bob Boydston, Abe Cohen, Richard Compeau, Ernest Escobar, Chet Ford, Paul Fussel, Ben Gelernter, Karen Giles, Brian Henry, Linda Hsieh, Rick Knight, Ray Love, Nina Machotka, Paul Mahar, Diana Peh, Richard Reiter, Geoff Riordan, Ron Skalski, Hiram Vega, and Pat Zylius.

We would also like to recognize two members from the Technical Support department --Lloyd Linklater and Eric Uber—for contributing utilities, which are included on the accompanying disk.

Chapter 1
Language Elements

dBASE for Windows is a *database management system* (*DBMS*), a software tool specifically designed for the collection, storage, organization, modification, and retrieval of electronic information. Like virtually all DBMS products, dBASE for Windows comes with a programming language for developing application programs.

At first glance, the dBASE for Windows language appears to have much in common with other programming languages that are used in the Windows environment, (such as C++ or Visual Basic). However, DBMS languages are specifically designed to perform tasks related to data management. Here are some examples:

- Print a report on all physicians who have 20 years of experience or more, are board-certified, live in the Miami area, and specialize in ophthalmology or dermatology.

- Purge all records on traffic citations that have been successfully resolved, are more than 10 years old, and imposed fines of $30 or less.

- Make an itemized list of the names and addresses of all our company's suppliers, plus each supplier's deliveries within the last three months.

Programs written in conventional programming languages can perform these tasks adequately; however, a DBMS language can reduce the time, labor, and expense necessary to develop such programs.

The language of dBASE for Windows has another important feature that sets it apart from most other languages: it is *object oriented*. Because of this feature, the language has power and flexibility undreamed of with previous versions of the dBASE language.

The Object-Oriented Approach

dBASE for Windows fully embraces a technique of application development known as *object-oriented programming* (or OOP, as it's affectionately known in the industry). As the name implies, an OOP language creates, utilizes, and manipulates entities known as *objects*. Objects are computer-generated tools that have attributes, respond to events, and perform actions.

OOP programming has several important advantages. First, it's incredibly efficient; it only takes a few hours to develop applications that once took weeks of work. Second, OOP is intuitive. Because most objects resemble tools, you can think of your programming tasks in the same way that you think of your ordinary, nonprogramming tasks. Third, OOP lets you develop applications that users like. OOP programs often appear self-explanatory even to new users, reducing the learning curve significantly. OOP increases the productivity of users and programmers alike.

Best of all, *OOP is easy*. This may seem a peculiar idea to some; after all, OOP uses strange new symbols and seemingly bizarre syntax. It introduces concepts that sometimes confuse experienced programmers who are used to the old ways. However, as you learn more about OOP, you'll discover that it actually saves you time and trouble. You'll be won over by its simplicity and elegance. You'll never want to go back.

The language of dBASE for Windows is a major departure from the dBASE language versions of the past. Although the language retains many--indeed, most--of its old semantic and syntactic features, its object-oriented capabilities make some of these features obsolete. In fact, a few of the old features were kept only for backward compatibility, and have little to do with the new technology. Whenever possible, this book introduces the new features and ignores the obsolete ones. Even so, we make full use of the many older features that are still a vital part of the language.

To learn how to program in the language of dBASE for Windows, you must understand its basic elements. Here is a brief introduction to those elements and the objects that use them.

Data Types and Control Objects

Like the previous versions of the dBASE programming language, dBASE for Windows makes and enforces distinctions between different kinds of information. For example, it's irrational for alphabetic names to be "added" to numeric salaries, or for chronological dates to be compared with true or false values. Clearly, different categories of information require different handling by a language. For this reason, virtually all languages on the market today, object-oriented or not, categorize their information by *data type*.

The applications you create with dBASE for Windows use *controls* (or *control objects*) to access and modify data elements (see Figure 1.1). A control is an object that provides an easy, intuitive way to manage data. Controls are displayed in *forms*, which are custom windows you design for your application (see Figure 1.1). The form is itself an object, just like the controls it contains.

We begin with the basic data types, all of which originated in the DOS versions of the dBASE language.

Basic Data Types

dBASE for Windows offers five basic data types: *character*, *date*, *float*, *logical*, and *numeric*. Because these data types differ in form and purpose, data elements made from different types might not be immediately compatible. Special handling is needed to make them combine or interact--a subject discussed later in this chapter.

Data elements of all basic data types (and a few others besides) can be accessed with a *browse object*, which displays multiple table records in row-and-column format, as shown in Figure 1.2. (Browse objects can also display data in single-record format.)

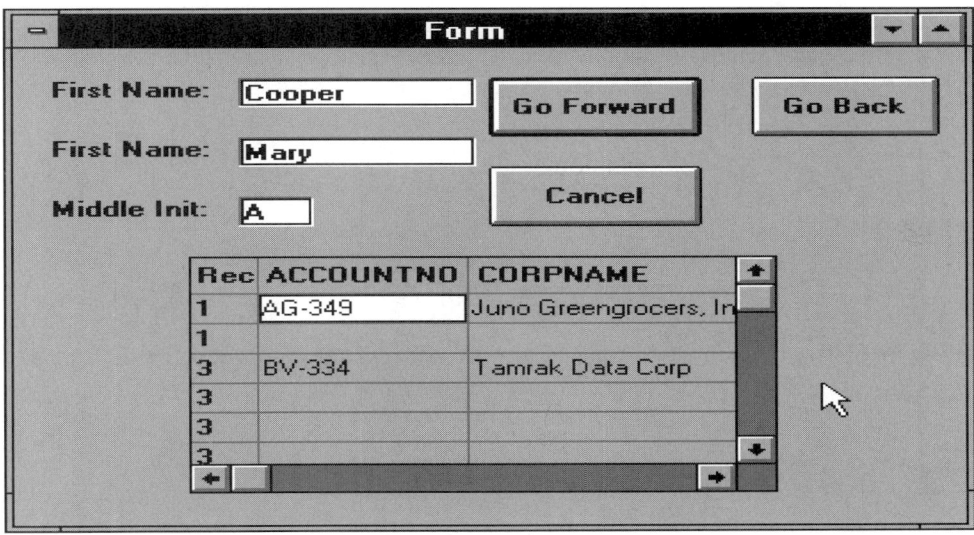

Figure 1.1   Controls in a Form

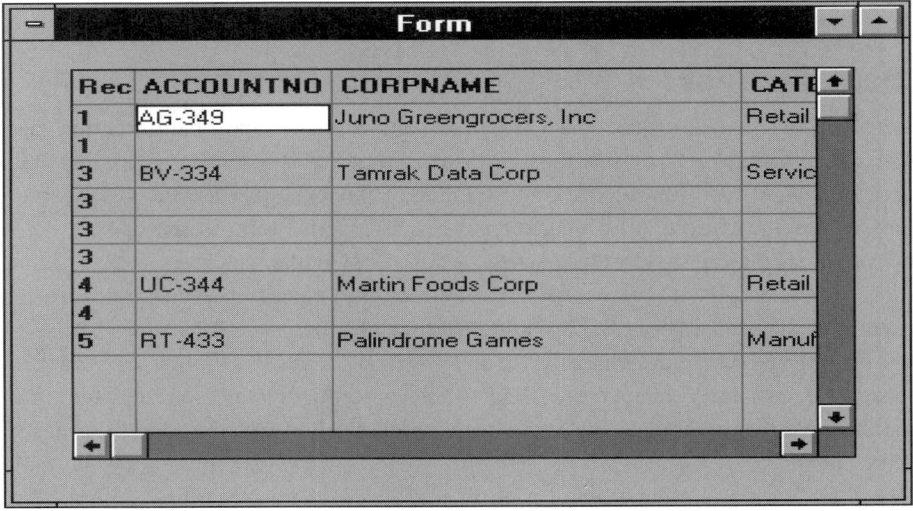

Figure 1.2   A Browse Object

Table 1.1 Typical Character Values

Proper names	`"Janet Tyler"`
	`"Mark Olivietsky"`
Serial numbers	`"TY-978I"`
	`"XX9TP00"`
Addresses	`"13829 West Park Terrace"`
	`"Riverside, CA, 92506"`
Company names	`"Janus Storage and Supply Corp."`
	`"International Dynamics"`
Job titles	`"Chief Operations Officer"`
	`"Corporate Communications Officer"`
Social Security numbers	`"556-96-0796"`

Character Type

Character data (also known as *text*) is perhaps the simplest kind of information managed by dBASE for Windows. Also the most prevalent type, it is useful for holding standard information such as words, names, codes, and symbols. Some examples are shown in Table 1.1.

Units of character information are often called *strings*. This term is appropriate, because a character value is merely a closely packed array of symbols, such as letters, numerals, punctuation marks, and blanks. Because of their simplicity, character values are not normally used for mathematical calculations or chronological timekeeping.

You can join two or more character strings together, a process known as *concatenation*. (Concatenation is introduced later in this chapter.) Because they can be concatenated, character values are the most commonly used data type for a process called *indexing*, a subject introduced in the next chapter.

dBASE for Windows offers several controls that access character strings. Figure 1.3 shows some examples:

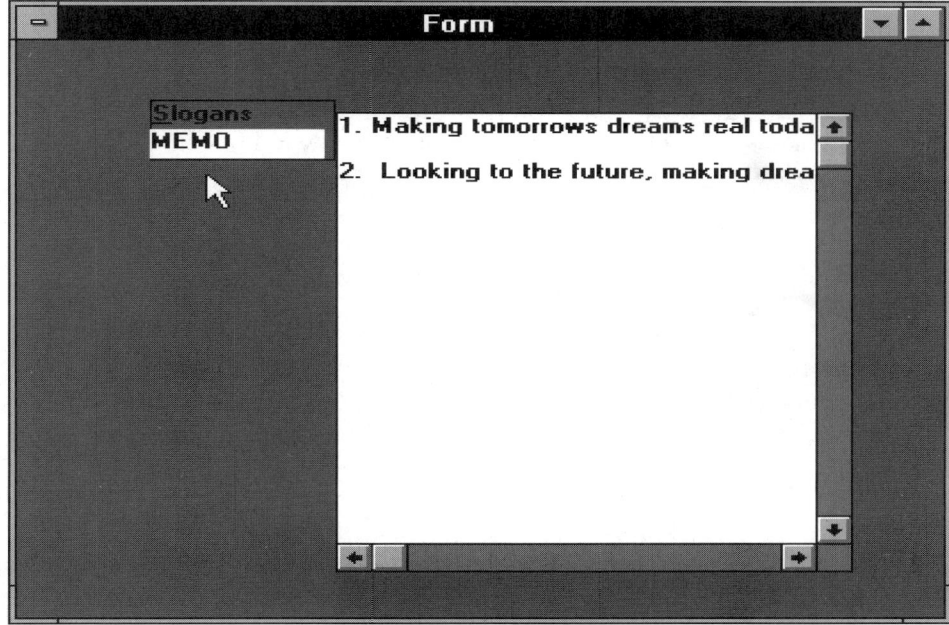

Figure 1.7 An Editor Object to view and change data

Figure 1.8 An Image Object

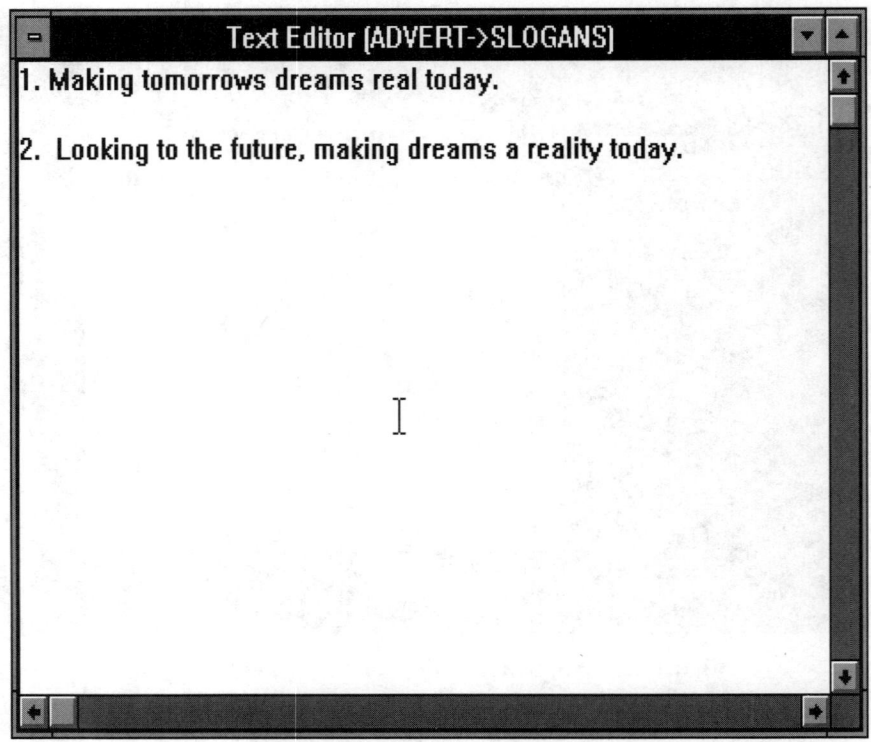

Figure 1.6 A Memo field

The best control object for providing access to memo fields is the *editor object*. An editor object lets the user view and change the data in a memo field in the same way that conventional text editors do (see Figure 1.7).

Binary Type

A *binary field* stores binary items like bitmap graphics and recorded sounds. For example, you can create images in Windows Paintbrush and store them in binary fields, or store images from bitmap files (.BMP).

The control that displays bitmap images stored in binary fields is the *image object*. An image object displays images in a read-only fashion; it doesn't let you change or edit the image (see Figure 1.8).

OLE Type

An *OLE field* initiates an action in an external Windows application, directing it to open and use an item known as an *OLE document*. An OLE document can be a graphic image, a spreadsheet, a digitized sound, or any other item usable by the external application. The document can be held in the OLE field itself or in a file.

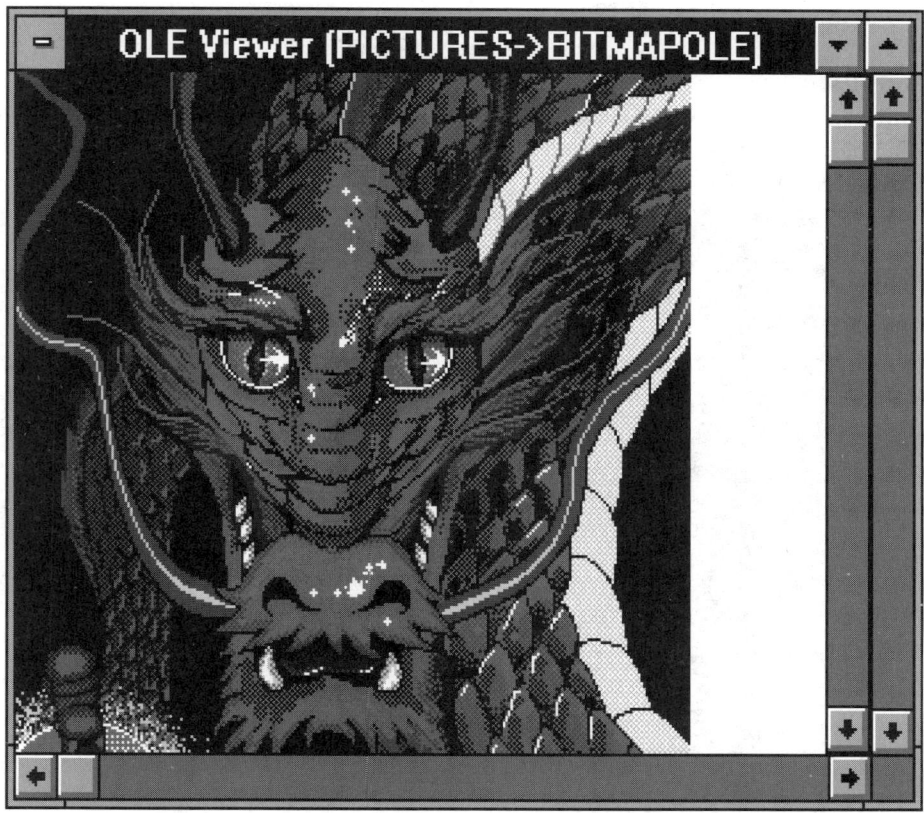

Figure 1.9 OLE Viewer window

In most cases, you can modify an OLE document by starting a session in the application that created it. In dBASE for Windows, you can start this external session by double-clicking on the OLE viewer window (see Figure 1.9) or on an *OLE object* (see Figure 1.10). The external application, known as the *server application*, must be specially designed to function as an OLE server. Borland's Quattro Pro for Windows (a spreadsheet application) and Paintbrush (a Windows accessory application) are good examples.

The OLE acronym stands for *Object Linking and Embedding*, a process by which an object is inserted into another object. When you *link* a document to an OLE field, the file containing the document is opened automatically when you start an OLE session. When you *embed* a document in an OLE field, only the contents of the OLE field itself are affected.

Object Management Data Types

When we say that the language of dBASE for Windows is *object-oriented*, we mean that it creates, modifies, and uses entities known as *objects* (some of which you've already been introduced to). Objects form the bedrock of any serious application. The subject of objects is too large to cover completely in this chapter; for now, it's enough to think of an object as a tool that has attributes, performs tasks, and reacts to events.

dBASE for Windows has three data types that identify objects or routines assigned to objects: object reference, codeblock, and function pointer. The control objects introduced above use all these data types.

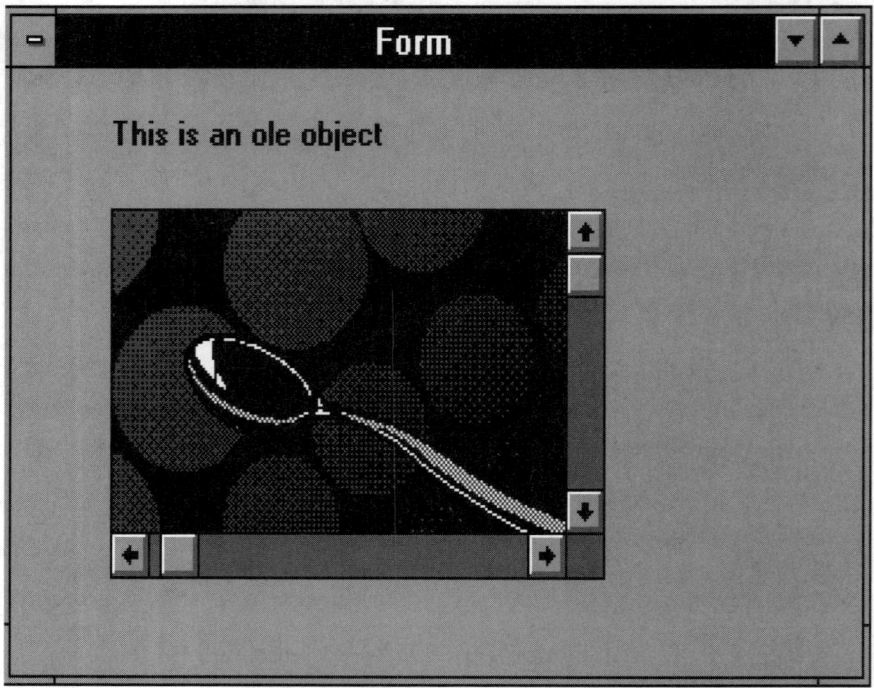

Figure 1.10   An OLE Object

Object Reference Type

Application programs access an object through an *object reference*. An object reference is like a handle or a link; it's the medium through which you, the programmer, take control of the object and tell it what to do. For this reason, an object reference is often said to *point* to the object. We use this terminology throughout this book.

Here is a command that creates a form--which is an object--and creates an object reference variable that points to it:

```
Form1 = NEW FORM("THIS IS A TEST FORM.")
```

Chapter 1 Language Elements

The new object reference variable is Form1. Through Form1, you can tell the new form to perform actions or to behave in various ways. For example, you can open the form with the following command:

```
Form1.Open()
```

(The form opens with "THIS IS A TEST FORM." on its caption bar. To close the form, double-click the box icon at the upper-left corner.)

Every object you create in dBASE for Windows has at least one object reference that points to it; otherwise, it would be inaccessible. In fact, when all object references that point to an object are destroyed, dBASE automatically removes the object from memory.

More than one object reference can point to the same object. For example, the following commands create a copy of the object reference variable Form1 and use it to open and close the form:

```
OtherRef = Form1
OtherRef.Open()
OtherRef.Close()
```

You'll become more familiar with object references as you progress through the exercises in this book.

Codeblock Type

A codeblock is a dBASE subroutine. This subroutine can consist of one command or multiple commands. Here's an example.

The following procedure contains two commands, one that performs a directory listing of all table files and one that emits a beeping sound:

```
PROCEDURE DirBeep
   DIR       && Directory listing of tables.
   ? CHR(7)  && Sounds a beep.
```

You can store this routine as a codeblock in a memory variable with a simple assignment statement:

```
MyCodeBl = {; DIR ; ? CHR(7)}
```

Note that each command in the routine is preceded by a semicolon, and the entire routine is surrounded by curly braces ({ and }). You can execute this routine in much the same way you execute a function call:

```
MyCodeBl()    && Does directory listing, sounds a beep
```

You usually use codeblocks to assign actions to objects, a process we introduce in later chapters.

```
* dBASE IV procedure and function.
PROCEDURE PRBeep
   DIR           && Directory listing of tables.
   ? CHR(7)      && Sounds a beep.

FUNCTION FNBeep
   DIR           && Directory listing of tables.
   RETURN CHR(7) && Sounds a beep.
```

Listing 1.1 A dBASE IV Procedure and UDF.

Function Pointer Type

A *function pointer* is the name of a user-defined function (UDF) or a procedure. As with codeblocks, you use function pointers to create custom methods. However, a function pointer doesn't *contain* a subroutine the way a codeblock variable does; a function pointer identifies (that is, *points to*) the subroutine.

That a function pointer points to a UDF *and* a procedure might seem a bit confusing at first, especially to an experienced dBASE IV programmer. For example, in dBASE IV, procedures and UDFs have distinctly different roles; a procedure is a subroutine that performs general-purpose actions, while a UDF is a subroutine that returns a single value. Furthermore, the syntax required to execute a procedure or a subroutine is more limited in dBASE IV.

For example, examine PROCEDURE PRBeep and FUNCTION FNBeep in Listing 1.1. In dBASE IV, you can execute PROCEDURE PRBeep with the following command:

```
DO PRBeep
```

You can execute the FNBeep UDF with the following command:

```
? FNBeep()
```

However, you can't execute the routines the opposite way:

```
? PRBeep()    && Can't do it that way! I'm a procedure.
DO FNBeep     && Can't do it that way! I'm a function.
```

dBASE for Windows has reduced the distinction between procedures and UDFs. For example, you can rewrite the PRBeep procedure and the FNBeep UDF as shown in Listing 1.2, and execute them with the following commands:

```
? PRBeep()    && No problem! This is dBASE for Windows.
DO FNBeep     && No problem! This is dBASE for Windows.
```

In other words, even though PRBeep is declared as a procedure, it can behave like a function. Conversely, although FNBeep is declared as a function, it can behave like a procedure. (The only requirement for a subroutine to be treated as a function is that it return a value with the RETURN command.)

dBASE for Windows considers the character strings FNBeep *and* PRBeep to be function pointers, and makes no real distinction between the two subroutines in that regard.

```
* dBASE IV procedure and function.
PROCEDURE PRBeep
DIR          && Directory listing of tables.
RETURN CHR(7)    && Sounds a beep.

FUNCTION FNBeep
   DIR        && Directory listing of tables.
   ? CHR(7)   && Sounds a beep.
```

Listing 1.2 Making UDFs Act Like Procedures, and Vice Versa

Expressions

Like a spoken language, the language of dBASE for Windows is made up of words arranged in phrases. These phrases are commonly known as *expressions*. Expressions are comprised of certain fundamental elements from which all comparisons and calculations are made:

- Variables
- Literals
- Field names
- Array objects
- Functions
- Operators

Variables

A *variable* (also known as a *memory variable*) is a value held in memory and given an identifying name. You use variables whenever you want to store a value temporarily. A variable can be any of the five basic data types (character, date, float, logical, or numeric) or any of the object management types (object reference, codeblock, or function pointer).

Variables are created in a variety of ways, but the most common are the **STORE** command and the assignment operator (=). Here are some examples:

```
STORE 10 TO AGE
STORE "PETE" TO NAME
STORE {12/12/81} TO DOB
```

or

```
AGE = 10
NAME = "PETE"
BIRTHDATE = {12/12/81}
```

AGE is type numeric, NAME is character, and BIRTHDATE is date. The contents of these variables may be changed at any time with the syntax shown above, or through data-entry objects like entry fields or radio buttons.

Table 1.3 Commands that Create or Modify Variables

Creates a variable or modifies its content during calculation

```
    AVERAGE       CALCULATE      COUNT         SUM
```

Creates a variable with a formal declaration

```
    PARAMETERS    PRIVATE       PUBLIC
```

Creates a variable or modifies its content directly

```
    STORE
```

As a general rule, variables of the basic data types don't play as significant a role in dBASE for Windows as in previous dBASE versions. In fact, it's entirely possible to create a complete application using only one or two such variables, or none at all. Most of the variables used in a dBASE OOP program are of object reference, codeblock, or function pointer type. In many cases, other data items called *properties* take over the role played by variables of the basic data types in the past. However, you still have the option of using them, and they sometimes come in handy.

Table 1.3 lists several commands that create or modify memory variables.

Literals

A *literal* is an unnamed value that is explicitly defined and not subject to change. Literals are most often used for comparison with other values, initialization of new variables, or insertion into fields and variables. Literals can be any of the five basic data types (character, date, float, logical, or numeric) or codeblock.

Character literals must be surrounded by quotes or brackets:

```
NAME = "SMITH"
NAME = 'SMITH'
NAME = [SMITH]
```

Literals of the date type must be surrounded by curly braces, although you can simulate a date literal with the **CTOD( )** function:

```
XDATE = {04/21/82}           && Uses a true literal.
```

```
XDATE = CTOD("04/21/82")   && Uses CTOD() instead.
```

Logical literals use the TRUE and FALSE symbols .T. and .F..

```
XVERDICT = .T.   && True
XVERDICT = .F.   && False
```

Numeric literals are not surrounded by any identifying mark:

```
SALARY = 34521.78
```

Literals of type codeblock must be surrounded with brackets, and all contained commands must be preceded by semicolons.

```
xRoutine = {;DIR ;? DISKSPACE()}
```

Note that in all of the examples shown here, the literal is placed on the right side of an assignment expression. This is no accident; any attempt to use a literal alone results in an error condition. Literals may appear on either side of a comparison expression but only on the right side of an assignment expression, as in the following program code:

```
IF (ID = "X") .OR. ("Y" = ANS) && Comparison expression
   @ 10,10 SAY "Go ahead"
ENDIF
PERSON = "Cooper"    && Assignment expression.
```

Assignment expressions are actually commands. They don't merely execute comparisons between entities, but perform actions. For example, the last line of code in the previous example created a new memory variable named PERSON (or perhaps only altered its contents). In some ways, it's better to call such an expression an assignment command.

Field Names

A *field name* identifies a field in a table file (.DBF). Table files are the most important data-carrying files used by dBASE for Windows. Fields may be any of the five basic data types described above or any of the three special field types, *binary*, *memo*, or *OLE*. Like memory variables, fields are given names, and their contents can be held in memory. Unlike memory variables, fields are also stored on disk and can't be created spontaneously with the commands shown in Table 1.3.

A common way to modify the contents of a field is with the **REPLACE** command:

```
REPLACE NAME WITH "TYLER", AGE WITH 20,;
        BIRTHDAY WITH {03/01/91}  && Changes 3 fields.
```

In a well-written dBASE for Windows application, control objects are much more likely to access fields than variables. This is due to the fact that most of these objects can store values on their own and don't need extra memory variables. You'll see many examples of this in later chapters.

Array Objects

An *array object* contains a series of storage units known as *elements*. These elements are usually arranged in a one-dimensional configuration resembling a single line, or a two-dimensional configuration resembling a grid. Each element resembles a conventional memory variable and can contain any of the five basic data types.

The number of dimensions and constituent elements is determined by the DECLARE command that defines the array object. For example, an array object with two dimensions might be declared like this:

```
DECLARE XLIST[10,20]
```

As with forms and other objects, you can create an array object with the *NEW operator* (described below):

```
XLIST = NEW ARRAY(10, 20)
```

Either way, the array object XLIST is a two-dimensional grid of elements with 10 rows and 20 columns. Individual elements of this array are referenced by the array name and the specific row and column coordinates:

```
RESULT = XLIST[5, 7]
XLIST[8, 19] = 100
```

The first command copies the element at Row 5, Column 7 to the memory variable RESULT. The second command places the number 100 at Row 8, Column 19.

Unlike most objects in dBASE for Windows, an array object is not contained by a form. It doesn't depend on a form for its existence, and can be created and used independently. Because an array object doesn't appear on a form and is invisible to the user, it isn't a control like an entry field, a list box, or a browse object.

Functions

A *function* is a subroutine that generates (or *returns*) a single value. You typically use a function to calculate a value, alter a value, test a condition, or retrieve a unit of information. For example, the following command, given at the Dot Prompt or included in a program, reveals today's date according to the system clock:

```
? DATE()
```

As with **DATE( )**, each function has a name that gives a clue as to its purpose, followed immediately by parentheses. These parentheses are known as *function call operators* and are described in the next section. Some functions require one or more values called *arguments* (also known as *parameters*) between the parentheses, and others do not. For instance, the **UPPER( )** function, which converts all lower case letters to upper case, requires a character argument:

```
NEWNAME = UPPER(OLDNAME)
```

Chapter 1 Language Elements

The **DATE( )** function needs no argument at all.

Operators

Operators are symbols that determine the relationships between elements of data. They come in five basic categories.

- Logical
- Mathematical
- Relational
- String
- Object management

Logical Operators

A *logical operator* makes a comparison between two complete expressions and returns a logical value of true (.T.) or false (.F.). For example, the following expressions compare variables (or fields) named LASTNAME and SALARY with the literals "COOPER" and 65000:

```
(LASTNAME = "COOPER")
(SALARY > 65000)
```

If you want to combine both of these expressions into one, you can connect them with the .AND. logical operator:

```
(LASTNAME = "COOPER") .AND. (SALARY > 65000)
```

This compound expression requires both its constituent parts to be true before the entire expression is true. Replacing .AND. with the .OR. operator requires that only one of the original expressions be true:

```
(LASTNAME = "COOPER") .OR. (SALARY > 65000)
```

The logical operators are shown in Table 1.4.

Table 1.4 Logical Operators

Symbol	Example	True only if
.AND.	DELETED() .AND. AGE = 20	Record is marked for deletion.
.OR.	SN = "56Y-3645" .OR. EOF()	Serial Number is "56Y-3645" OR we are past end of file.
.NOT.	.NOT. DELETED()	Record is NOT deleted.

Mathematical Operators

A *mathematical operator* performs a numerical comparison or calculation. For example, the following line of program code adds two variables, SALARY and BONUSES, and inserts the result into a third variable, INCOME:

```
INCOME = SALARY + BONUSES
```

The following command calculates 500 to the 2/3 power:

```
RESULT = 500 ** (2/3)
```

The mathematical operators are shown in Table 1.5.

Table 1.5 Mathematical Operators

Symbol	Example	Effect
+ (add)	SCORE + HC	Adds a handicap to a golf score
	DATE() + 31	Adds 31 days to today's date
- (subtract)	REVENUE - COST	Calculates PROFIT
	DATE() - 365	Subtracts one year from today's date
* (multiply)	PRINC * 1.05	Applies 5% interest
/ (divide)	RATE / TIME	Calculates SPEED
*, ^ (power)	231.56 ** 2	Calculates 231.56 squared

Relational Operators

A *relational operator* makes a comparison between two values and returns .T. (true) or .F. (false). The following expression, which uses the relational operator (=), returns .T. if the field AGE is equal to 10:

```
? AGE = 10
```

The following expression returns true (.T.) if the date field DUEDATE is later than today's date:

```
? DUEDATE > DATE()
```

Chapter 1 Language Elements

When a relational operator is used in an expression, both of the compared values must have the same data type, or an error condition is generated.

The relational operators are shown in Table 1.6.

Table 1.6 Relational Operators

Operator	Example	Effect
< (less than)	< "Bert"	Before "Bert" alphabetically
	< 45.60	Less than 45.60
	< {05/18/52}	Before May 18, 1952
> (Greater than)	> "MANFRED"	After "MANFRED" alphabetically
	> 45.60	Greater than 45.60
	> {05/18/52}	After May 18, 1952
= (Equal to)	= "JONES"	Contains "JONES"
	= 4325.78	Exactly 4325.78
	= {05/18/52}	On May 18, 1952
	= .F.	FALSE
	= .T.	TRUE
<> (Not equal to)	<> "DOE"	Anything but "DOE"
	<> {05/18/52}	Not May 18, 1952
	<> .F.	TRUE
>= (Greater than/equal to)	>= "G"	"G" and above alphabetically

	>= 0	0 or higher
	>= {05/18/52}	May 18, 1952 or after
<= (Less than/equal to)	<= "VERNA"	"VERNA" or lower alphabetically
	<= {05/18/52}	May 18, 1952 or before
$ (Contains)	$ "Jr."	Contains "Jr."

Table 1.6 Relational Operators (contd.)

String Operators

A *string operator* joins two character strings into one, a process known as *concatenation*. The following line of program code uses the string operator "+" to create a character variable named RESULT from two other character variables named FIRSTNAME and LASTNAME:

```
RESULT = FIRSTNAME+LASTNAME
```

Assuming that FIRSTNAME contains the string "CHUCK   ", and LASTNAME contains the string "BENTLEY", RESULT should now contain the concatenated string "CHUCK   BENTLEY ."

Notice that the trailing blanks of FIRSTNAME are left where they were, creating a gap between the names. This gap can be prevented by using the other string operator, "-", instead:

```
RESULT = FIRSTNAME-LASTNAME
```

yielding a value of "CHUCKBENTLEY   ." Notice that the spaces are not eliminated, but moved to the end of the resulting string.

Function Call Operators

You've already seen several examples of function call operators; they are the parentheses that follow the name of a function and that surround the arguments you pass to the function. For example, the following command uses both function call operators:

```
? UPPER(LASTNAME)
```

In this case, the function call operators surround a single argument, a field or variable named LASTNAME. Of course, function call operators do not necessarily surround arguments; for example, the **DATE( )** function requires no arguments at all. However, the function call operators are still required, as with:

```
? DATE()
```

Function call operators are also used to execute codeblocks and user-defined functions. For example, you've already seen an example of codeblock execution where function call operators were used:

```
MyCodeBl = {; DIR ; ? CHR(7)}   && Create the codeblock.
MyCodeBl()                      && Execute it.
```

Object Operators

dBASE for Windows uses three operators to create or use objects: the NEW operator, the dot operator, and the index operator.

The NEW Operator

The *NEW operator* creates a new object. You've already seen an example of a command that uses NEW to create a new form object:

```
Form1 = NEW FORM("THIS IS A TEST FORM.")
```

Contrary to appearances, the keyword NEW is *not* a command, but an operator. This sometimes causes confusion; can a word be an operator? And isn't the equals sign an operator? Is it really proper to have two operators side by side?

Actually, the equals sign isn't really an operator in this command. To see why, let's break the command down into its component parts, starting at the left.

- Form1 is a new object reference variable pointing to the new form object.
- = is sometimes known as the *assignment operator*. However, this is a little misleading. When you use an equals sign to create a new variable, it really serves as a command, not an operator. It isn't relating two expressions (a characteristic of an operator); it's *performing an action* (a characteristic of a command). In fact, when used as the so-called assignment operator, an equals sign is the equivalent of the dBASE command STORE, which creates or changes memory variables.
- NEW is the real operator.
- FORM is the *class* of the new object. All objects belong to a class; for example, entry fields belong to the *Entryfield class*, browse objects belong to *Browse class*, and so on.
- "THIS IS A TEST FORM." is a parameter that determines what appears on the caption bar of the new form. It's entirely optional, and could have been omitted from the command.

Each object you create with the NEW operator is said to be an *instance of a class*. A class is a template, in the same way that a cookie cutter is a template; you create an instance of a cookie with the cookie cutter, and you create an instance of an object with its object class. For example, the form created by the command above creates an instance of the Form class--in other words, a form.

The Dot Operator

You've already seen an example of a command that uses the dot operator (which is also known as the *member access operator*):

```
Form1.Open()
```

On the left of the dot operator is Form1, the object reference variable that points to the form object. On the right of the dot operator is Open( ), a *property* of the form object. (This property causes the form to open and become available to the user.)

Properties are variables that are stored in an object. Some properties, like Open( ), perform actions; such properties are called *methods*. Some properties react to events; such properties are called *event handlers*. Some properties determine the characteristics of an object; in this book we refer to them as *attributes* (although it's not an official term in dBASE for Windows). There are over 170 properties. We'll look at properties more closely in Chapter 3.

Properties are sometimes known as *members*. Each object class has its own set of members, and each instance you create from a class automatically acquires the members of that class. For example, each time you create a form object, it automatically acquires all the members (that is, the properties) of the Form object class.

For the sake of consistency, we refer to members as properties in this book.

The Index Operator

The index operator consists of square brackets ([and]), and is most often used to access an element in an array object. For example, the following commands create an array object, insert a value into one of its elements, and then display the new contents:

```
SArray = NEW ARRAY(10)    && New array with 10 elements
SArray[3] = 100           && Put 100 in element 3
? SArray[3]               && Echo contents (100)
```

The index operators are the square brackets surrounding the number 3.

You aren't limited to using index operators on array objects alone; for example, you can create what is known as a *custom property* and access it with an index operator.

```
NewForm = NEW FORM()      && Creates a new form.
NewForm[3] = 450          && Creates a custom property.
? NewForm[3]              && Displays its contents.
```

Incidentally, this isn't the only way to add a custom property to an object. Custom properties are discussed further in Chapter 3.

Two Syntax Styles

The language elements used in program code must be arranged according to rules of the language. Any deviation from these rules can cause an error condition that prevents the application from compiling and running. The rules of any language regarding the arrangement of its fundamental elements is called *syntax*.

The language of dBASE for Windows provides two different syntaxes for many OOP programming tasks. The most important of these tasks is the creation and modification of objects. One syntax uses the NEW and dot operators. For the sake of discussion, we call this *NEW operator syntax*. The other syntax uses more traditional keywords and commands; we call this *DEFINE object syntax*.

You've already seen an example of NEW operator syntax. Here's a variation:

```
Form1 = NEW FORM()          && Create the form.
Form1.ColorNormal = "W+/B"  && Set its color.
Form1.Open()                && Open the form.
```

DEFINE object syntax doesn't use the NEW operator or the dot operator. Instead, it uses commands and keywords. DEFINE object syntax resembles that of previous versions of the dBASE language. For example, the following commands use DEFINE object syntax:

```
DEFINE FORM Form1 PROPERTY ColorNormal "W+/B"
OPEN FORM Form1
```

These commands are equivalent to the commands in the previous example; both code samples accomplish the same thing.

- Create a form object (that is, create an *instance* of the Form object class)
- Create an object reference variable named Form1 that points to the form object
- Set the color characteristics of the form
- Open the form

Fortunately, you don't have to choose between the two syntax styles; you can use them in combination. For example, the following code samples use mixed syntax, and work just as well:

```
DEFINE FORM Form1 PROPERTY ColorNormal "W+/B"
Form1.Open()

Form1 = NEW FORM()
Form1.ColorNormal = "W+/B"
OPEN FORM Form1
```

You'll use both styles throughout this book.

What Next?

Now that you've been introduced to the basic elements of the dBASE for Windows language, you're ready to start writing applications. But first you'll need some data to work on, so the next chapter introduces tables, indexes, and queries. You'll create two tables and a query that extracts data from both. This query will be the main source of data for the applications you develop in subsequent exercises and chapters. Be sure to create these items, even if you're already familiar with table and query development.

Chapter 2
Tables, Indexes, and Queries

The most common data storage medium in dBASE is the *table file*, which has the file name extension .DBF. A table file consists of *records*, and records are made up of *fields*, which hold individual units of information. A table file also contains a special header region that holds information on record structure, record count, record size, date of last update, and so on. Virtually all dBASE applications are based on the creation, management, and access of table files.

The records in a table file can be viewed or listed in their *natural order* (that is, the physical order in which they are stored on disk) or in *logical order*. Logical order is provided by an *index*, which is held in memory and stored in an index file (file extension .MDX or .NDX). Index files with extensions of .MDX are called *multiple-index files*. A multiple-index file can contain up to 47 indexes; these indexes are called *tags*. Index files with extensions of .NDX are called *single-index files*, and can contain only one index at a time. (The exercises and examples in the book use multiple-index files only, since they are far more versatile and convenient than single-index files.)

The easiest way to retrieve the data contained in tables and present it in a useful format is with *query by example* (QBE). A QBE is a program you generate with a convenient, menu-driven tool known as the *Query Designer*.

Tables

The dBASE product line has always adhered to the *relational model*, which mandates that all data managed by a system be stored, accessed, and retrieved in table form. A table is a two-dimensional grid of data, as shown in Figure 2.1. The terminology used to describe this grid has changed since the release of dBASE for Windows.

Using dBASE Terminology

Until dBASE for Windows was released, most programmers called individual dBASE table files "databases". In fact, many programmers still call them that; unfortunately, it's a misnomer that often causes confusion among new dBASE programmers. In most DBMSs (like ORACLE and DB2), a table is a collection of one or more separate table files that can be joined to one another on various fields or attributes and viewed as one. In the old dBASE terminology, "databases" are individual data storage files which, like "tables" in other systems, can be related to each other and viewed as one. In this book we refer to individual storage files with the more up-to-date terminology--as tables.

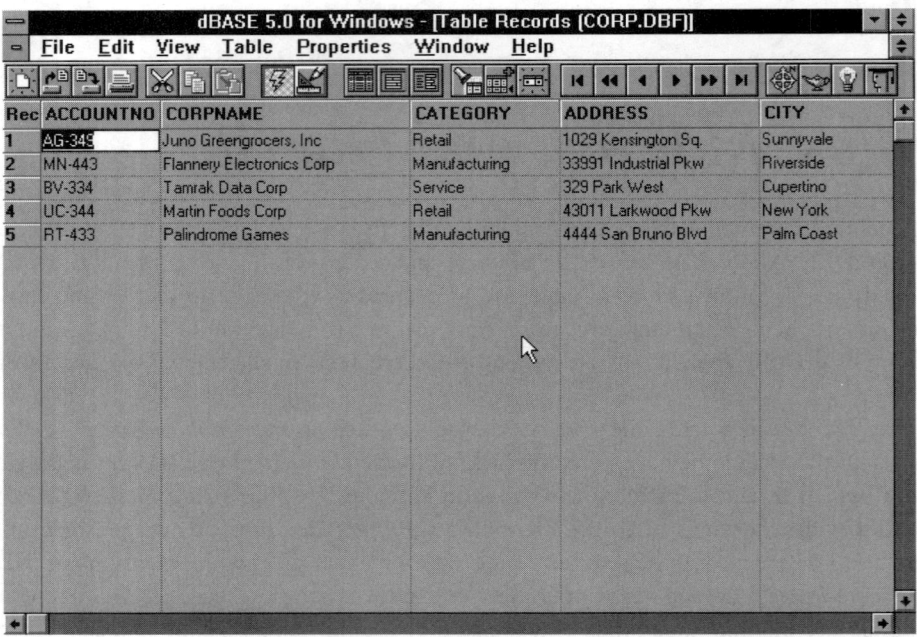

Figure 2.1 A table

The terms *record* and *field* are also sources of confusion. For example, examine the table in Figure 2.1. In most DBMSs, each horizontal line of data is called a *row*. Similarly, each vertical line of data is called a *column*. In the dBASE product line, it is more traditional to refer to rows as records and columns as fields. We follow that convention in this book.

Creating and Using Table Files

In the following exercises you create two table files, CORP.DBF and ADVERT.DBF, which hold information for a mythical advertising agency named AdverData Corporation. CORP.DBF will hold records on client corporations that have advertising accounts with the agency. ADVERT.DBF will hold records on advertising campaigns for the client corporations. Each client corporation will have only one record in CORP.DBF, but each might have multiple records in ADVERT.DBF.

If you're already familiar with table file creation, you needn't go through the exercises step by step. However, you still need to create the files, since you'll be using them in subsequent chapters to develop sample applications.

Exercise 1

In this exercise you create CORP.DBF. In the process, you become acquainted with the *Table Designer*, a tool that creates fields, designates their data type, and determines their size. Together, these attributes make up the *structure* of the table.

Chapter 2 Tables, Indexes, and Queries

Figure 2.2 The Navigator and the Command windows

1. Start a session in dBASE for Windows. If the windows shown in Figure 2.2 are not visible, click their icons (which should be located near the bottom-left of the screen.)

   The two-paned window at the right is called the *Command window*. The upper pane is called the *input pane*, and the lower pane is called the *result pane*. As the names imply, you enter commands in the input pane and see the results in the result pane. Together, these panes let you interact with dBASE on an ad hoc basis, performing tests, executing programs, and experimenting with various commands.

2. Click the input pane and enter the following command:

   CREATE CORP

   The Table Designer appears, as shown in Figure 2.3. This window lets you define what data items--that is, fields--are contained by each record in the new table you create. Note that the highlight is in the **Name** column, next to the number 1.

3. Enter the following character string under the **Name** column, then press <Enter>:

   ACCOUNTNO

   The highlight moves to the **Type** column. Note that a button with an arrow appears at the right.

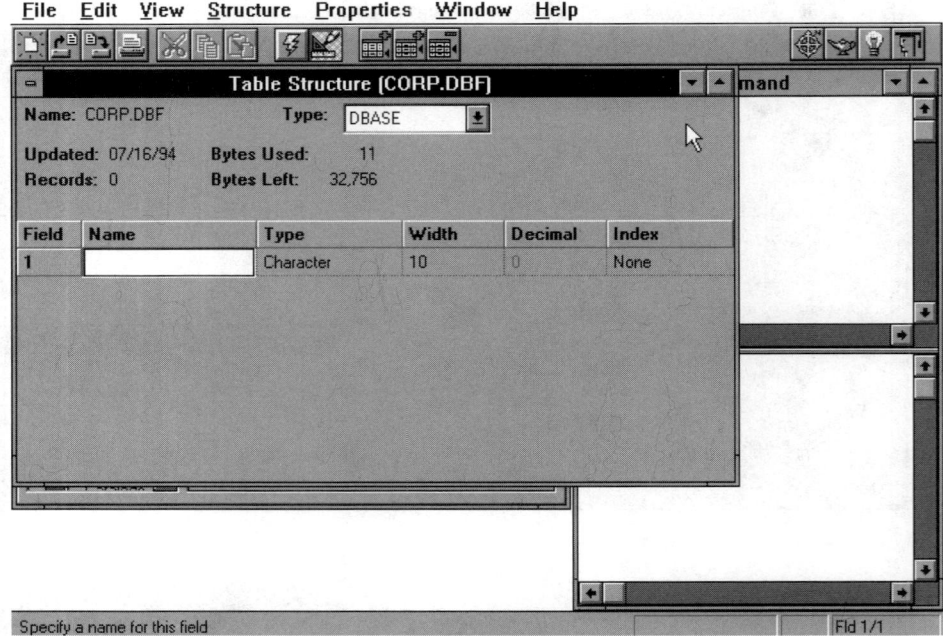

Figure 2.3 The Table Designer appears

4. Click the arrow button.

   A list of field type options appears. This is called a *dropdown list*. The highlighted box at the top of the list is called a *text box*. Together, they make up a common Windows object known as a *combo box*. You'll create combo boxes in dBASE applications later in this book.

5. Click on **Numeric**.

   The field is now designated as numeric. However, that isn't what we want. Fields containing unique, identifying values like account numbers, serial numbers, and social security numbers are usually of the character type, since character fields can be more easily indexed (as you'll see later in this chapter).

6. Click on the arrow button again.

   The dropdown list reappears.

7. Click on **Character** (or enter the letter **C**.)

   The ACCOUNTNO field is now of type character.

8. Press <Tab>.

Chapter 2 Tables, Indexes, and Queries

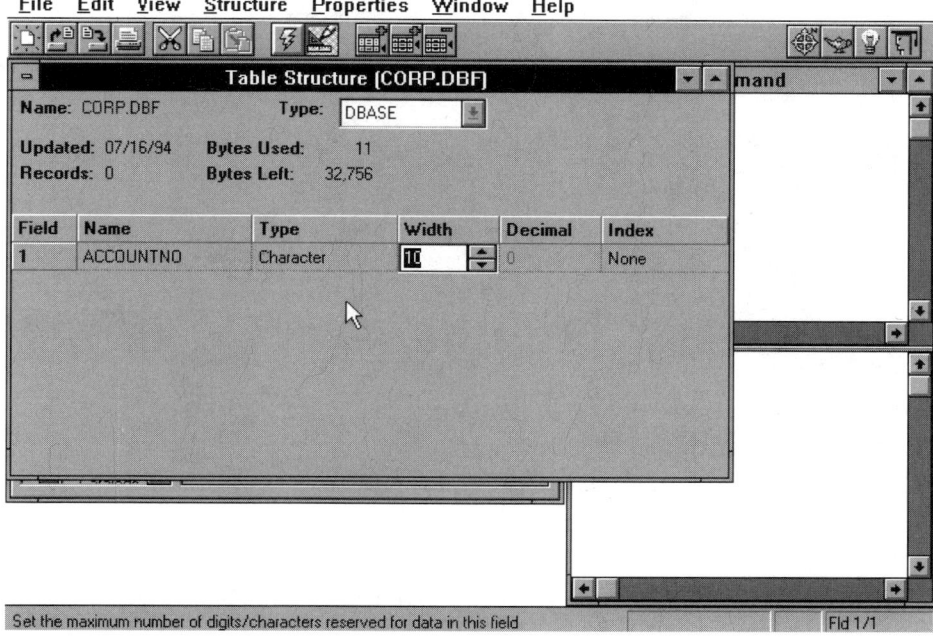

Figure 2.4 Width value is set to 10 by default

The highlight moves to the **Width** column.

9. Press <Shift-Tab>.

   The highlight moves back to the **Type** column.

10. Press <Tab> again.

    The highlight moves back to the **Width** column. <Tab> and <Shift-Tab> are highly useful key presses, since they let you retrace your steps and correct errors. (You can also use the mouse to change columns.)

    Note that the **Width** value is set to 10 by default. Note also that an UpArrow button and a DownArrow button appear to the right see Figure 2.4.)

12. Enter the number 6 in the **Width** column. You can do this in one of two ways:

    - Enter the number 6 manually, via the keyboard.
    - Decrement the value to 6 by clicking on the DownArrow four times.

    As with the combo box mentioned in Step 4, the area where you enter the number manually is called a *text box*. Together, the text box and the arrow keys make up a common Windows object known as a *spin box*. You'll create spin boxes in dBASE applications later in this book.

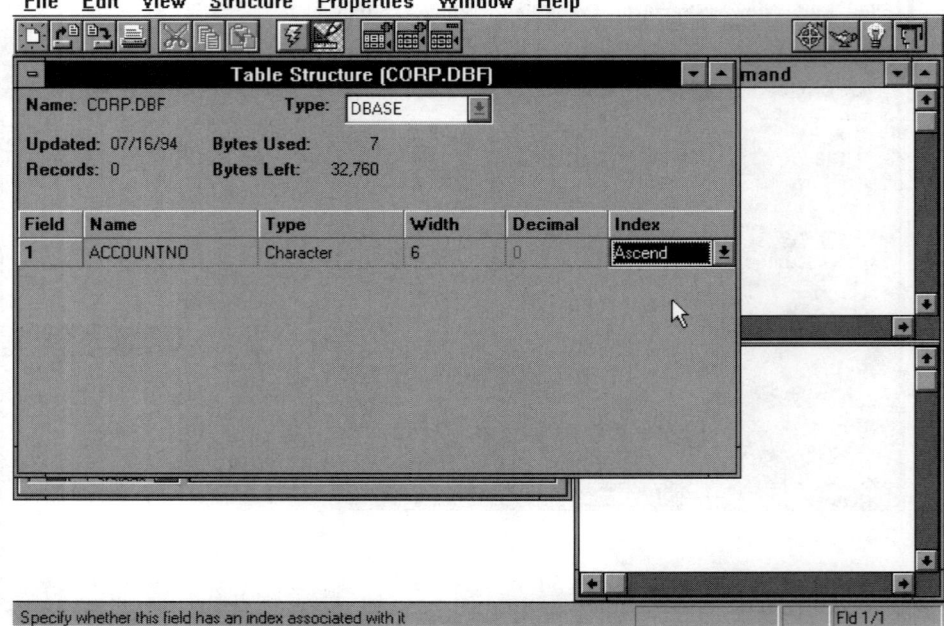

Figure 2.5 Adding fields to the table structure

13. Press <Enter>.

    The highlight moves to the **Index** column, skipping the **Decimal** column. This makes sense; character fields don't have decimal places like numeric and float fields do.

    As with the **Type** column, you select an **Index** setting with a combo box. The **Index** setting determines if the field you're creating will determine the order of records. Such fields are known as *key fields*.

14. Click the arrow button, then click on **Ascend** from the dropdown list (or enter the letter **A**.)

    You just created a character field named ACCOUNTNO, six characters wide, and designated it as a key field. The screen should now look like Figure 2.5.

15. That's enough for now. Double-click on the box at the upper left corner of the table design window.

    The table design window disappears and a dialog box is displayed, asking: **Save current changes?**

16. Click the **Yes** button.

    Another dialog box appears, saying **You may append records to the table**.

Chapter 2 Tables, Indexes, and Queries   33

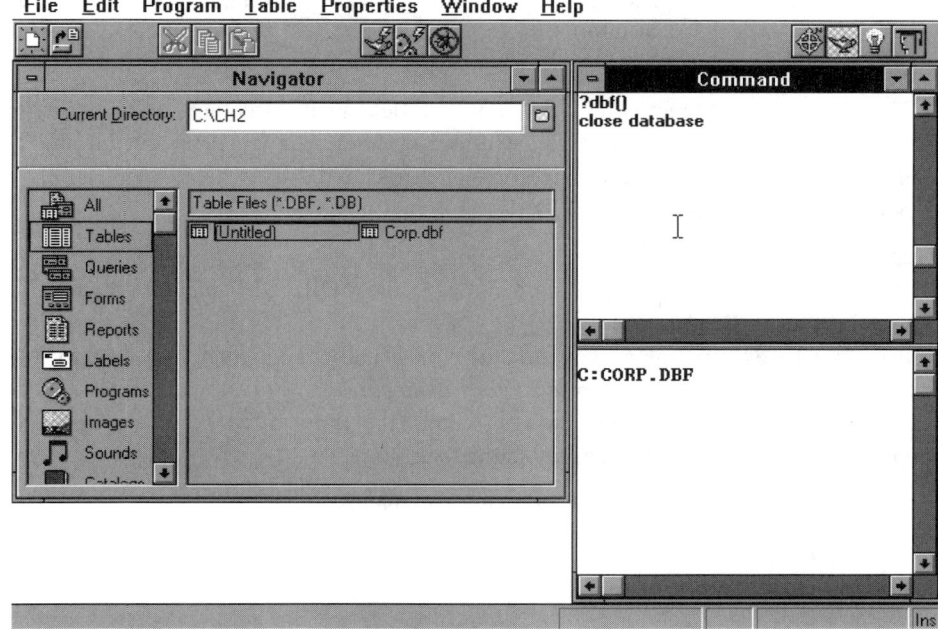

Figure 2.6   Corp.dbf appears in the File Viewer

17. Click the **Done** button.

    The dialog box and the table design window disappear. The cursor returns to the input pane.

18. Confirm the existence of the table you just created by entering the following command in the input pane:

    ? DBF()

    The following character string appears in the Results pane:

    C:CORP.DBF

    This not only confirms that the table exists, but that it is open and available. The DBF() function only returns the name of an open table file.

19. Close CORP.DBF with the following command:

    CLOSE DATABASE

Note that an icon labeled "Corp.dbf" now appears in the File Viewer (see Figure 2.6). After you enter data into the table, this icon lets you access the data. You'll use this icon in Exercise 4.

The table you just created now contains one field in its structure: ACCOUNTNO, type character, six characters wide, and designated as a key field. As you'll see later in this chapter, key fields are vital when you search for records or extract and display data.

Now let's finish designing CORP.DBF.

Exercise 2

In this exercise you add eight more fields to the CORP.DBF table structure. (You add records to the table in Exercise 3.)

Feel free to experiment as you go; there is usually more than one way to achieve a particular result with dBASE design tools. For example, many of the things you do with key presses can also be done with the mouse. Taking the time to familiarize yourself with all techniques can increase your productivity in the long run.

1. In the input pane, enter the following commands:

   ```
   USE CORP EXCLUSIVE
   MODIFY STRUCTURE
   ```

   The table design screen reappears. (Whenever you open a table to modify it, you must open it in EXCLUSIVE mode.)

2. Press <DownArrow> once.

   A blank field appears below ACCOUNTNO, with the highlight in the **Name** column.

3. Using the techniques you learned in the previous exercise, create a character field named CORPNAME, 25 characters wide, non-indexed.

4. Now complete the record structure shown in Figure 2.7.

   Be sure that all field types are correct, and that their sizes match those in Figure 2.7. For now, don't designate any field other than ACCOUNTNO as an index field.

5. When you're finished, double-click on the control box at the upper left corner of the Table Designer. When the dialog box asks for confirmation, click the **Yes** button.

   The Table Designer disappears and the cursor returns to the input pane.

6. Click the Maximize button at the upper right corner of the Command window.

   The input pane and the Results pane now cover the entire screen.

7. Execute the following command:

Chapter 2 Tables, Indexes, and Queries

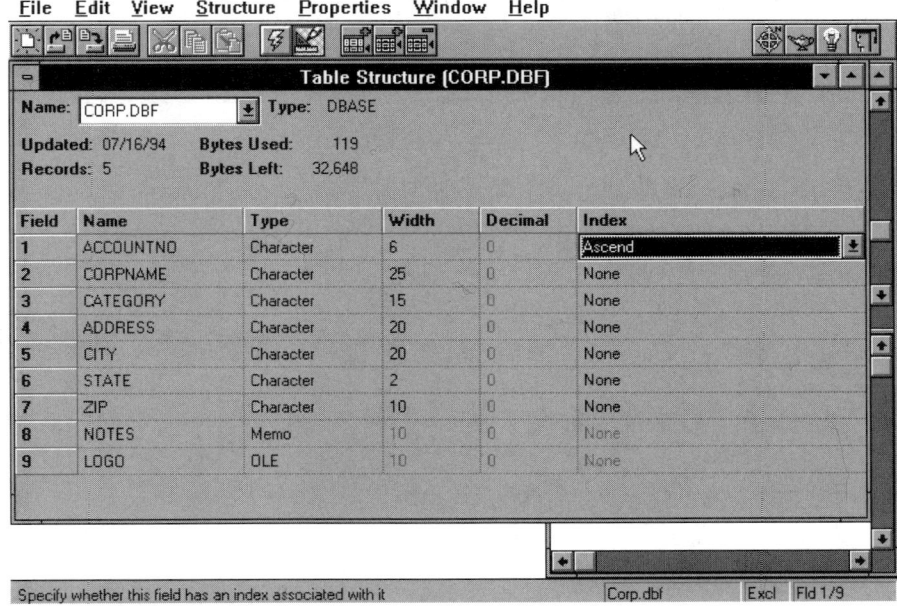

Figure 2.7   Record structure for Corp.dbf

```
DISPLAY STRUCTURE
```

A table appears in the Results pane showing the name, type, size, and indexing status of each field you created.

8. Return the Command window to its original size by clicking the Restore button at the upper-right corner.

9. Close CORP.DBF with the following command:

```
CLOSE DATABASE
```

When you executed DISPLAY STRUCTURE, you displayed the new table's *structure*--the fields, field types, field sizes, and so on that determine the characteristics of records in the table. A table's structure determines what kind of data you store in the file.

The sample applications you build in later chapters use the fields of CORP.DBF for the following purposes:

- ACCOUNTNO - The account number of each corporation. This number will be unique for each corporation. In other words, no two corporations will have the same account number.

- CORPNAME - The name of each corporation.

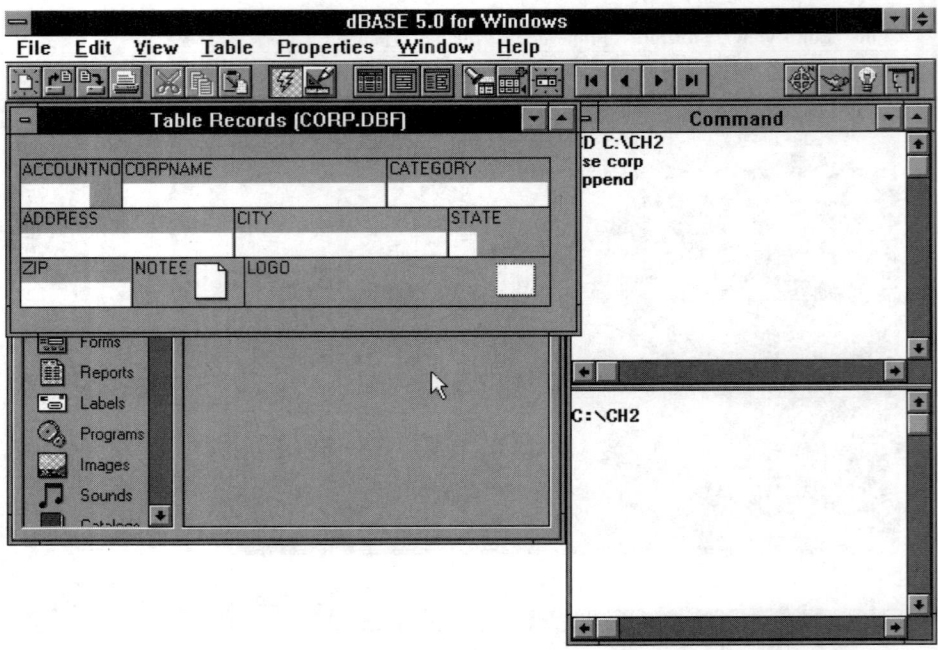

Figure 2.8 The Table Edit window is presented

- CATEGORY - The type of corporation: retail, manufacturing, and so on.
- ADDRESS, CITY, STATE, and ZIP - The corporation's mailing address.
- NOTES - Miscellaneous notes and comments on the corporation.
- LOGO - The official logo of each corporation.

Exercise 3

In this exercise you enter data into CORP.DBF. You also create another table, ADVERT.DBF, that holds records on individual advertising campaigns commissioned by the corporations.

1. Enter the following commands in the input pane:

   ```
   USE CORP
   APPEND
   ```

   The Table Edit window is presented, as shown in Figure 2.8.

2. Enter the data shown in Listing 2.1.

   CORP.DBF should now contain one record.

```
ACCOUNTNO   AG-349
CORPNAME    Juno Greengrocers, Inc
CATEGORY    Retail
ADDRESS     1029 Kensington Sq.
CITY        Sunnyvale
STATE       CA
ZIP         94087
NOTES       <Leave empty for now>
LOGO        <Leave empty for now>
```

Listing 2.1 The First Record of CORP.DBF

```
ACCOUNTNO   MN-443
CORPNAME    Flannery Electronics Corp
CATEGORY    Manufacturing
ADDRESS     33991 Industrial Pkw
CITY        Riverside
STATE       CA
ZIP         92507

ACCOUNTNO   BV-334
CORPNAME    Tamrak Data Corp
CATEGORY    Service
ADDRESS     329 Park West
CITY        Cupertino
STATE       CA
ZIP         94087

ACCOUNTNO   UC-344
CORPNAME    Martin Foods Corp
CATEGORY    Retail
ADDRESS     43011 Larkwood Pkw
CITY        New York
STATE       NY
ZIP         10003

ACCOUNTNO   RT-433
CORPNAME    Palindrome Games
CATEGORY    Manufacturing
ADDRESS     4444 San Bruno Blvd
CITY        Palm Coast
STATE       FL
ZIP         32142
```

Listing 2.2 Add These Records to CORP.DBF

3. Press <PgDn>.

    A blank record is displayed in the Table Edit window.

4. Enter the records shown in Listing 2.2 by repeating Steps 3 and 4 four times.

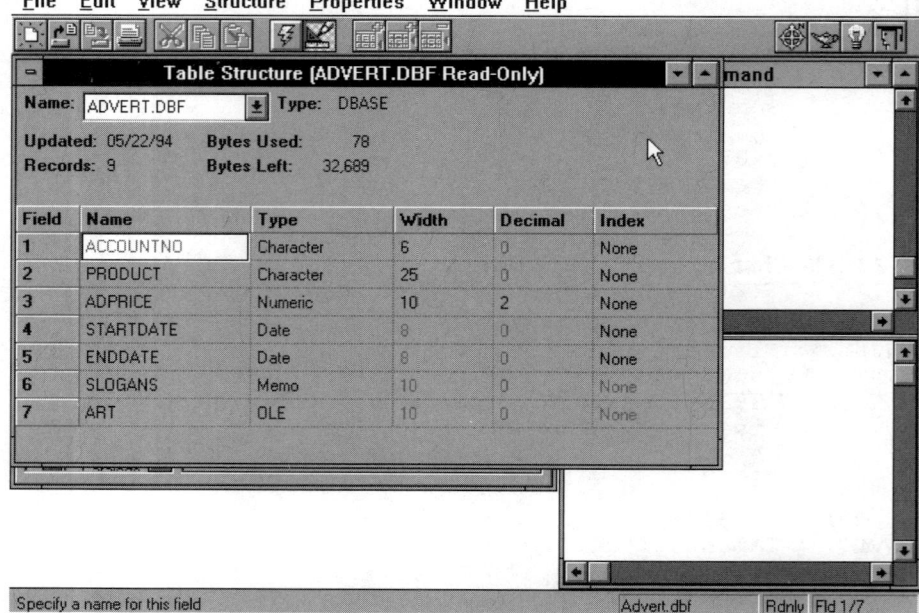

Figure 2.9 Record structure for Advert.dbf

CORP.DBF should now contain five records.

5. When you're finished, double-click on the control box at the upper left corner of the table design window. (If the dialog box asks for confirmation, click the **Yes** button.)

The cursor returns to the input pane.

6. Close CORP.DBF.

7. Using what you now know about table creation, make ADVERT.DBF. Give it the record structure shown in Figure 2.9.

8. Using the APPEND command as demonstrated in Steps 2 and 3, enter the records shown in Listing 2.3. Don't put anything in the fields named SLOGANS and ART; you'll work with these fields in later chapters.

9. When you're finished, save your work (as in Step 6) and return to the input pane.

10. Close ADVERT.DBF.

Notice that both CORP.DBF and ADVERT.DBF share an identical field, ACCOUNTNO, in common. Later in this chapter, you'll use a QBE to join the two files on this field to view the two tables as a common entity. Notice also that the ACCOUNTNO values in CORP.DBF are

Chapter 2 Tables, Indexes, and Queries

unique, while the ACCOUNTNO values in ADVERT.DBF are not. This has important implications for data access.

```
ACCOUNTNO    PRODUCT               ADPRICE     START    DATEENDDATE
BV-334       Software             433399.00   01/10/94   03/12/98
UC-344       Dairyproducts        322929.00   02/11/94   12/12/97
BV-334       Software             884430.00   11/11/95   12/18/99
RT-433       Videogames           596000.00   10/12/95   01/01/99
AG-349       Healthfood            99443.00   12/30/94   01/01/98
BV-334       Computerboards        43000.00   06/16/94   09/01/96
AG-349       Vitamins              88000.00   12/12/95   01/01/99
BV-334       Software            3200000.00   08/28/95   12/12/98
UC-344       Dairyproducts         45000.00   07/21/95   08/12/95
```

Listing 2.3 Add These Records to ADVERT.DBF

Now let's look at some ways to view and edit the data you've created.

Exercise 4

In this exercise you edit data in a browse window. Browse windows let you access data in multi-record format or single-record format.

1. From the input pane, open ADVERT.DBF:

   `USE ADVERT`

2. Enter the following command:

   `BROWSE`

   The browse window is displayed, as shown in Figure 2.10. Notice that some fields are obscured because the window isn't large enough to display them all. Let's maximize the window to make viewing a bit easier.

3. Click on Maximize button at the upper right corner of the window.

   The browse window now fills the entire work area of the dBASE application window, as shown in Figure 2.11. (The dBASE application window is the window that opens when you start a dBASE session.)

   Now let's edit a record.

4. Find the record with "Video games" in its PRODUCT field and click on the field.

   The field is now highlighted.

5. Change the contents to "Electronic entertainment."

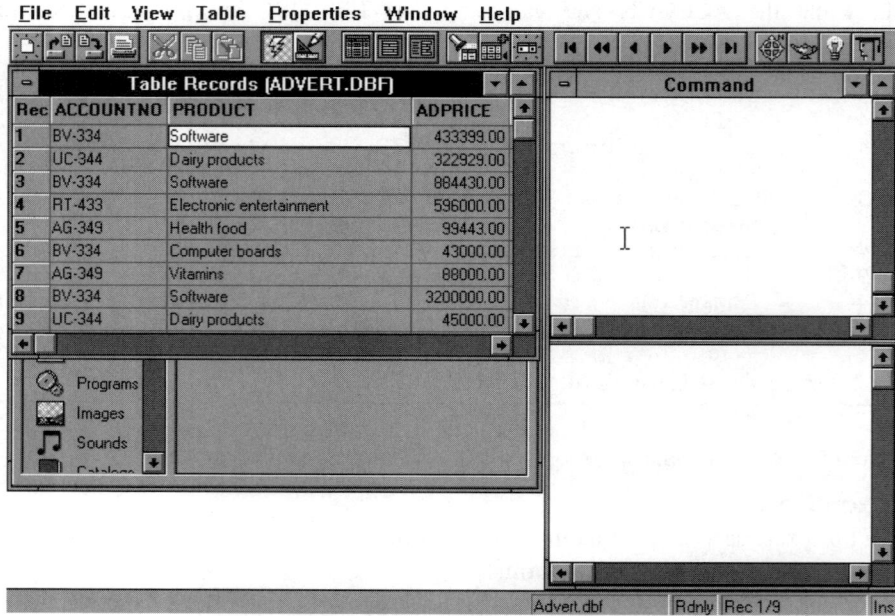

Figure 2.10 The browse window is displayed

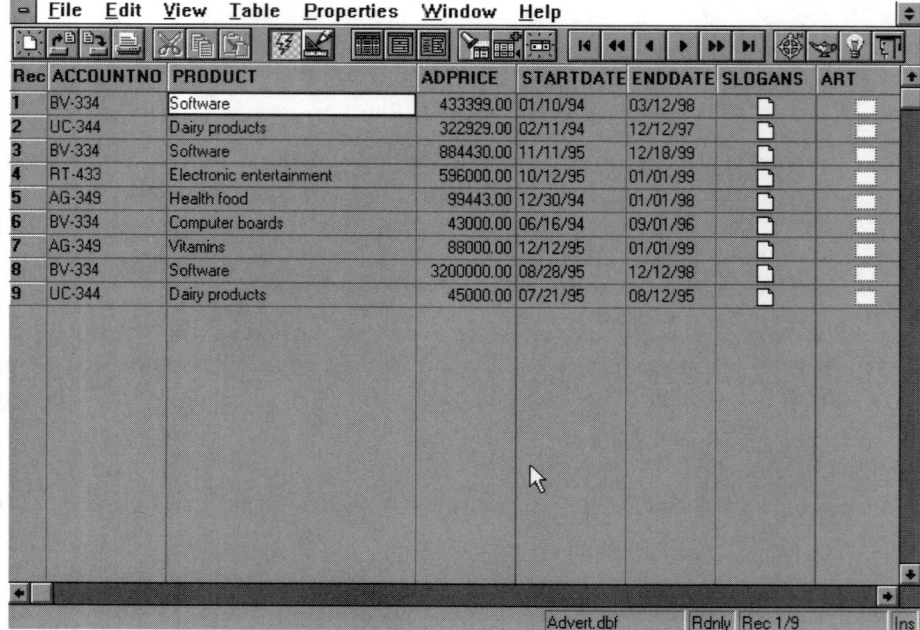

Figure 2.11 The browse window fills the entire screen

You can delete letters in a field in three ways.

- Place the mouse pointer at the far left of the field. Hold down the left mouse button and drag the pointer over the field, highlighting it. Delete the letters by pressing <Del>.
- Place the cursor at the far left of the field, then press <Del> until all characters are deleted.
- Place the cursor at the far right of the field, then press <Backspace> until all characters are deleted.

Once you delete the characters, type in the characters you want.

Now let's restore the browse window to its original size.

6. Click on the Restore button at the upper right corner of the browse window.

   The window reverts to its original size, and fields at the right are obscured again. However, you can still view the missing fields with the window's scroll bars.

7. Click once on the scroll bar at the bottom of the browse window.

   Two things happen:

   - The fields scroll to the left and fields at the right are displayed.
   - The scroll bar's slider button (also known as the *thumb*) moves to the right (see Figure 2.12).

   Now let's use the slider button to view fields.

8. Place the mouse pointer on the slider button and hold down the left mouse button.

9. Drag the slider button all the way to the right and release the mouse button.

   The fields are shifted to the left.

10. Now drag the slider button all the way to the left.

    The fields are shifted to the right.

    So far you've looked at records in *multiple-record format*, in which the records were displayed in a two-dimensional grid, one stacked on another. You can also view records individually, in *single-record format*.

11. Press <F2>.

    The browse window now shows one record. You might find this format a little less informative, since you can't see the other records. However, you can still navigate from field to field and from record to record.

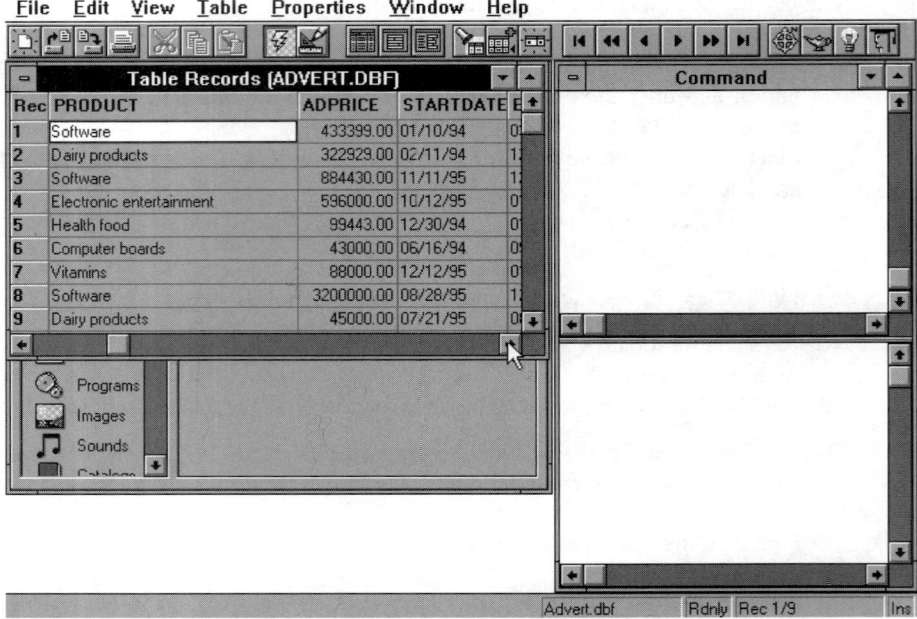

Figure 2.12 The slider button moves to the right

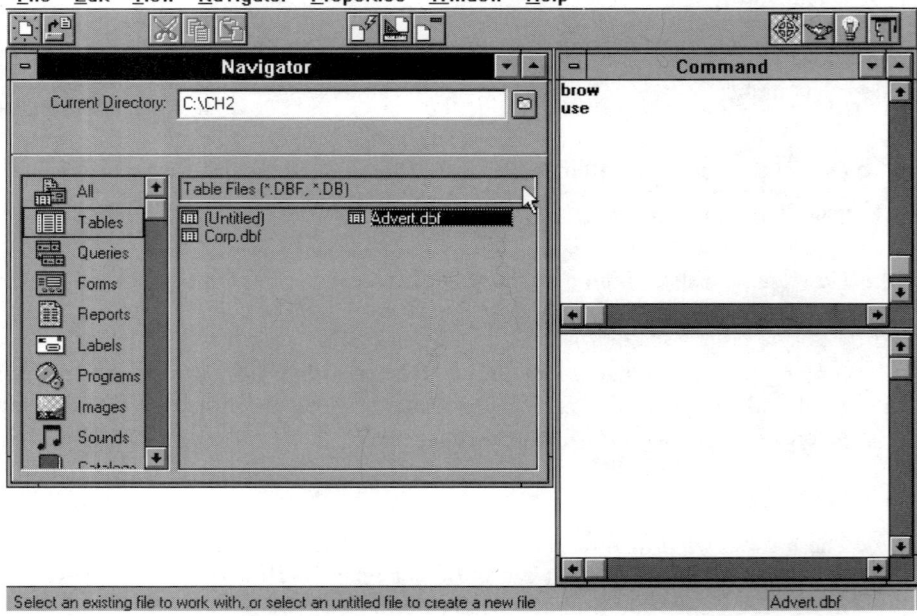

Figure 2.13 Icon labeled Advert.dbf in the Navigator

Chapter 2 Tables, Indexes, and Queries 43

12. Press <Tab> twice, then press <Shift-Tab> twice.

    The highlight moves from field to field in two directions.

13. Press <PgDn> twice, then press <PgUp> twice.

    Each time, a different record appears in the display. Pressing <PgDn> moves the record pointer forward by one record, and pressing <PgUp> moves the record pointer back by one record.

12. Now press <Ctrl-F4>.

    The browse window disappears and control returns to the input pane.

13. Close ADVERT.DBF.

    Now let's demonstrate a simpler way to open a table and view it in a browse window.

14. Double-click the icon labeled **Advert.dbf** in the Navigator (see Figure 2.13).

    In a few seconds, the browse window appears. You can open and view any table you wish by double-clicking its icon.

15. Close the browse window by pressing <Ctrl-F4>.

    The table is closed automatically.

As a programmer you'll find the browse window invaluable, since it provides a quick way of examining data and confirming the effects of your programs. For example, if your program inserts new data into a table or changes the contents of a record, viewing the table in the browse window makes it easy to see what really happened.

In later chapters you'll be introduced to the *browse object*, a powerful data-entry tool with all the capabilities of a browse window--and more.

Indexes

So far you've created and examined records in a rather random fashion. For example, the records you viewed with the browse window in Exercise 4 were not sorted on any field. This often interferes with viewing and editing, since finding the desired record is difficult, especially when a table has many records. dBASE solves this problem with *indexing*.

Exercise 5

In this exercise you create indexes and view the results.

1. From the input pane, open ADVERT.DBF:

    ```
    USE ADVERT EXCLUSIVE
    ```

```
Record#    accountno
      1    BV-334
      2    UC-344
      3    BV-334
      4    RT-433
      5    AG-349
      6    BV-334
      7    AG-349
      8    BV-334
      9    UC-344
```

Listing 2.4 Unordered Contents of the ACCOUNTNO Field

2. Execute the following command:

    `LIST ACCOUNTNO`

    The ACCOUNTNO values appear in the Results Pane, as shown in Listing 2.4. Note that they are not arranged in a sequential manner.

3. Now execute the following command:

    `INDEX ON ACCOUNTNO TAG ACTNO`

4. Repeat Step 2.

    This time, the records are ordered alphabetically, as shown in Listing 2.5. Notice that the record numbers are no longer sequential. This is because the record numbers represent the physical order of the records, and the physical order is unchanged. Only the *logical order* has changed.

    Executing the INDEX ON command created two things:

    - An *index file* named ADVERT.MDX
    - An *index tag* named ACTNO, which is stored in ADVERT.MDX

    Index tags order records on one or more fields in a table. Any field that serves as an indexing field is called a *key field*. In this case, ACCOUNTNO was the key field.

5. Execute the following commands:

    ```
    GO TOP
    BROWSE
    ```

    The browse window appears, as shown in Figure 2.14. Note that the records are still ordered on the ACCOUNTNO field.

    The GO TOP command placed the record pointer at the first record. (GO BOTTOM places the record pointer at the last record.)

```
Record#  accountno
      5  AG-349
      7  AG-349
      1  BV-334
      3  BV-334
      6  BV-334
      8  BV-334
      4  RT-433
      2  UC-344
      9  UC-344
```

Listing 2.5 Indexed Contents of the ACCOUNTNO Field

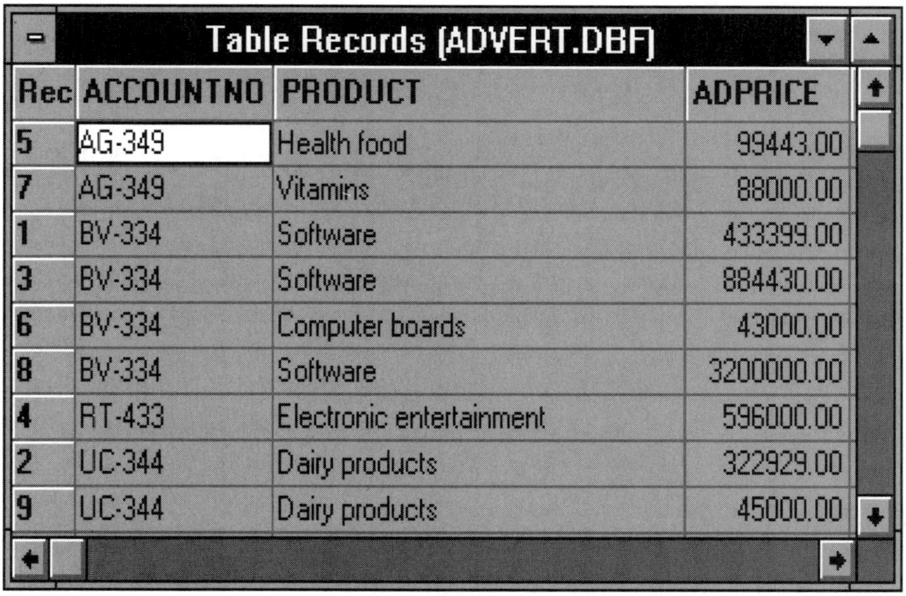

Table Records (ADVERT.DBF)

Rec	ACCOUNTNO	PRODUCT	ADPRICE
5	AG-349	Health food	99443.00
7	AG-349	Vitamins	88000.00
1	BV-334	Software	433399.00
3	BV-334	Software	884430.00
6	BV-334	Computer boards	43000.00
8	BV-334	Software	3200000.00
4	RT-433	Electronic entertainment	596000.00
2	UC-344	Dairy products	322929.00
9	UC-344	Dairy products	45000.00

Figure 2.14 The browse window appears

6. Quit the browse object by pressing <Ctrl-F4>.

7. Close ADVERT.DBF.

An index tag determines the order in which records are presented when you list them or search through them. It bears repeating that an index doesn't physically rearrange the order of records in a table file; it provides *logical order* instead of *physical order*. Giving a table logical order provides more benefits than sorting the table physically (as with the SORT command).

- Record searches can execute much faster when the table is indexed. This is important when your table gets very large or your computer isn't particularly fast.
- Indexes can be changed at a moment's notice. For example, an .MDX file can contain as many as 47 tags, each with a different ordering scheme. With a single command (SET ORDER), you can change the active index and reorder the records instantly.

Basic Index Types

You can create three basic categories of index: *simple*, *modified*, and *compound*. Which type of index you use depends on the complexity of the record-ordering task.

Simple Indexes

A simple index is built on one key field. It uses only the raw data contained in that one field, and makes no analysis or interpretation of its contents. Even so, simple indexes offer some flexibility.

You've already seen one example of a simple index. The command in Step 3 of the previous exercise created an index tag named ACTNO:

```
INDEX ON ACCOUNTNO TAG ACTNO
```

This index included all records, regardless of duplications (see Listing 2.5). For example, the listing includes two records with ACCOUNTNO values of AG-349 and four records with ACCOUNTNO values of BV-334. However, there may be times when only the first occurrence of a record with a particular value in the key field should be accessible. When this happens, use the UNIQUE option.

The records were ordered from low to high on the ACCOUNTNO field. However, there may be times when the records should be indexed in reverse order. When this happens, use the DESCENDING option.

Note also that, although the records were ordered differently, all of them were available. The INDEX ON command has an optional FOR clause that makes some records available for processing while hiding others.

Exercise 6

In this exercise you create UNIQUE and DESCENDING indexes. You also use a FOR clause to select which records are accessible when an index tag is active.

1. From the input pane, open ADVERT.DBF:

    ```
    USE ADVERT EXCLUSIVE
    ```

2. Execute the following commands:

    ```
    INDEX ON ACCOUNTNO TAG ACTNO2 UNIQUE
    LIST ACCOUNTNO
    ```

```
Record#    accountno
     5     AG-349
     1     BV-334
     4     RT-433
     2     UC-344
```

Listing 2.6 Using the UNIQUE Option

```
Record#    accountno
     2     UC-344
     9     UC-344
     4     RT-433
     1     BV-334
     3     BV-334
     6     BV-334
     8     BV-334
     5     AG-349
     7     AG-349
```

Listing 2.7 Using the DESCENDING Option

This time only the first occurrences of records with duplicate key values are visible, as shown in Listing 2.6. The records still exist in the table file, but as long as index tag ACTNO2 is active, they are inaccessible.

3. Execute the following commands:

   ```
   INDEX ON ACCOUNTNO TAG ACTNO3 DESCENDING
   LIST ACCOUNTNO
   ```

   This time, the records are listed in reverse order (see Listing 2.7).

4. Execute the following commands:

   ```
   INDEX ON ACCOUNTNO TAG CD FOR STARTDATE < {01/01/95}
   LIST ACCOUNTNO, STARTDATE
   ```

   Note that only records with STARTDATE values earlier than January 1, 1995 are listed, as shown in Listing 2.8).

5. Close ADVERT.DBF.

Simple indexes have their limitations. For example, key fields often contain information in a form unsuitable for the desired indexing order. When this happens, you can temporarily modify the key field while building the index, without actually changing the data itself. An index created with this method is said to be *modified*.

```
Record#    ACCOUNTNO    STARTDATE
     5     AG-349       12/30/94
```

```
    1  BV-334    01/10/94
    6  BV-334    06/16/94
    2  UC-344    02/11/94
```

Listing 2.8 Excluding Certain Records with the FOR Clause

```
Record#  product
      7  E vitamins
      6  computer boards
      2  dairy products
      9  dairy products
      4  electronic entertainment
      5  health food
      1  software
      3  software
      8  software
```

Listing 2.9 The Effect of Case Sensitivity

Modified Indexes

A modified index uses one or more of the dBASE IV functions to temporarily modify values in the key field during indexing. This makes it possible to alter the logical order of the index without actually changing the contents of the key field itself.

Exercise 7

In this exercise you use dBASE functions to create modified indexes.

1. From the input pane, open ADVERT.DBF:

   ```
   USE ADVERT EXCLUSIVE
   ```

2. Execute the following commands:

   ```
   INDEX ON PRODUCT TAG XPROD
   LIST PRODUCT
   ```

   The listing generated is shown in Listing 2.9. Something is obviously wrong. The records are not ordered alphabetically as expected; the record with "E vitamins" in its PRODUCT field comes first, even though this is alphabetically incorrect.

   This happened because indexing in dBASE is case-sensitive. Among other things, case sensitivity means that upper case letters have a lower significance than lowercase letters, and always come first when the indexing order is ASCENDING (as it is by default). The solution is a modified indexing scheme.

3. Execute the following commands:

   ```
   INDEX ON UPPER(PRODUCT) TAG XPROD2
   ```

Chapter 2 Tables, Indexes, and Queries

```
LIST PRODUCT
```

The records are listed correctly, as shown in Listing 2.10.

```
Record#    product
      6    computer boards
      2    dairy products
      9    dairy products
      7    E vitamins
      4    electronic entertainment
      5    health food
      1    software
      3    software
      8    software
```

Listing 2.10 Case Sensitivity Problem Solved

```
Record#    accountno
      1    BV-334
      3    BV-334
      6    BV-334
      8    BV-334
      2    UC-344
      9    UC-344
      5    AG-349
      7    AG-349
      4    RT-433
```

Listing 2.11 Ordered on the Last Three Characters of ACCOUNTNO

4. Now execute the following commands:

   ```
   INDEX ON LOWER(PRODUCT) TAG XPROD3
   LIST PRODUCT
   ```

   As in Step 3, the records are listed correctly. As the index was being built, the UPPER() or LOWER() function temporarily converted all of the characters in the PRODUCT field to upper-case or lower-case, respectively, making the index's logical order case-insensitive.

   Recall that in Exercise 5 you created an index named ACTNO that correctly ordered records on the ACCOUNTNO field. It didn't need conversion with the UPPER() or LOWER() function because all letters in the ACCOUNTNO field are upper case.

5. Execute the following commands:

   ```
   INDEX ON RIGHT(ACCOUNTNO, 3) TAG ACTNO4
   LIST ACCOUNTNO
   ```

   This time, the records are listed in order of the last three characters of the ACCOUNTNO field, as shown in Listing 2.11.

6. Execute the following commands:

```
INDEX ON SUBSTR(ACCOUNTNO, 2, 1) TAG ACTNO5
LIST ACCOUNTNO
```

This time, the records are listed in order of the second letter of the ACCOUNTNO field, as shown in Listing 2.12.

7. Close ADVERT.DBF.

```
Record#    accountno
     2     UC-344
     9     UC-344
     5     AG-349
     7     AG-349
     4     RT-433
     1     BV-334
     3     BV-334
     6     BV-334
     8     BV-334
```

Listing 2.12 Ordered on the Second Character of ACCOUNTNO

Modified indexes offer greater flexibility and control than simple indexes. However, like simple indexes, they have limitations. Sometimes it's necessary to order records according to the contents of more than one field. The *compound index* offers a solution to this problem.

Compound Indexes

A compound index (also called a *complex index*) uses two or more fields to create an indexing order. In most cases the fields must be joined together in a process known as *concatenation*. Only character fields can be concatenated; when any key field is not character type, you must temporarily convert it to character type with a function.

Exercise 8

In this exercise you create indexes that use two or more fields.

1. From the input pane, open ADVERT.DBF:

```
USE ADVERT EXCLUSIVE
```

2. Execute the following commands:

```
SET ORDER TO TAG ACTNO
LIST ACCOUNTNO, PRODUCT
```

The SET ORDER TO command invoked the index tag ACTNO, which you created in Exercise 5. This index is based on the key field ACCOUNTNO (see Listing 2.13).

Chapter 2 Tables, Indexes, and Queries

Note that, although the records are correctly ordered on ACCOUNTNO, they are not correctly ordered on the PRODUCT field.

```
Record#    accountno  product
     5     AG-349     health food
     7     AG-349     E vitamins
     1     BV-334     software
     3     BV-334     software
     6     BV-334     computer boards
     8     BV-334     software
     4     RT-433     electronic entertainment
     2     UC-344     dairy products
     9     UC-344     dairy products
```

Listing 2.13 Ordered on ACCOUNTNO, but Not on PRODUCT

```
Record#    accountno  product
     7     AG-349     E vitamins
     5     AG-349     health food
     6     BV-334     computer boards
     1     BV-334     software
     3     BV-334     software
     8     BV-334     software
     4     RT-433     electronic entertainment
     2     UC-344     dairy products
     9     UC-344     dairy products
```

Listing 2.14 Ordered on ACCOUNTNO and PRODUCT

3. Execute the following commands:

    ```
    INDEX ON ACCOUNTNO+UPPER(PRODUCT) TAG NAME
    LIST ACCOUNTNO, PRODUCT
    ```

   Now the records are ordered correctly, as shown in Listing 2.14. Note that each PRODUCT field is ordered properly within each group of identical ACCOUNTNO fields.

   This INDEX ON command concatenated the ACCOUNTNO field with the PRODUCT field, making them one key value. The ACCOUNTNO field is the *primary key*, the first field in the index expression. The PRODUCT field is the *secondary key*. Had there been a third field in the indexing scheme, it would have been the *tertiary key*, and so on.

   Let's look at an example of a tertiary key.

4. Execute the following command:

    ```
    LIST ACCOUNTNO, PRODUCT, ADPRICE
    ```

Note that the records are ordered correctly on ACCOUNTNO and PRODUCT, but not on ADPRICE (see Listing 2.15).

Record#	accountno	product	adprice
7	AG-349	E vitamins	88000.00
5	AG-349	health food	99443.00
6	BV-334	computer boards	43000.00
1	BV-334	software	433399.00
3	BV-334	software	884430.00
8	BV-334	software	3245.00
4	RT-433	electronic entertainment	596000.00
2	UC-344	dairy products	322929.00
9	UC-344	dairy products	45000.00

Listing 2.15 Not Ordered on ADPRICE

Record#	accountno	product	adprice
7	AG-349	E vitamins	88000.00
5	AG-349	health food	99443.00
6	BV-334	computer boards	43000.00
8	BV-334	software	3245.00
1	BV-334	software	433399.00
3	BV-334	software	884430.00
4	RT-433	electronic entertainment	596000.00
9	UC-344	dairy products	45000.00
2	UC-344	dairy products	322929.00

Listing 2.16 Ordered on All Three Fields

5. Execute the following command:

```
INDEX ON ACCOUNTNO+UPPER(PRODUCT) + STR(ADPRICE,10,2)
    TAG ACTNO6
```

(This is one command; you can enter it all on one line.)

6. Now list out the records.

```
LIST ACCOUNTNO, PRODUCT, ADPRICE
```

The records are ordered as shown in Listing 2.16. The new index tag orders records according to ACCOUNTNO first (the primary index), PRODUCT second (the secondary index), and ADPRICE last (the tertiary index). Note that, just as each PRODUCT field is ordered within each group of identical ACCOUNTNO fields, each ADPRICE field is ordered within each group of identical PRODUCT fields.

7. Close ADVERT.DBF.

Theoretically, you can make compound indexes as complicated as you like. However, the authors suggest restraint. Simple indexes should be used whenever possible because of their

Chapter 2 Tables, Indexes, and Queries   53

relative speed, economy, and resistance to corruption. Even when you create modified and compound indexes, you should keep them as simple as possible. Use all the complexity you need, but no more.

Creating Indexes With the Expression Builder

dBASE for Windows offers tools that create indexes without using commands. The most important of these tools is the *Expression Builder*, a dialog box in which you create key expressions from items in dropdown lists.

Exercise 9

In this exercise you create an index tag that uses the fields ACCOUNTNO and ENDDATE. You design the key expression for this index tag with the Expression Builder.

1. From the input pane, execute the following command:

   USE ADVERT EXCLUSIVE

2. Execute the following command:

   MODIFY STRUCTURE

   The Table Structure dialog box appears.

3. Click **Structure | Manage Indexes**.

   The Manage Indexes dialog box appears, as shown in Figure 2.15.

4. Click the **Create** button.

   The Create Index dialog box appears, as shown in Figure 2.16.

5. Enter MYINDEX in the **Index Name** input field, then press <Tab>.

   The cursor moves to the **Key Expression** input field.

6. Click the tool button at the right of the **Key Expression** input field.

   The Expression Builder appears, as shown in Figure 2.17. The Expression Builder automates the construction of expressions like the one in Step 5 of Exercise 7.

7. Click on the word **Field** in the **Category** box.

   The word is highlighted, and the fields in ADVERT.DBF are displayed in the **Paste** list (see Figure 2.17).

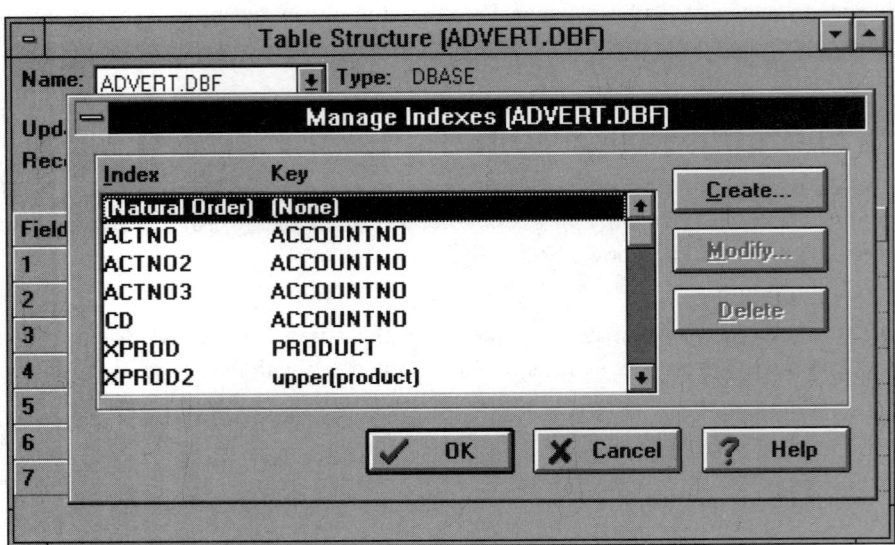

Figure 2.15 The Manage Indexes box appears

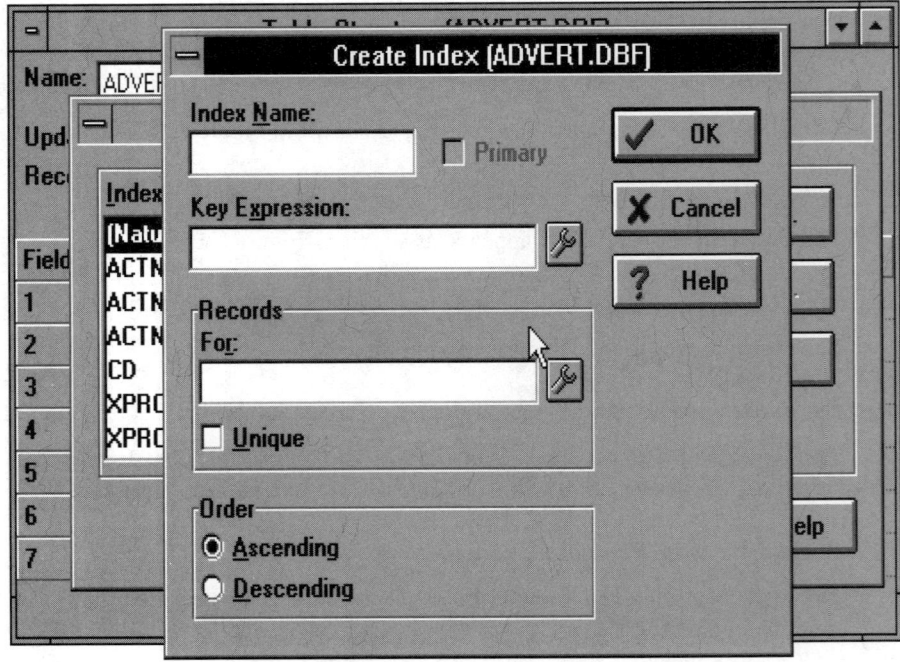

Figure 2.16 The Create Index box appears

Chapter 2 Tables, Indexes, and Queries

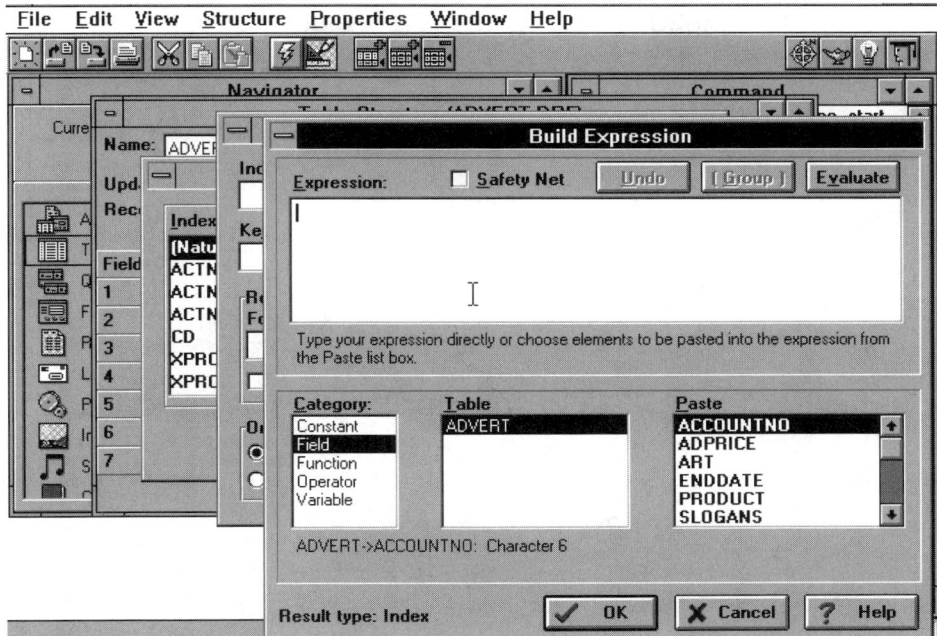

Figure 2.17 The Expression Builder appears

8. Double-click on ACCOUNTNO under the **Paste** heading.

    The following entry appears in the **Expression** box:

    ```
    ADVERT->ACCOUNTNO
    ```

9. Now click on the word **Function** in the **Category** box.

    The word is highlighted and dBASE function names, starting with **ABS( )**, are displayed in the **Paste** list (see Figure 2.18).

10. Click on the scroll bar at the right of the **Paste** list until **DTOS** comes into view, then double-click on it.

    The following entry now appears in the **Expression** box:

    ```
    ADVERT->ACCOUNTNODTOS(expD)
    ```

11. Using the mouse, place the cursor between ADVERT->ACCOUNTNO and DTOS(expD), then enter a plus sign (+).

    The entry should now look like:

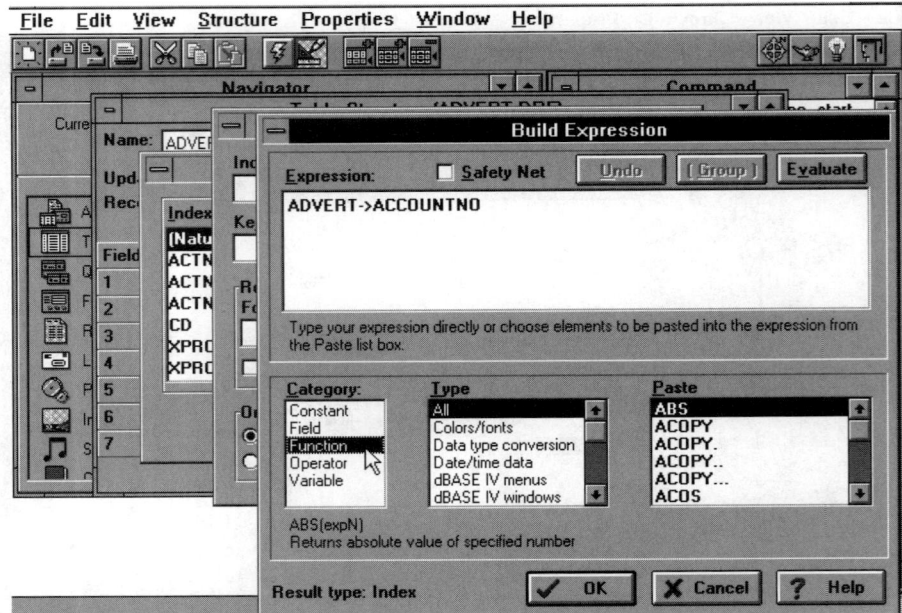

Figure 2.18   dBASE functions appear in the Paste list

```
ADVERT->ACCOUNTNO+DTOS(expD)
```

12. Replace **expD** with ENDDATE.

    The entry should now look like:

    ```
    ADVERT->ACCOUNTNO+DTOS(ENDDATE)
    ```

13. Click OK.

    The Create Index dialog box reappears. Notice that the key expression appears in the **Key Expression** entry field. (If you wish, you can enter key expressions in this field directly.)

14. Click OK.

    The Manage Indexes dialog box reappears.

15. Click on the scroll bar until you can see the new index tag and its key expression, as shown in Figure 2.19.

16. Click OK.

    The Table Structure dialog box reappears.

Chapter 2 Tables, Indexes, and Queries   57

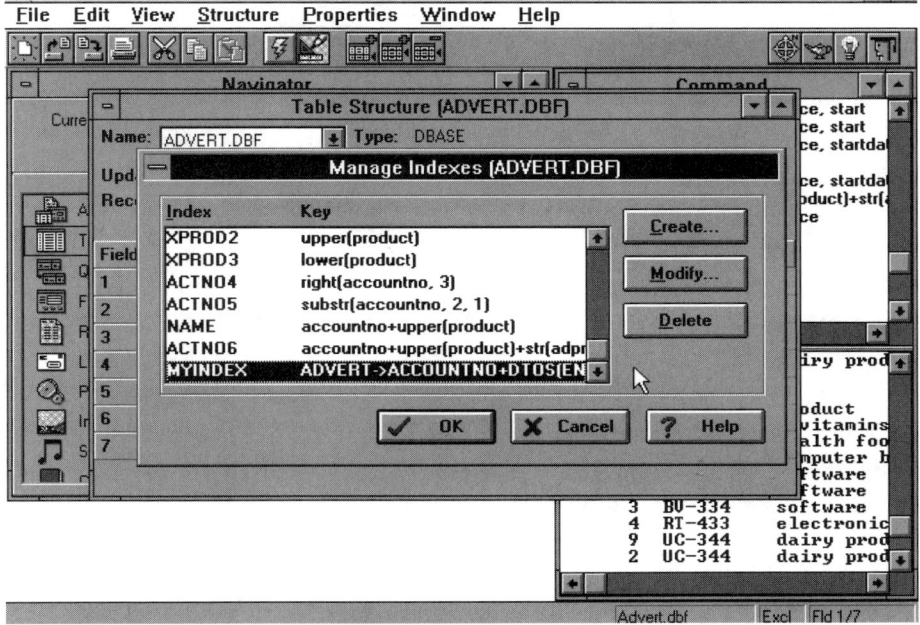

Figure 2.19 MYINDEX tag appears in the Manage Indexes box

17. Double-click on the button at the upper left corner of the Table Structure dialog box.

18. Execute the following commands:

    ```
    SET ORDER TO TAG MYINDEX
    BROWSE
    ```

    Notice that the records are sorted first on ACCOUNTNO (the primary index) and second on ENDDATE (the secondary index).

19. Quit the browse window and close ADVERT.DBF.

QBE

A QBE is a special dBASE program that extracts data from one or more tables and rearranges it into an entity known as an *answer table*. An answer table presents data in an orderly, rational format well suited for report generation and on-screen inquiry. It does this in accordance with the *relational model*, which mandates that all data be extracted and viewed in table form.

A QBE performs the following tasks:

- *Joins two or more table files*--A QBE can join the two or more .DBF files through a connection known as a *link*. A link makes a logical connection between the files on the contents of one or more common fields, known as *key fields*. This joining is called a *relation*. A relation allows the collective information held in all related tables to be viewed as one entity. (A QBE can also access data in a single table.)

- *Imposes a logical order on the data*--A QBE can present information in sorted order. This is comparable, in many ways, to the order provided by an index file; in fact, QBEs can create new indexes or use existing indexes.

- *Hides irrelevant records*--A QBE can make some records visible and hide others. It makes these decisions by comparing the values contained in one or more fields with values specified in the QBE itself.

- *Hides irrelevant fields*--A QBE decides which fields to make visible and which to hide. You can use this feature to provide data security by protecting sensitive fields from unwanted scrutiny.

Although you can write a QBE with the text editor (as with any other dBASE program), the easiest way is to use the *Query Designer*, a powerful tool that does most of the hard work for you. The Query Designer presents a convenient, intuitive design interface that lets you create sophisticated QBEs in minutes. When you finish designing a QBE with the Query Designer, dBASE generates the program code automatically and stores it in a program file with an extension of .QBE.

Exercise 10

In this exercise you join CORP.DBF and ADVERT.DBF in a QBE. In this relation, CORP.DBF is the *parent* and ADVERT.DBF is the *child*, and the relation is said to be *one-to-many*. The one-to-many relation is by far the most common relation in the real world of data management

1. First, be sure all table files are closed by entering the following command:

   CLOSE DATABASES

2. Now enter the following command:

   CREATE VIEW ACCOUNTS

   A dialog box appears, as shown in Figure 2.20.

3. Click on **corp.dbf**, then click the OK button.

   The Query Designer window is displayed as shown in Figure 2.21. Note that the fields in CORP.DBF are displayed horizontally, although only a few are visible because of the size of the Query Designer window.

4. Maximize the Query Designer window by clicking its Maximize button.

Chapter 2 Tables, Indexes, and Queries

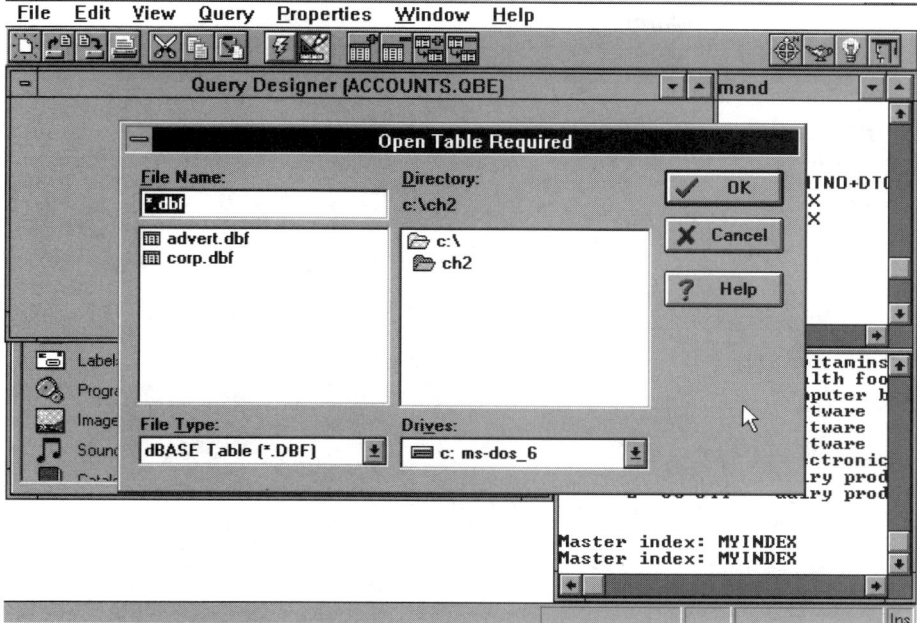

Figure 2.20 The Open Table Required box appears

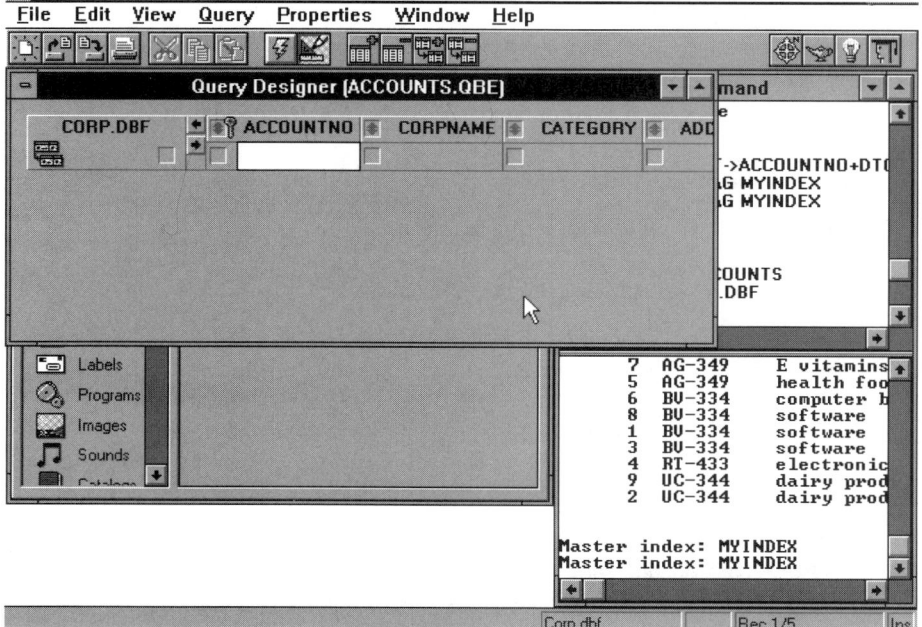

Figure 2.21 The Query Designer window is displayed

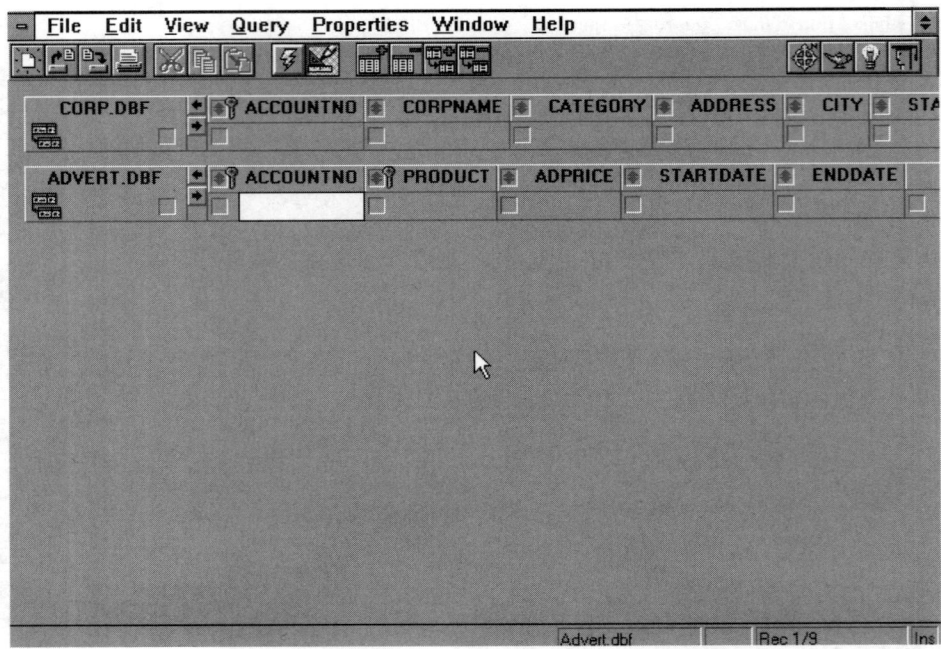

Figure 2.22 Record structures of both tables are displayed

The window now fills the dBASE application window, and more fields are visible.

5. Now click once on the **Query** menu item near the top of the screen.

   The Query menu is displayed.

6. Click on the **Add Table...** option.

   The dialog box you saw in Step 2 reappears.

7. Click on **advert.dbf**, then click the OK button.

   Now the record structures of both tables are displayed horizontally in the Query Designer, as shown in Figure 2.22. Each horizontal display is called a *skeleton*.

8. Place the mouse pointer on the icon at the far left of the CORP.DBF skeleton and hold down the mouse key. Drag the pointer down to the corresponding icon in the ADVERT.DBF skeleton, then release.

   The Define Relation dialog box appears, as shown in Figure 2.23. Note that CORP.DBF appears under **Parent Table** and ADVERT.DBF appears under **Child Table**. Note also that ACCOUNTNO appears under **Field**, and that the **One To Many** check box is tagged. This is what we want.

Chapter 2 Tables, Indexes, and Queries

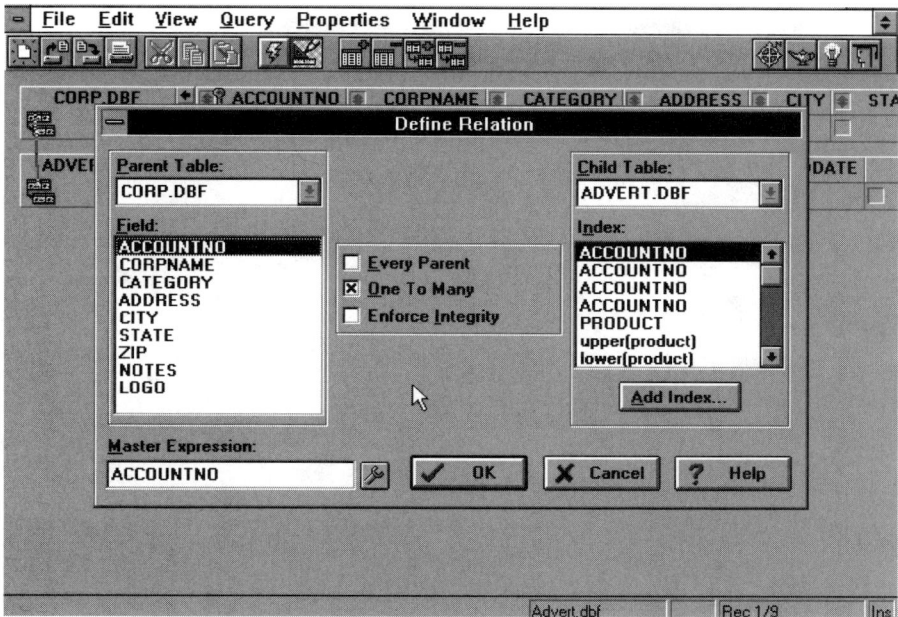

Figure 2.23 The Define Relation box appears

9. Click the OK button.

   Notice that a line runs from the CORP.DBF skeleton to the ADVERT.DBF skeleton, ending with an arrow.

10. Click on the box to the lower right of **CORP.DBF** at the far left of the CORP.DBF skeleton.

    Green check marks appear under each field in the skeleton. Each mark signifies that its field will be included in the answer table of the QBE. However, this isn't what we want for now; we only want a few fields from CORP.DBF to be included.

11. Click on the box again.

    The green check marks disappear.

12. Now click on the boxes of the following fields:

    - ACCOUNTNO
    - CORPNAME
    - CATEGORY

    All three fields (and no others) should now have green check marks.

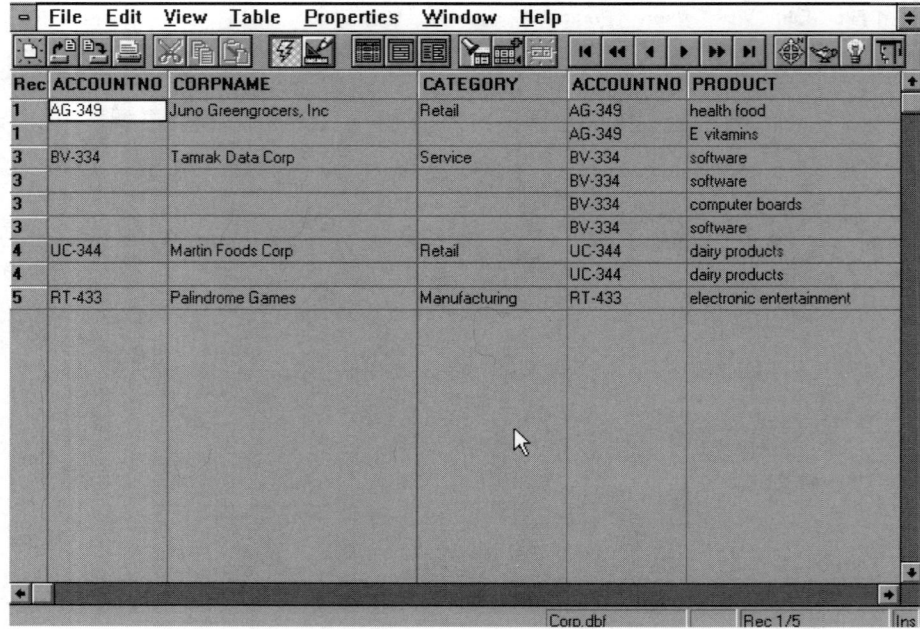

Figure 2.24 The browse window covers the entire screen

13. Now give green check marks to the following fields in the ADVERT.DBF skeleton:

    - ACCOUNTNO
    - PRODUCT
    - ADPRICE
    - STARTDATE

    Now let's run the query to see what we get.

14. Click on the *View table data* icon (the one with the lightning bolt).

    In a few seconds, a browse window appears.

15. Maximize the browse window by clicking on its Maximize button.

    The browse window now covers the dBASE application window, as shown in Figure 2.24.

    Note that all rows are ordered on the ACCOUNTNO field. Note also the ACCOUNTNO field of ADVERT.DBF is duplicated on several records. This is an example of a one-to-many relationship, the most common arrangement when tables are correctly related in a QBE. A QBE with a one-to-many relationship displays each record in the child table (ADVERT.DBF) that has a key value matching a key value in the parent table (CORP.DBF).

16. Restore the browse window by clicking the Restore button at the upper right corner of the window.

17. Quit the browse window.

    A dialog box appears, asking confirmation.

18. Click the **Yes** button.

    The Command window reappears.

19. Close all open tables with the following command:

    CLOSE DATABASES

It is usually best to have only one record per key field value in the parent file if the relationship is one-to-many. For example, it's appropriate that CORP.DBF has only one record with an ACCOUNTNO value of AG-349. The child file, however, can have any number of records with key fields containing duplicated values, just as ADVERT.DBF has two records with ACCOUNTNO values of AG-349.

The tables and the query you created in this chapter are the foundation of the sample applications you develop in the remaining chapters of this book. Before going on to the next chapter, you might want to check your work to make sure it conforms to the instructions contained in the exercises.

What Next?

Now that you have data and a query to extract it, you're ready to manipulate and control it with the elegant OOP language of dBASE for Windows. dBASE for Windows offers the *Form Designer*, a powerful tool that generates dBASE OOP programs automatically. However, the Form Designer can insulate you from the new language, keeping you from learning its secrets. For this reason, we introduce the Form Designer in a later chapter. First, we demonstrate the basics of the OOP language--and get you thinking like an OOP programmer.

Chapter 3
Introduction to OOP

It's not uncommon for experienced dBASE DOS programmers to be more intimidated and confused by object-oriented programming than new programmers who enter the profession with no previous experiences on which to draw. Steeped in the habits and practices of the past, DOS programmers often view the object-oriented paradigm as bizarre, confusing, and unintuitive.

Fortunately, it's a false perception. The fundamental purpose of this book is to show that programming with the dBASE OOP language is actually *easier* than programming in the original dBASE command language. The OOP language of dBASE for Windows lets you develop, in hours, applications that would have taken weeks of conventional programming. In fact, OOP lets you create applications that would have been impossible with the command language of dBASE IV and its predecessors. It puts you in control of the task ahead. It lets you perceive your programming task the way humans perceive ordinary tasks in everyday life.

What Is OOP?

Object-oriented programming is a method of application development that creates, utilizes, and manipulates entities known as *objects*. Objects are convenient tools that save you, the programmer, much time and effort. They provide a framework around which sophisticated and powerful applications are written.

Introducing Objects

Think of an object as a device that you use to accomplish a task. A device has certain features, qualities, and capabilities that make it useful to its owner. In dBASE OOP terminology, these are known as *properties*.

Properties

Your telephone is like an object. It has certain properties that make it different from other devices and (in some ways) from other telephones.

- *It has attributes*. A telephone is white, blue, or some other color. It has a spin-dial or touch-tone buttons. It's mounted on the wall or rests on a surface. In general OOP terminology, such characteristics are often called *attribute properties*. (Although this isn't an official dBASE term, we use it in this book because it's accurate and descriptive.)

- *It responds to events*. A telephone gives a dial tone when you pick up the receiver. It sends a signal to the telephone network when you spin the dial or push a button. It terminates the connection when you hang up. In OOP terminology, such tasks are performed by *event properties*.

- *It performs actions*. A telephone translates your voice into electronic signals. It translates electrical signals into sound waves. In OOP terminology, such tasks are performed by *methods*.

The vast majority of the OOP applications you create with dBASE for Windows use objects as the primary means of managing data. Objects also serve as the main interface between your users and the data they work with.

To understand how objects are made and used, you must understand the concept of object class.

Table 3.1 The dBASE Stock Classes

ARRAY	BROWSE	COMBOBOX	CHECKBOX	DDELINK
DDETOPIC	EDITOR	ENTRYFIELD	FORM	IMAGE
LISTBOX	LINE	MENU	OBJECT	OLE
PUSHBUTTON	RADIOBUTTON	RECTANGLE	SCROLLBAR	SPINBOX
TEXT				

Object Classes

An object class is a category. Each category has a set of properties common to all objects that belong to the category. For example, telephones belong to a very recognizable class of devices; the properties of this class (such as dial tone and signal translation) clearly distinguish telephones over other devices like bicycles, egg beaters, or calculators.

Most object classes have all three property types: attribute properties, event properties, and methods. Some properties are shared in common between most or all classes, while others are unique to one class. For example, the telephone is not the only device class with the color property; in fact, every device class--car, refrigerator, or airplane--has that property. However, very few devices give a dial tone. This property is largely restricted to the telephone class (and perhaps the modem class).

Each object you create in dBASE for Windows belongs to a class. Each class has a different purpose, and each has its own unique set of properties.

Table 3.1 lists the object classes of dBASE for Windows. (There are two other object classes, APPLICATION and FRAMEWINDOW, but they're atypical.) The classes listed in Table 3.1 are known as *stock classes*, since they are intrinsic to the dBASE language and need not be created. There is another type of class called *custom*, which you create according to your own specifications. This subject is introduced in the next chapter.

Creating Objects and Using Properties

In addition to thinking of a class as a category, it's appropriate to think of it as a template; in fact, you create objects from a class in much the same way you create cookies with a cookie cutter. The next exercise shows how.

Exercise 1

In this exercise, you create two objects and view their properties. One object will be of class Form, and the other will be of class Pushbutton. The pushbutton object will be *contained* in the form object, a concept discussed further in Chapter 4.

1. Click the input pane of the Command window.

   The cursor moves to the input pane.

2. Now clear all existing items from memory with the following command:

   ```
   CLEAR ALL
   ```

   It is often wise to execute this command before you perform certain experiments; it eliminates the possibility of interference from previously created items in memory.

3. Enter the following command:

   ```
   xForm = NEW FORM("HI! I'M A FORM OBJECT!")
   ```

   You just created a form object. Its definition is stored in memory, and the object reference variable xForm points to it. (Form objects are also known simply as *forms*, and we'll use this term from here on.)

   In OOP terminology, the command created an *instance* of the Form object class. In fact, whenever you create an object of any type, you create an instance of its object class.

4. Enter the following command:

   ```
   xForm.PushMe = NEW PUSHBUTTON(xForm)
   ```

   You just created a pushbutton (that is, an instance of the Pushbutton object class). The pushbutton is *contained* in the form pointed to by xForm. Among other things, *containership* means that the pushbutton can't be seen or used unless the form is active.

5. Activate the form with the following command:

   ```
   xForm.Open()
   ```

   The form appears, as shown in Figure 3.1. Note that it contains the pushbutton you created in Step 4, and that it's label says "PushButton". Let's change it.

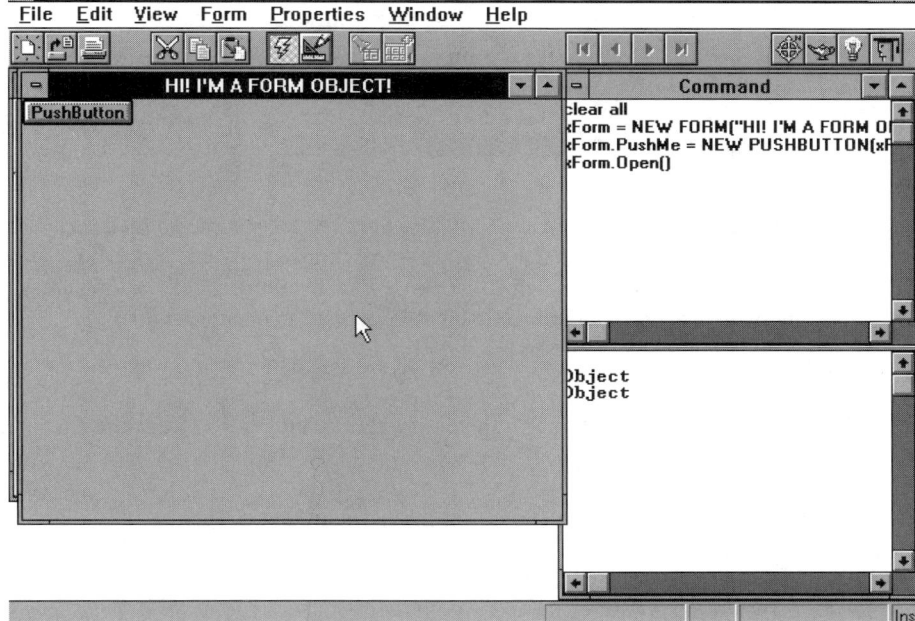

Figure 3.1   The form is opened

6. Click on the input pane of the Command window.

   The Command window moves to the foreground. In dBASE for Windows, the window (or form) in the foreground is said to have *focus*.

7. Change the pushbutton's label with the following command:

   ```
   xForm.PushMe.Text = "Push me!"
   ```

   Note that the change is reflected in the pushbutton instantly.

   The Pushbutton object class has a property called Text that determines what label a pushbutton displays. Other objects, including forms, also have the Text property; in fact, the label at the top of the form (**HI! I'M A FORM OBJECT!**) is contained in the Text property of the form (see Figure 3.1.)

   The Text property is an example of an attribute property. Attribute properties are passive; they don't respond to events or execute actions. They simply change the characteristics of the object.

   Now let's take a look at a more active property.

8. Enter the following command:

```
xForm.PushMe.OnClick = {; ? CHR(7); ? "Thanks!"}
```

You just created a subroutine known as a *codeblock*. Codeblocks are quick and convenient ways of creating short, simple programs and attaching them to objects. This particular codeblock sounds a beep (with the command ? CHR(7)) and displays the character string **Thanks!** in the results pane (with the command ? "Thanks").

You stored the codeblock in the OnClick property of the pushbutton. OnClick is an example of an event property. As the term implies, event properties respond to events. An event is a thing that happens, like a mouse click, a key press, or the closing of a form. The codeblock itself is known as an *event handler*.

9. Click the pushbutton.

   The beep sounds, and **Thanks!** appears in the Results pane. You just executed your first OOP application.

10. Now execute the following commands in the input pane:

    ```
    xForm.MeToo = NEW PUSHBUTTON(xForm)
    xForm.MeToo.Top = 5
    xForm.MeToo.Text = "Close Form."
    ```

    A new pushbutton appears, as shown in Figure 3.2. Note that the new pushbutton is lower than the first one; this is due to the setting you gave the pushbutton's Top property. Top is one of several properties that determine the position and size of objects in a form.

11. Execute the following command:

    ```
    xForm.MeToo.OnClick = {; Form.Close()}
    ```

    This codeblock uses a method (Close(), a property of the Form object class). A method is a property that performs an action, which makes it similar to an event property; however, a method doesn't respond to an event, but must be explicitly executed, much like a procedure or a function.

    The word Form is an object reference that points to the form which contains the pushbutton. dBASE creates this object reference automatically whenever you create an object contained by a form.

12. Click the Close Form button.

    The form disappears. However, its definition and the definitions of the pushbuttons it contains still exist in memory.

    Let's look at another way to close a form.

Chapter 3 Introduction to OOP

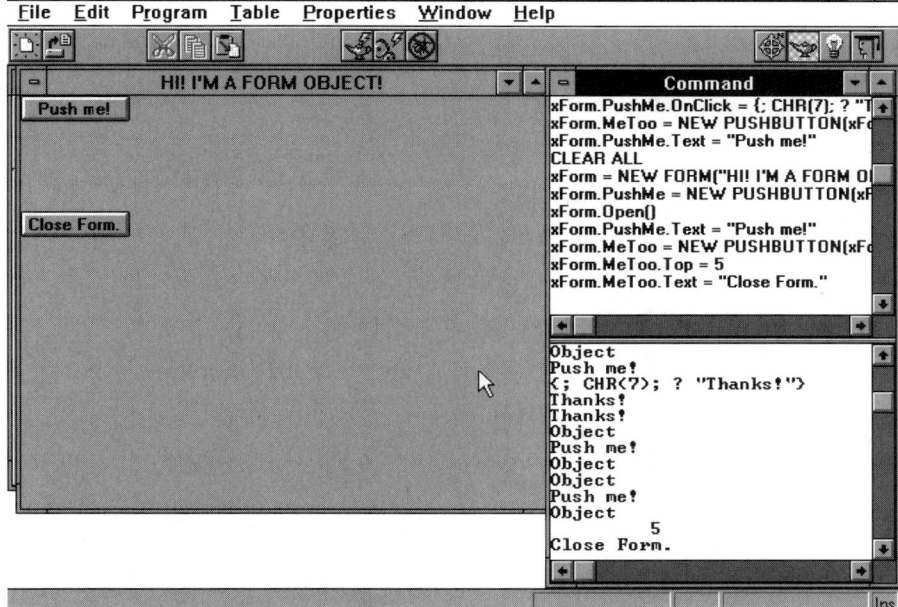

Figure 3.2 A new pushbutton appears

13. Open the form again with the following command:

    ```
    xForm.Open()
    ```

14. Close the form by double-clicking the Control box at the upper left corner.

    The form disappears. As before, all object definitions still exist. The next exercise uses these objects, so don't remove them from memory.

It should already be apparent that OOP programming with dBASE for Windows isn't terribly difficult. It mostly consists of creating objects (which dBASE generates for you) and manipulating their properties. This is a much simpler task than writing code to produce your own user-interface objects. With OOP, you simply create an object from its object class, then tell it what to do!

Using the Object Inspector

dBASE for Windows provides many tools designed to make your job as easy as possible. One of the most important of these tools is the *Object Inspector*, a window that provides access to all of an object's properties. You can use the Object Inspector to view the current settings of the object's attribute properties, or you can change the settings directly and see the results immediately.

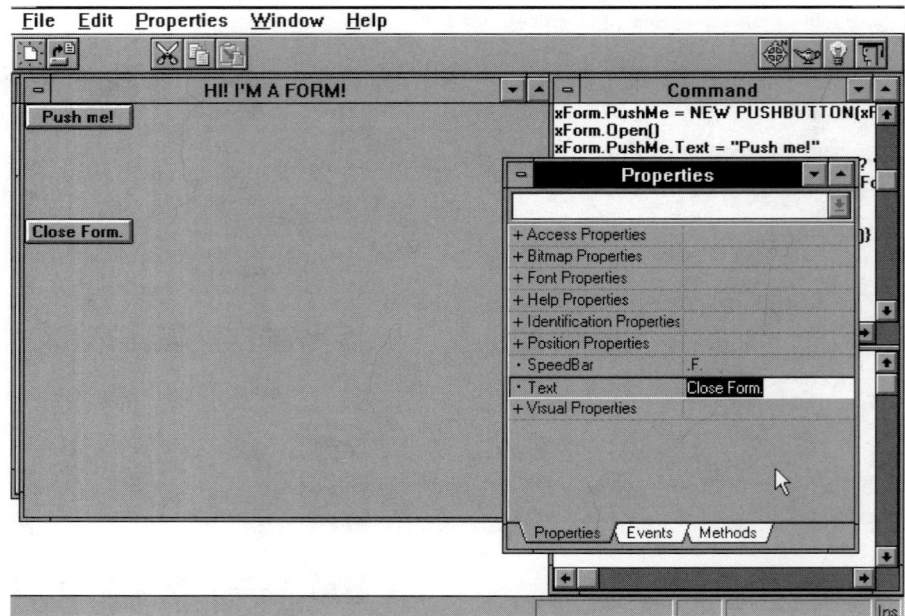

Figure 3.3 The Object Inspector

When you use the Form Designer, you can also use the Object Inspector to write subroutines for the object's event properties. You'll do this in subsequent chapters.

Exercise 2

In this exercise you modify the properties of the form and its pushbuttons with the Object Inspector.

1. Enter the following command in the input pane:

   `xForm.Open()`

   The form you created in the previous exercise appears.

2. Enter the following command in the input pane:

   `INSPECT(xForm.MeToo)`

   The Object Inspector appears, as shown in Figure 3.3.

   Notice the notebook tabs at the bottom of the Object Inspector window, labeled **Properties**, **Events**, and **Methods**. These tabs let you move from page to page, accessing each category of properties.

   The **Properties** page is currently selected. This page provides access to all attribute properties of the object.

Chapter 3   Introduction to OOP   71

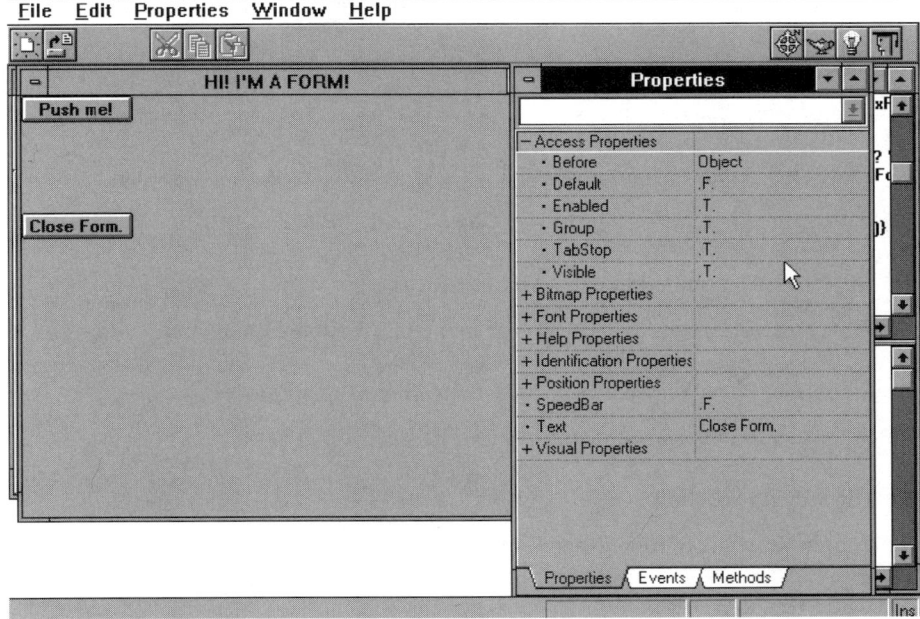

Figure 3.4   A list of properties off the Access Properties menu

3. Double-click on **Access Properties**.

   A list of properties appears under the heading, as shown in Figure 3.4.

4. Click on **Visible**.

   A *tool button* appears at the right.

5. Click the tool button.

   A dropdown list appears, offering .T. (true) or .F. (false).

6. Click on .F.

   Note that the pushbutton disappears. The Visible property, then, determines whether an object can be seen. But does it mean that the object is merely invisible, or does it also mean you can't use it?

7. Attempt to close the form by clicking in the place where the pushbutton once appeared. If you're not sure where it was exactly, make several attempts in several locations.

   The answer is that you can't use an object whose Visible property is set to false (.F.).

8. Using the techniques of Steps 9 and 10, set the Visible property back to true (.T.).

9. Double-click on **Access Properties** again.

    The property list disappears.

10. Now click **Text**.

    The contents of the Text property, **Close Form**, are highlighted.

11. Replace the current contents with **Shutdown**.

    Note that your changes are reflected in the pushbutton automatically.

12. Double-click on **Visual Properties**, then click **MousePointer**.

    A tool button appears at the right.

13. Click the tool button.

    A dropdown list of mouse pointer types appears.

14. Click **10 UpArrow**.

15. Now move the mouse pointer over the pushbutton.

    The mouse pointer changes to an arrow pointing straight up.

16. That's enough for now. Close the form by double-clicking the Control box at the upper left corner.

Covering all of the attribute properties of any object class would take many pages, and goes far beyond the scope of this book. However, you can always use the Object Inspector to experiment with attribute properties to see the effect. The authors encourage you to experiment whenever possible; it's the easiest and quickest way to gain knowledge.

If you're stumped by a property, you can always get immediate assistance through the on-line Help system. Just select the property from the Property Inspector and press <F1>. In a second or two, a description of the property appears, complete with jumps to other related topics. This is known as *context-sensitive Help*, since the Help topic that appears matches the item you selected. In fact, dBASE for Windows provides context-sensitive Help in many other tools besides the Object Inspector.

Programming with Objects and Properties

Now that you're acquainted with objects, you're ready to write your first OOP program. In DOS versions of dBASE, most programs are written with the Text Editor (commonly referred to

Chapter 3 Introduction to OOP

as the *MODIFY COMMAND editor*, or *MODI COMM editor* for short). You can still do it this way, as the next exercise demonstrates.

Creating Event Handlers

Arguably the most outstanding characteristic of objects is that they can be programmed to react to events. In fact, *event* is a key OOP term which means *anything that happens which an object is designed to detect*. For example, form objects (and many others) have a property named OnLeftMouseDown that detects a left mouse click and executes a subroutine in response. Events like mouse clicks or keyboard input are user actions, and they make up the majority of events in dBASE for Windows. However, some events have nothing to do with user actions; for example, if a program moves the record pointer in a table, the OnNavigate property (demonstrated in Exercise 5) detects the event and executes its routine.

Exercise 3

In this exercise you write a simple OOP program that creates a form and several objects to display in it. Instead of using codeblocks, this program uses user-defined functions (*UDFs*) as event handlers. Before you write this program, be sure that the query described in Chapter 2 (ACCOUNTS.QBE) and the two table files it uses (CORP.DBF and ADVERT.DBF) exist in the default directory. If not, perform the exercises in that chapter, and then return to this exercise.

1. Open the MODIFY COMMAND editor and start a program file named NEWFORM.PRG.

   MODIFY COMMAND NEWFORM

2. Enter the program shown in Listing 3.1, save by pressing <Ctrl-W>, and then click the Input pane to give it focus.

```
* A simple OOP program.
CLEAR ALL

AForm = NEW FORM()
AForm.Text = "Click the button!"

AForm.ClickMe = NEW PUSHBUTTON(AForm)
AForm.ClickMe.Top = 5
AForm.ClickMe.Left = 7
AForm.ClickMe.Text = "Click me!"
AForm.ClickMe.OnClick = DoThis

AForm.GetOut = NEW PUSHBUTTON(AForm)
AForm.GetOut.Top = 5
AForm.GetOut.Left = 30
AForm.GetOut.Text = "Quit"
AForm.GetOut.OnClick = GetLost

AForm.Open()
```

```
PROCEDURE DoThis
  CLEAR
  SET VIEW TO ACCOUNTS.QBE
  BROWSE
RETURN

PROCEDURE GetLost
  ? "Goodbye!"
  Form.Close()
  Form.Release()
RETURN
```

Listing 3.1 An OOP Program that Accesses Data

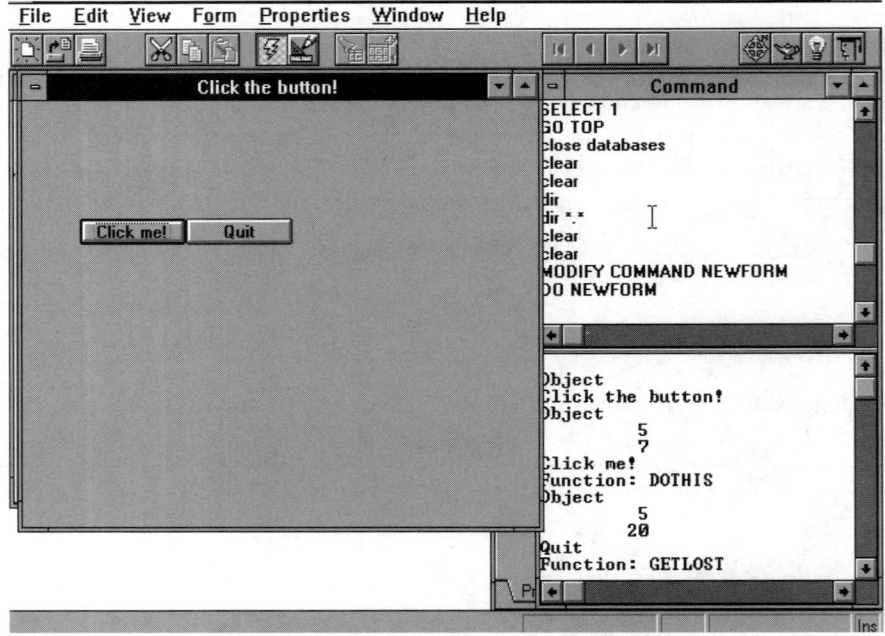

Figure 3.5 Result of running program NEWFORM

3. Run the program with the following command:

   DO NEWFORM

   The form shown in Figure 3.5 appears.

4. Click the **Click me!** pushbutton.

Chapter 3 Introduction to OOP

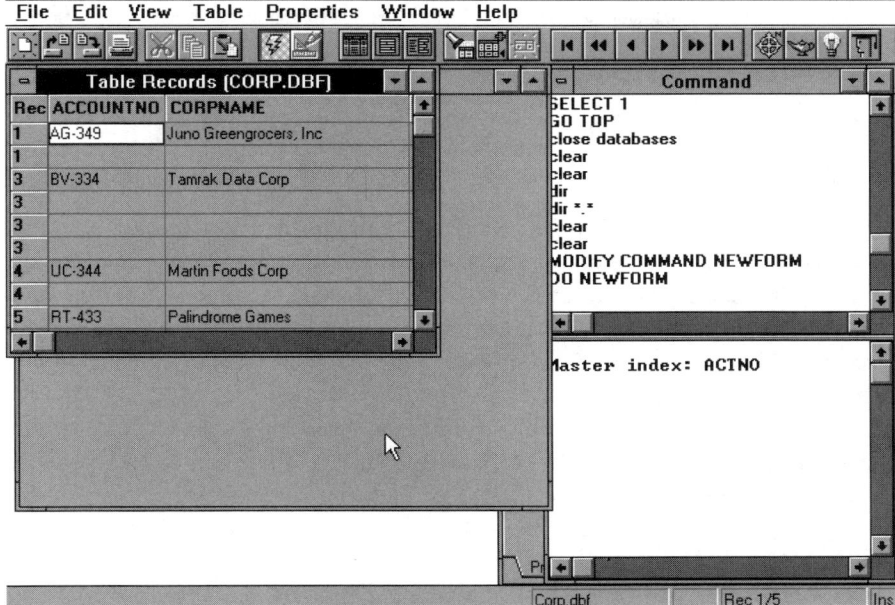

Figure 3.6 Output of ACCOUNTS.QBE

In a few seconds, the browse screen appears, displaying the output of the ACCOUNTS.QBE query (see Figure 3.6).

5. Close the browse screen by double-clicking the Control box at the upper left corner.

6. Click the **Quit** pushbutton.

   The form disappears.

Let's examine the program you just ran (see Listing 3.1). The first line of code following CLEAR ALL creates a new form and an object reference variable (AForm) that points to it.

```
AForm = NEW FORM()
```

Note that every command in the main body of the program (the region after CLEAR ALL and up to but not including PROCEDURE DoThis) uses this variable to reference the form and the objects it contains.

The program created a new pushbutton using the dot operator and the NEW operator:

```
AForm.ClickMe = NEW PUSHBUTTON(AForm)
```

ClickMe is actually two things simultaneously:

- *A new property of the form object*--The command designated ClickMe as a new property. As with any other property of the form, you can access it through the AForm variable and the dot operator.

- *An object reference pointing to the pushbutton*--Just as the AForm variable is an object reference that points to the form, the new ClickMe property is an object reference that points to the pushbutton.

The new pushbutton is said to be *contained* by the form. Containership is an extremely important concept in OOP. When one object is contained by another object, the contained object can exist only when the containing object exists. Furthermore, a contained object can only be used when the container object is active. For example, when you close a form, you make the objects contained in it unreachable and unusable, even though they still exist in memory.

At first, it might seem strange that a property can be added to an object so easily. However, it isn't any stranger than the fact that you can create variables spontaneously, a capability of the dBASE language since the first version of dBASE II. In fact, a property is nothing more than a variable that's tied to an object. For example, the following commands create a new form, and then create a new property named HiThere containing the character string "Hello, Bunky!"

```
Friendly = NEW FORM()
Friendly.HiThere = "Hello, Bunky!"
```

The new property is just as easily accessible as any of the form's built-in properties. For example, you could display the contents of the property in the Results pane with the **?** command, as with:

```
? Friendly.HiThere   && Displays "Hello, Bunky!"
```

The property ClickMe is very similar to HiThere; the only difference is that it contains an object reference instead of a character string.

The browse window you saw in this exercise is a very handy device for viewing and editing data. However, it isn't an *object*; it doesn't belong to an object class, and it doesn't have properties that you can alter. However, dBASE for Windows has an object class named Browse. The objects you create from this class resemble browse windows, but they are actually much more powerful.

Exercise 4

In this exercise you create a browse object. But first, you prepare the form by linking it with a QBE (ACCOUNTS.QBE, which is described in Chapter 2). If you haven't created this query, go back to Chapter 2 and create it, and then return to this exercise.

1. First, be sure that there is nothing in memory that might interfere with the execution of a test program. Enter the following command:

    ```
    CLEAR ALL
    ```

Chapter 3 Introduction to OOP

2. Open the MODIFY COMMAND editor and start a program file named BRFORM.PRG.

   MODIFY COMMAND BRFORM

3. Enter the program shown in Listing 3.2; then save it by pressing <Ctrl-W>, and then click the Input pane to give it focus.

```
* A data entry program.
CLEAR ALL

BForm = NEW FORM("DATA ENTRY FORM")
BForm.Height = 20
BForm.Width = 60
BForm.View = "ACCOUNTS.QBE"

BForm.xBrowse = NEW BROWSE(BForm)
BForm.xBrowse.Height = 15
BForm.xBrowse.Width = 56
BForm.xBrowse.Top = 2
BForm.xBrowse.Left = 2

BForm.Open()
```

Listing 3.2 An OOP Program that Creates a Browse Object

4. Run the program with the following command:

   DO BRFORM

   The form shown in Figure 3.7 appears. It contains a large, gridlike object that resembles the browse window of Exercise 3. In dBASE for Windows terminology, this is called a *browse object*. In its current state, the browse object is said to be in *multiple-record format*, since it displays more than one record at a time.

5. Press <F2>.

   The display format changes to a single-record format known as *form* (see Figure 3.8).

6. Press <F2> again.

   The display format changes to another single-record format known as *columnar* (see Figure 3.9).

7. Change the form back to multiple-record format by pressing <F2> again.

8. Click the scroll bar at the bottom of the browse object three times.

   Note that the fields scroll to the left each time.

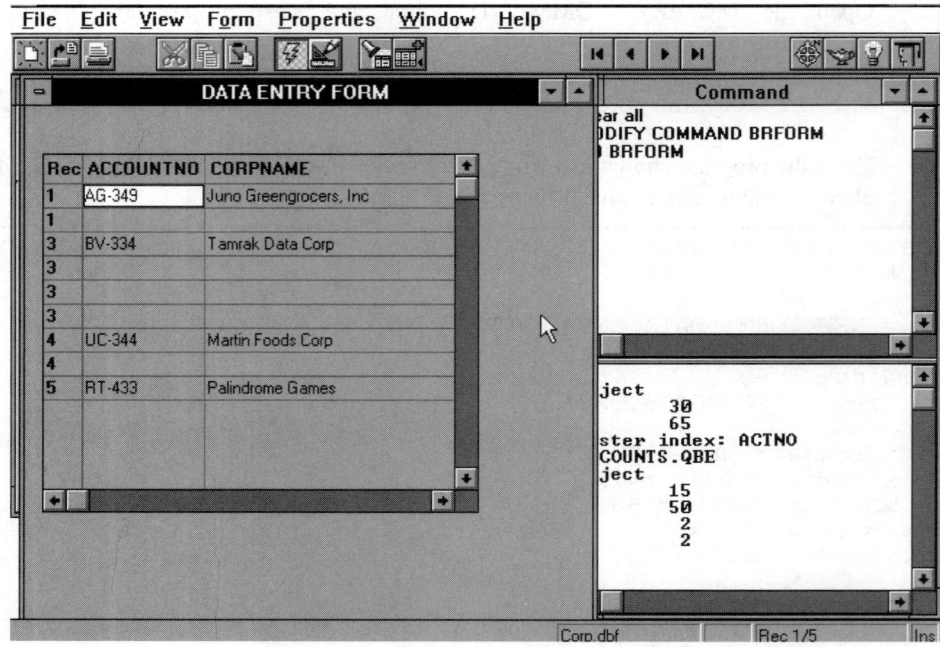

Figure 3.7 The form appears with a browse object

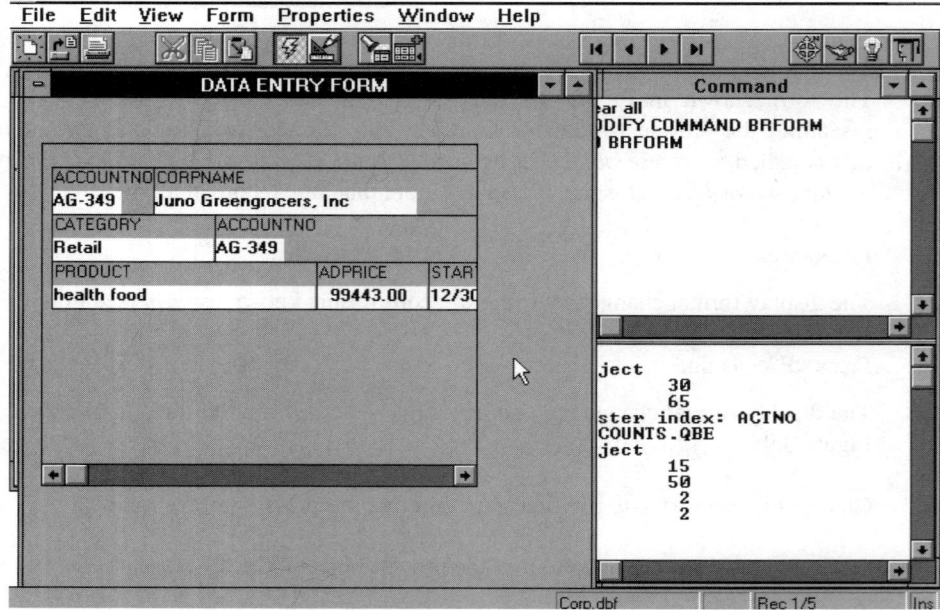

Figure 3.8 The display changes to a single-record format

Chapter 3 Introduction to OOP

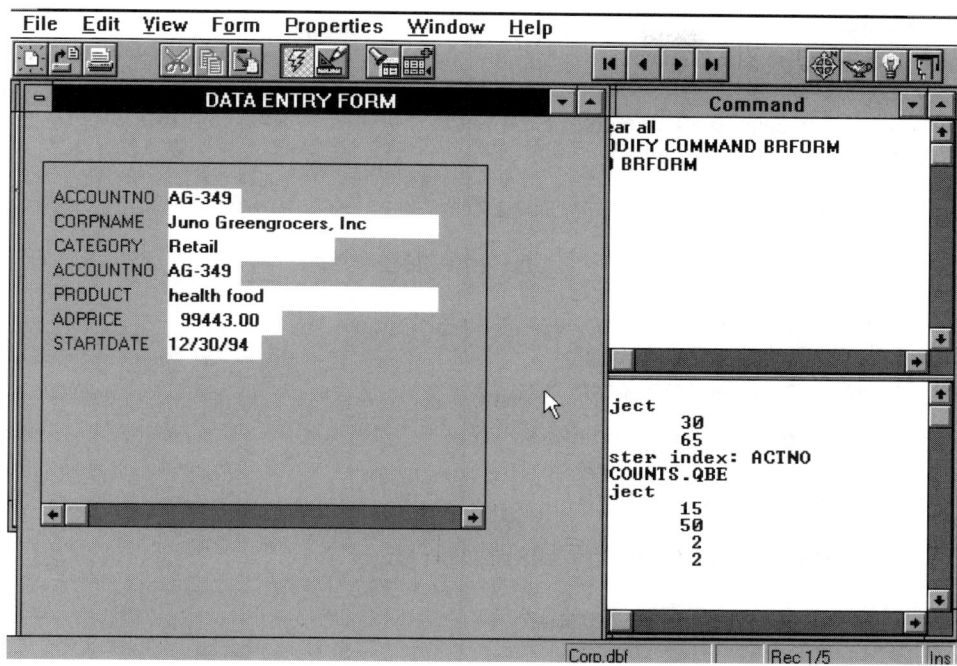

Figure 3.9 **The form changes to yet another single-record format**

9. Now click any field in any record.

   The highlight goes to the field you click on, just as with the browse window of the previous exercise.

10. Experiment with moving from field to field and from record to record a few times. When you're finished experimenting, close the form by double-clicking the Control box at the upper left corner.

Browse objects are arguably the most important data-access objects offered by dBASE for Windows. Like browse windows, they show more data at a time and, when used to alter data, they provide the greatest opportunity to make changes. However, the greatest source of their power comes from the fact that they are *objects*; unlike browse windows, you can enhance browse objects through their properties, and even assign new properties to them. The next exercises provides a brief introduction.

The data that appeared in the browse object was obtained from ACCOUNTS.QBE, which you specified with the View property of a form. When you specify a QBE with the View property, the form is said to be *based* on the QBE. All control objects you place in the form, including browse objects, can access data from this QBE.

Exercise 5

In this exercise you enhance the program you created in the previous exercise. After you make this enhancement, the browse object responds each time you move from record to record in the browse object display. (The name of the record's company is written to a text file named LOGFILE.TXT.)

1. First, make a copy of the program you wrote in Exercise 4.

   COPY FILE BRFORM.PRG TO BRFORM2.PRG

2. Now create LOGFILE.TXT with the Text Editor.

   MODIFY COMMAND LOGFILE.TXT

   Don't enter anything into this new file.

3. Save by pressing <Ctrl-W>.

4. Now open BRFORM2.PRG with the Text Editor.

   MODIFY COMMAND BRFORM2

5. Under the following line of program code:

   BForm.xBrowse.Left = 2

   add the following line:

   BForm.xBrowse.OnNavigate = LogThis

6. Now add the PROCEDURE LogThis the to very end of the program, as shown in Listing 3.3.

```
* A data entry program.
CLEAR ALL

BForm = NEW FORM("DATA ENTRY FORM")
BForm.Height = 20
BForm.Width = 60
BForm.View = "ACCOUNTS.QBE"

BForm.xBrowse = NEW BROWSE(BForm)
BForm.xBrowse.Height = 15
BForm.xBrowse.Width = 56
BForm.xBrowse.Top = 2
BForm.xBrowse.Left = 2
BForm.xBrowse.OnNavigate = LogThis

BForm.Open()
```

Chapter 3 Introduction to OOP

```
PROCEDURE LogThis
  PTR = FOPEN("LOGFILE.TXT", "A")
  FWRITE(PTR, CORP->CORPNAME+TIME()+CHR(13))
  FCLOSE(PTR)
RETURN
```

Listing 3.3 Demonstration of the OnNavigate Method

7. Run BRFORM2.PRG.

   DO BRFORM2

   As before, the form opens and displays the browse object.

8. Click on several different records (at least three).

   As before, the highlight goes from record to record.

9. When you're finished clicking on records, close the form.

10. Now examine the result in LOGFILE.TXT.

    MODIFY COMMAND LOGFILE.TXT

    The contents should look something like Listing 3.4.

```
Palindrome Games           09:51:17
Tamrak Data Corp           09:51:17
Palindrome Games           09:51:17
Flannery Electronics Corp         09:51:17
Palindrome Games           09:51:17
Tamrak Data Corp           09:51:17
Palindrome Games           09:51:17
Martin Foods Corp          09:51:17
```

Listing 3.4 Corporation Names Logged with the FWRITE() Function

Let's examine the subroutine you just wrote and the method that executed it. The event property OnNavigate (a property of browse objects) executes a subroutine each time you move from record to record. In this case, that subroutine was PROCEDURE LogThis.

The first command in PROCEDURE LogThis uses the FOPEN() function to open LOGFILE.TXT, preparing it to receive data.

    PTR = FOPEN("LOGFILE.TXT", "A")

The "A" argument tells dBASE that any new data subsequently entered into the file is appended instead of written over old data in the file. The PTR variable is numeric, and contains a number that identifies the file for subsequent commands.

The next command sends the contents of the CORPNAME field, which is concatenated with the TIME() function and a carriage return character (generated by the CHR(13) function call).

```
FWRITE(PTR, CORP->CORPNAME+TIME()+CHR(13))
```

The carriage return character makes each entry appear on its own line.

The last command closes LOGFILE.TXT, saving the new entries by writing them to the disk

```
FCLOSE(PTR)
```

However, there's a problem with this program: a lack of efficiency. Each time you move to another field, the OnNavigate subroutine opens and closes LOGFILE.TXT. This eats up processor time and reduces the elegance of your application. It would be better to somehow open the file once when the form is opened and then close the file when the form is closed. You'll do that in the next exercise.

Exercise 6

In this exercise you make the form do the work of opening and closing LOGFILE.TXT. You do this with two form properties, OnOpen and OnClose.

1. First, make a copy of the program you modified in Exercise 5.

   ```
   COPY FILE BRFORM2.PRG TO BRFORM3.PRG
   ```

2. Open BRFORM3.PRG with the MODIFY COMMAND editor.

   ```
   MODIFY COMMAND BRFORM3
   ```

3. Add the following line:

   ```
   PUBLIC PTR
   ```

   beneath the following line:

   ```
   CLEAR ALL
   ```

4. Remove the following lines from PROCEDURE LogThis:

   ```
   PTR = FOPEN("LOGFILE.TXT", "A")
   FCLOSE(PTR)
   ```

5. Now add the following two lines:

   ```
   BForm.OnOpen = {; PTR = FOPEN("LOGFILE.TXT", "A")}
   BForm.OnClose = {; FCLOSE(PTR)}
   ```

Chapter 3 Introduction to OOP 83

after this line:

```
BForm.View = "ACCOUNTS.QBE"
```

The program should now look like Listing 3.5.

```
* A data entry program.
CLEAR ALL
PUBLIC PTR

BForm = NEW FORM("DATA ENTRY FORM")
BForm.Height = 20
BForm.Width = 60
BForm.View = "ACCOUNTS.QBE"
BForm.OnOpen = {; PTR = FOPEN("LOGFILE.TXT", "A")}
BForm.OnClose = {; FCLOSE(PTR)}

BForm.xBrowse = NEW BROWSE(BForm)
BForm.xBrowse.Height = 15
BForm.xBrowse.Width = 56
BForm.xBrowse.Top = 2
BForm.xBrowse.Left = 2
BForm.xBrowse.OnNavigate = LogThis

BForm.Open()

PROCEDURE LogThis
   FWRITE(PTR, CORP->CORPNAME+TIME()+CHR(13))
RETURN
```

Listing 3.5 A More Efficient Way to Open and Close LOGFILE.TXT

6. Now execute the program:

   ```
   DO BRFORM3
   ```

   Again, the form is displayed.

7. Click on various records. When you're through, close the form.

8. View the contents of LOGFILE.TXT.

   ```
   TYPE LOGFILE.TXT
   ```

   The new entries are displayed.

Let's examine the changes you made (see Listing 3.5). The OnOpen method (a property of forms) executes a subroutine when a form is opened. The subroutine you used in this example was a codeblock:

```
{; PTR = FOPEN("LOGFILE.TXT", "A")}
```

This codeblock is executed only once during the entire execution of the application--when the form is originally opened. The OnClose method (also a property of forms) executes a subroutine when a form is closed:

```
{; FCLOSE(PTR)}
```

As with the OnOpen codeblock, this codeblock is executed only once.

This is a perfect example of a problem that can be solved more than one way. The fundamental issue is, which properties of which objects should be used to solve a given problem? It's a dilemma you'll encounter many times, and it's often a difficult call, but two considerations always apply:

- To what extent does a particular solution reduce the efficiency of the application? Does it require more steps than another solution? If so, are those steps justified?

- To what extent does the solution box you into a corner, forcing you to write other routines inefficiently? For example, the first solution (in Exercise 5) closed LOGFILE.TXT each time you moved from record to record, making the file unavailable to other any other routines you might write. These routines would also have been required to open LOGFILE.TXT on their own, reducing their efficiency as well.

It's almost always a good exercise to evaluate each solution after you make it. Ask yourself whether another solution might be smarter, and try it. As always, experimentation is the key. The more solutions you try, the likelier you'll hit on the best answer--and the faster you'll master the language.

Creating Custom Properties

You've already seen how you can create new properties for objects spontaneously. Let's take a closer look at this concept now. In the next exercise, you create a new method for the form and execute it.

Exercise 7

In this exercise you create a new property named Greetings(). This property will display some friendly salutations on the caption bar of the form and sound the bell each time.

1. First, make a copy of the program you modified in Exercise 6.

   ```
   COPY FILE BRFORM3.PRG TO BRFORM4.PRG
   ```

2. Open BRFORM4.PRG with the MODIFY COMMAND editor.

   ```
   MODIFY COMMAND BRFORM4
   ```

3. Add the following line:

Chapter 3 Introduction to OOP

```
BForm.Greetings = HelloUser
```

after this line:

```
BForm.OnClose = {; FCLOSE(PTR)}
```

4. Add the following line:

```
BForm.Greetings()
```

after this line:

```
BForm.Open()
```

5. Add PROCEDURE HelloUser, shown in Listing 3.6.

The entire application should now look as it does in this listing.

```
* A data entry program.
CLEAR ALL
PUBLIC PTR

BForm = NEW FORM("DATA ENTRY FORM")
BForm.Height = 20
BForm.Width = 60
BForm.View = "ACCOUNTS.QBE"
BForm.OnOpen = {; PTR = FOPEN("LOGFILE.TXT", "A")}
BForm.OnClose = {; FCLOSE(PTR)}
BForm.Greetings = HelloUser

BForm.xBrowse = NEW BROWSE(BForm)
BForm.xBrowse.Height = 15
BForm.xBrowse.Width = 56
BForm.xBrowse.Top = 2
BForm.xBrowse.Left = 2
BForm.xBrowse.OnNavigate = LogThis

BForm.Open()
BForm.Greetings()

PROCEDURE LogThis
  FWRITE(PTR, CORP->CORPNAME+TIME()+CHR(13))
RETURN

PROCEDURE HelloUser
  INKEY(2)
  ? CHR(7)
  BForm.Text = "HELLO THERE!"
  INKEY(2)
  ? CHR(7)
  BForm.Text = "I'M VERY GLAD YOU'RE LEARNING"
  INKEY(2)
```

```
    ? CHR(7)
    BForm.Text = "OBJECT-ORIENTED PROGRAMMING"
    INKEY(2)
    ? CHR(7)
    BForm.Text = "ENJOY!"
RETURN
```

Listing 3.6 Adding a Greeting Routine to the Application

6. Now execute the program.

   DO BRFORM4

   For the next few seconds, the bell sounds and delivers portions of a greeting message.

7. Close the form.

Let's review the PROCEDURE HelloUser subroutine executed by the new Greetings( ) method (see Listing 3.6). The INKEY( ) function delays execution of the next command for the number of seconds you specify. In our example, INKEY(2) delays execution for two seconds. After the delay, the CHR(7) function call sounds a beep. The Text property of the form is changed, displaying a portion of the greeting message in the form's caption bar. The process is repeated until the entire message is delivered.

Unlike the other routines you've created so far, the Greetings() method was executed explicitly from the body of the program after the form was opened. By contrast, event properties (like OnClick, OnNavigate, OnOpen, and OnClose) execute when specific events take place.

You've seen how the user can interact with objects, and how objects can respond to events. However, objects can also interact with each other, and the actions taken by one object can affect the appearance and behavior of another object. The next exercise demonstrates this ability.

Exercise 8

In this exercise you add two pushbuttons to the form. One pushbutton moves the record pointer forward by one record, and the other moves the record pointer backward by one record. Each movement is automatically reflected in the browse object.

1. First, make a copy of the program you wrote in Exercise 7.

   COPY FILE BRFORM4.PRG TO BRFORM5.PRG

2. Open BRFORM5.PRG with the MODIFY COMMAND editor.

   MODIFY COMMAND BRFORM5

3. Insert the following lines of program code:

   BForm.MoveOn = NEW PUSHBUTTON(BForm)
   BForm.MoveOn.Top = 18

Chapter 3 Introduction to OOP

```
BForm.MoveOn.Left = 15
BForm.MoveOn.Text = "Forward!"
BForm.MoveOn.OnClick = GoAhead
```

beneath this line:

```
BForm.xBrowse.OnNavigate = LogThis
```

These new lines create a pushbutton and position it below the browse object. The OnClick event property of the pushbutton will execute a procedure named GoAhead each time you click the pushbutton.

4. Insert the following lines of program code beneath the code you just inserted:

```
BForm.MoveBack = NEW PUSHBUTTON(BForm)
BForm.MoveBack.Top = 18
BForm.MoveBack.Left = 35
BForm.MoveBack.Text = "Back!"
BForm.MoveBack.OnClick = GoBack
```

These lines create another pushbutton and position it below the browse object and to the right of the other pushbutton. The OnClick event property of the pushbutton will execute a procedure named GoBack each time you click the pushbutton.

5. Now go to the end of the program and add PROCEDURE GoAhead and PROCEDURE GoBack, shown in Listing 3.7.

The program should now resemble this listing.

```
* A data entry program.
CLEAR ALL
PUBLIC PTR

BForm = NEW FORM("DATA ENTRY FORM")
BForm.Height = 20
BForm.Width = 60
BForm.View = "ACCOUNTS.QBE"
BForm.OnOpen = {; PTR = FOPEN("LOGFILE.TXT", "A")}
BForm.OnClose = {; FCLOSE(PTR)}
BForm.Greetings = HelloUser

BForm.xBrowse = NEW BROWSE(BForm)
BForm.xBrowse.Height = 15
BForm.xBrowse.Width = 56
BForm.xBrowse.Top = 2
BForm.xBrowse.Left = 2
BForm.xBrowse.OnNavigate = LogThis

BForm.MoveOn = NEW PUSHBUTTON(BForm)
BForm.MoveOn.Top = 18
```

```
BForm.MoveOn.Left = 15
BForm.MoveOn.Text = "Forward!"
BForm.MoveOn.OnClick = GoAhead

BForm.MoveBack = NEW PUSHBUTTON(BForm)
BForm.MoveBack.Top = 18
BForm.MoveBack.Left = 35
BForm.MoveBack.Text = "Back!"
BForm.MoveBack.OnClick = GoBack

BForm.Open()
* BForm.Greetings()

PROCEDURE LogThis
   FWRITE(PTR, CORP->CORPNAME+TIME()+CHR(13))
RETURN

PROCEDURE HelloUser
   INKEY(2)
   ? CHR(7)
   BForm.Text = "HELLO THERE!"
   INKEY(2)
   ? CHR(7)
   BForm.Text = "I'M VERY GLAD YOU'RE LEARNING"
   INKEY(2)
   ? CHR(7)
   BForm.Text = "OBJECT-ORIENTED PROGRAMMING"
   INKEY(2)
   ? CHR(7)
   BForm.Text = "ENJOY!"
RETURN

PROCEDURE GoBack
   IF .NOT. BOF()
      SKIP -1
   ENDIF
RETURN

PROCEDURE GoAhead
   IF .NOT. EOF()
      SKIP
   ENDIF
RETURN
```

Listing 3.7 Procedures for Moving Forward and Backward Through Records

Chapter 3 Introduction to OOP

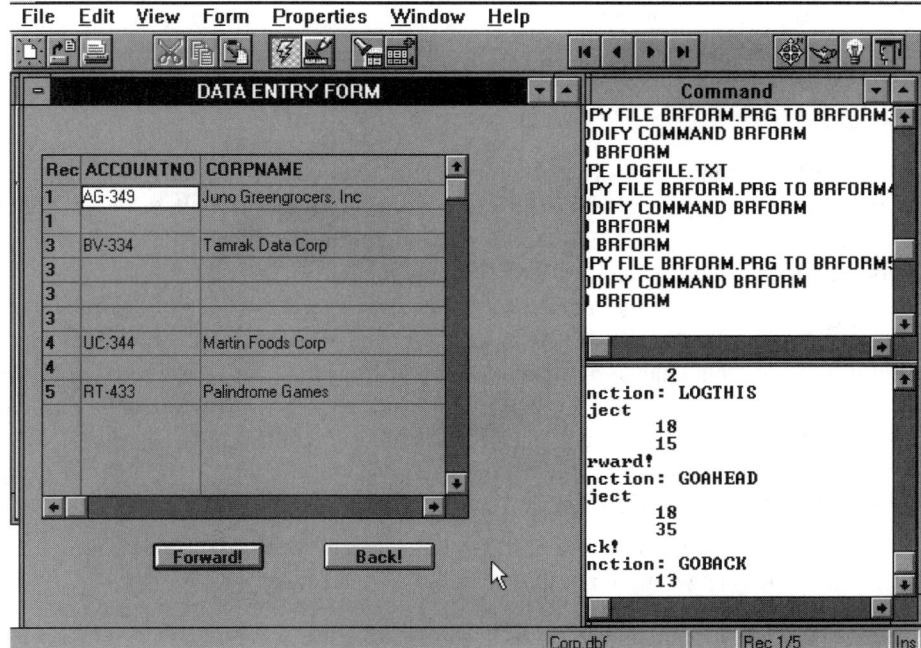

Figure 3.10 Two pushbuttons appear below the browse object

6. This step is optional. You may wish to prevent the opening greeting from appearing the next time you run the program; if so, comment out the following line by placing an asterisk in front of it:

```
BForm.Greetings()
```

7. Save your work by pressing <Ctrl-W>, and then click the Input pane to give it focus.

8. Run the program.

   ```
   DO BRFORM5
   ```

   The two pushbuttons appear below the browse object, as shown in Figure 3.10.

9. Examine the browse object, and note that the highlight is on the first field in the first record. Leave it there for now.

10. Click the **Forward!** pushbutton twice.

    The highlight jumps to the next record each time.

11. Click the **Back!** pushbutton twice.

    The highlight jumps to the previous record each time.

12. Close the form.

This SKIP command moves you from one record to another by resetting the record pointer of the table. PROCEDURE GoBack used the command **SKIP - 1**, which moves the record pointer back by one record. PROCEDURE GoAhead used the command **SKIP**, which moves the record pointer forward by one record.

Each time the record pointer moved forward or backward, the change was reflected in the browse object display. This is an example of how events that occur in one object (say, a click on a pushbutton) can cause a change in another object (the highlight in a browse object). This is a highly important aspect of objects. Because of their ability to interact with each other, you can develop applications that are truly integrated, consistent, and intuitive.

Using the DEFINE Command

So far you have used NEW operator syntax to create forms and other objects. Let's see how the program you just wrote can be rewritten in DEFINE object syntax.

Exercise 9

In this exercise you rewrite the program you wrote in Exercise 8. This time, you use DEFINE object syntax, without using the NEW operator.

1. First, make a copy of the program you wrote in Exercise 8.

    ```
    COPY FILE BRFORM5.PRG TO BRFORM6.PRG
    ```

2. Open BRFORM6.PRG with the MODIFY COMMAND editor.

    ```
    MODIFY COMMAND BRFORM6
    ```

3. Remove the following lines of program code:

    ```
    BForm = NEW FORM("DATA ENTRY FORM")
    BForm.Height = 20
    BForm.Width = 60
    BForm.View = "ACCOUNTS.QBE"
    BForm.OnOpen = {; PTR = FOPEN("LOGFILE.TXT", "A")}
    BForm.OnClose = {; FCLOSE(PTR)}
    BForm.Greetings = HelloUser
    ```

4. Now insert the following lines of program code where the old ones were:

    ```
    DEFINE FORM BForm;
    ```

Chapter 3 Introduction to OOP

```
        PROPERTY;
   Height              20,;
   Width               60,;
   View                "ACCOUNTS.QBE"
   BForm.OnOpen   =    StartLog
   BForm.OnClose  =    EndLog
   BForm.Greetings =   HelloUser
```

Note that the last three lines still use the dot operator. This is fine; dBASE for Windows lets you mix syntax styles.

5. Remove the following lines of program code:

```
BForm.xBrowse = NEW BROWSE(BForm)
BForm.xBrowse.Height = 15
BForm.xBrowse.Width = 56
BForm.xBrowse.Top = 2
BForm.xBrowse.Left = 2
```

6. Now insert the following lines of program code where the old ones were:

```
DEFINE BROWSE xBrowse OF BForm;
   PROPERTY;
   Height              15,;
   Width               56,;
   Top                  2,;
   Left                 2
```

7. Remove the following lines of program code:

```
BForm.MoveOn = NEW PUSHBUTTON(BForm)
BForm.MoveOn.Top = 18
BForm.MoveOn.Left = 15
BForm.MoveOn.Text = "Forward!"
```

8. Now insert the following lines of program code where the old ones were:

```
DEFINE PUSHBUTTON MoveOn OF BForm;
   PROPERTY;
   Top                 18,;
   Left                15,;
   Text                "Forward!"
```

9. Remove the following lines of program code:

```
BForm.MoveBack = NEW PUSHBUTTON(BForm)
BForm.MoveBack.Top = 18
BForm.MoveBack.Left = 35
BForm.MoveBack.Text = "Back!"
```

10. Insert the following lines of program code where the old ones were:

```
DEFINE PUSHBUTTON MoveBack OF BForm;
    PROPERTY;
    Top                 18,;
    Left                35,;
    Text                "Back!"
```

11. Finally, add the following procedure declarations at the very end of the program:

```
PROCEDURE StartLog
    PTR = FOPEN("LOGFILE.TXT", "A")
RETURN

PROCEDURE EndLog
    FCLOSE(PTR)
RETURN
```

The program should now look like Listing 3.8.

```
* A data entry program.
CLEAR ALL
PUBLIC PTR

DEFINE FORM BForm;
    PROPERTY;
    Height              20,;
    Width               60,;
    View                "ACCOUNTS.QBE"
    BForm.OnOpen =      StartLog
    BForm.OnClose =     EndLog
    BForm.Greetings =   HelloUser

DEFINE BROWSE xBrowse OF BForm;
    PROPERTY;
    Height              15,;
    Width               56,;
    Top                  2,;
    Left                 2
    BForm.xBrowse.OnNavigate = LogThis
```

Chapter 3 Introduction to OOP   93

```
DEFINE PUSHBUTTON MoveOn OF BForm;
  PROPERTY;
  Top                     18,;
  Left                    15,;
  Text                    "Forward!"
  BForm.MoveOn.OnClick = GoAhead

DEFINE PUSHBUTTON MoveBack OF BForm;
  PROPERTY;
  Top                     18,;
  Left                    35,;
  Text                    "Back!"
  BForm.MoveBack.OnClick = GoBack


BForm.Open()
* BForm.Greetings()

PROCEDURE LogThis
  FWRITE(PTR, CORP->CORPNAME+TIME()+CHR(13))
RETURN

PROCEDURE HelloUser
  INKEY(2)
  ? CHR(7)
  BForm.Text = "HELLO THERE!"
  INKEY(2)
  ? CHR(7)
  BForm.Text = "I'M VERY GLAD YOU'RE LEARNING"
  INKEY(2)
  ? CHR(7)
  BForm.Text = "OBJECT-ORIENTED PROGRAMMING"
  INKEY(2)
  ? CHR(7)
  BForm.Text = "ENJOY!"
RETURN

PROCEDURE GoBack
  IF .NOT. BOF()
     SKIP -1
  ENDIF
RETURN

PROCEDURE GoAhead
  IF .NOT. EOF()
     SKIP
  ENDIF
RETURN

PROCEDURE StartLog
  PTR = FOPEN("LOGFILE.TXT", "A")
RETURN

PROCEDURE EndLog
```

```
   FCLOSE(PTR)
RETURN
```

Listing 3.8 Using DEFINE Object Syntax

12. Save your work and exit by pressing <Ctrl-W>.

13. Run BRFORM6.PRG

    ```
    DO BRFORM6
    ```

    The program runs as it did before.

The DEFINE object syntax is simply an alternative way to create and modify objects. Many programmers consider it more elegant and easy to use than NEW object syntax. Let's examine the DEFINE command that created one of the pushbuttons.

```
DEFINE PUSHBUTTON MoveBack OF BForm;
   PROPERTY;
   Top              18,;
   Left             35,;
   Text             "Back!"
```

Believe it or not, this is a single command, even though it consists of five lines. Note that all but the last line of code end with a semicolon; in the dBASE language, this means that the command is continued on the next line.

The first line of the command declares the name of the object reference variable (MoveBack) that points to the pushbutton. It also identifies BForm as the object reference pointing to the form in which the pushbutton is contained. Since the form contains the pushbutton, the BForm object reference points to the MoveBack object reference. Note, for example, that you were able to use both variables to assign actions to the pushbutton:

```
BForm.MoveBack.OnClick = GoBack
```

The second line of the command uses the PROPERTY keyword to tell dBASE that the next lines make property settings. The last three lines of the command set the values for three properties, Top, Left, and Text. The Top property determines the vertical positioning of the pushbutton; setting Top to 18 places the top of the pushbutton at the 18th line in the form. The Left property determines the horizontal position of the pushbutton; setting Left to 35 places the left border of the object at the 35th column. The Text property specifies the label to display on the pushbutton (in this case, **Back!**).

What Next?

The classes you've worked with so far are powerful and easy to work with. However, just as you can design custom properties, you can also design custom classes. This amazing OOP feature is introduced in the next chapter.

Chapter 4
Custom Classes

The previous chapter demonstrated how easy it is to create an instance of a class (that is, an object with the characteristics of that class). But what if the object you need differs from the 21 stock classes offered by dBASE for Windows? Is there any way to create a class that suits your needs exactly?

Fortunately, you almost always can. dBASE for Windows lets you use the stock classes to create new classes according to your own specifications. Such classes are known as custom classes. Custom classes give you an extra measure of power and control; they are resources that you design to solve specific problems.

Once you create a custom class, you can create instances of the class just as easily as an instance of a stock class. As with stock classes, each new instance of a custom class automatically takes on the attributes of the class.

Creating Custom Classes

You create a custom class with the CLASS...ENDCLASS command, which specifies the characteristics of the new class and gives it a name. It doesn't have to stop there; you can use CLASS...ENDCLASS to create new classes from the custom class just as easily. This capability gives the dBASE for Windows language incredible power, since it puts you in control of the resources available to you.

The key to this power is an OOP concept known as *inheritance*.

Inheritance

Inheritance is the automatic acquisition of a class's properties by a new custom class. That is, when you create a custom class from another class, the new class has all the properties of the old one (plus all custom properties you declare for the new class).

Exercise 1

In this exercise you derive a new class from the Form class. Objects derived from this new class identify you as its owner through six custom properties.

1. First, clear memory of any extraneous items.

    ```
    CLEAR ALL
    ```

2. Start a program named MYFORM with the Text Editor.

Chapter 4 Custom Classes

MODI COMM MYFORM

Executing MODIFY COMMAND like this is legal; you can input only the first four letters of commands and functions in dBASE. However, you can't abbreviate property names.

3. Write the program shown in Listing 4.1.

   The program displays the name and address of a mythical person named Chris Nelson in the Results pane of the Command window. However, you might want to put your own name and address in the program instead.

```
* A form that identifies its owner!
CLEAR
SET TALK OFF
AForm = NEW NEWFORM()
AForm.Open()
? TRIM(AForm.FName), AForm.LName
? AForm.Street
? TRIM(AForm.City)+", "+;
  AForm.State+" "+AForm.Zip

CLASS NewForm OF FORM
   Height = 20
   Width = 30
   this.FName = "Chris"
   this.LName = "Nelson"
   this.Street = "5784 Newlark Dr."
   this.City = "Sunnyvale"
   this.State = "CA"
   this.Zip = "94087"
ENDCLASS
```

Listing 4.1 A Custom Class (NewForm) Derived from the Form Class

4. Save the program and exit with <Ctrl-W>.

5. Run the program.

   DO MYFORM

   An empty form appears, as shown in Figure 4.1. Note also that the name and address appear in the results pane of the Command window.

6. Close the form by double-clicking it in the upper left corner.

The program you just wrote and executed created a new custom class with the CLASS...ENDCLASS command (see Listing 4.1). The commands between the first line of the command (CLASS NewForm OF FORM) and the last line (ENDCLASS) are called *contructor code*. Constructor code defines the properties and the default property settings of the new class. For example, the first line of constructor code sets the default height of each form derived from the class at 20 rows:

```
this.Height = 20
```

In other words, when you create a form from this class it is initially 20 rows high. Likewise, the form is 30 columns wide due to the Width specification. Both Height and Width are stock properties of the Form object class (and others), and were inherited from the Form object class. In fact, because of inheritance, the new class has all the properties of the Form class.

The new class also has six custom properties: FName, LName Street, City, State, and Zip. (These are attribute properties, since they only contain inactive values; that is, they perform no actions and don't react to events.)

Of course, you could just as easily store the values contained in these custom properties in memory variables instead, as with:

```
FName = "Chris"
LName = "Nelson"
Street = "5784 Newlark Dr."
City = "Sunnyvale"
State = "CA"
Zip = "94087"
```

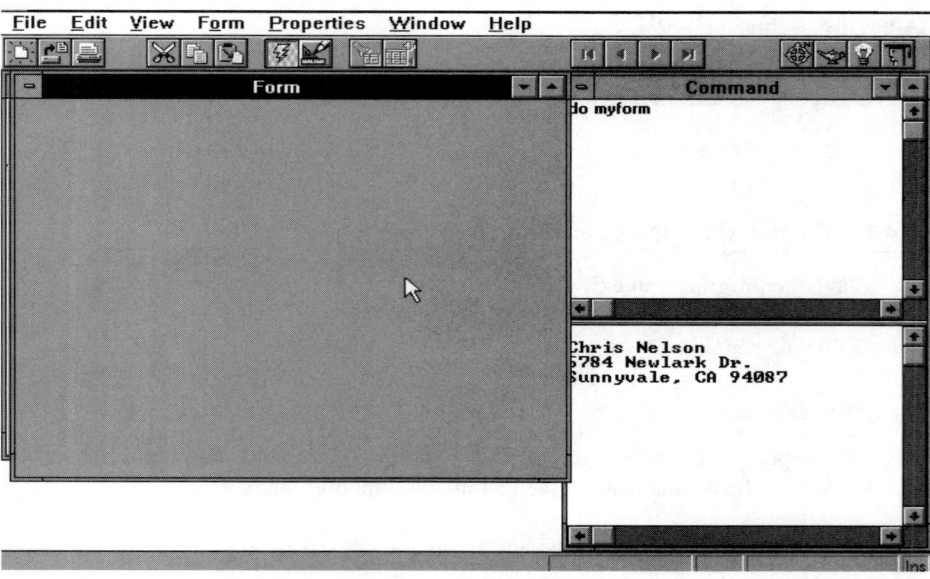

Figure 4.1 An empty form appears

However, storing information this way is obsolete and misses out on much of the power of OOP. By storing values in properties instead of memory variables, you insulate them from the rest of the program, in effect hiding them. Consequently, you can reuse the names of each property by assigning them to other objects. For example, the following commands create two new forms, then add a new custom property to each:

```
OneForm = NEW form()
TwoForm = NEW Form()
OneForm.LName = "Beatty"
TwoForm.LName = "Smith"
```

Although each property has the same name, they are different entities because they belong to different objects.

Storing values in properties instead of memory variables is known as *encapsulation*. Encapsulation is usually the preferred method for storing values in memory. In fact, there are many dBASE for Windows applications that, except for the variable that contains the object reference for the main form, don't use a single conventional memory variable!

Notice that the keyword *this* is used in the class description wherever a custom property is declared. *this* is often referred to as the *member call operator*. dBASE treats this operator as an object reference pointing to a custom property of the new class. Any time you declare a new object class and create a custom property, use *this* to reference it.

You created an instance of this class with the NEW operator:

```
AForm = NEW NewForm()
```

Since the NewForm object class inherited all the properties of the Form object class, the new instance has the Open( ) property:

```
AForm.Open()
```

In OOP terminology, the Form object class is the *base class*, since it was the class that the NewForm object class was derived from. The NewForm object class is the *sub class*, since it was derived from another class. Some programmers use different terminology for the base class; to them, FORM is the *superclass*. This book uses the term base class for any class from which other classes are derived.

Custom Methods

You've already been introduced to the concept of custom properties; simply put, a custom property is a property you design. In the previous exercise you added custom attribute properties to a custom class. You can also add method properties to a custom class and execute them.

In the previous program, the contents of the six custom properties were displayed. This was done by commands outside of the CLASS...ENDCLASS declaration and after the creation of an object from the class. It's usually better to place such commands in a subroutine inside of the class declaration itself, transforming the commands into a custom method. The next exercise shows how.

Exercise 2

In this exercise you convert a section of program code to a custom method. You declare this method within the CLASS...ENDCLASS command, so any new object derived from the class has this method as one of its properties.

1. First, make a backup copy of the program you created in Exercise 1.

   ```
   COPY FILE MYFORM.PRG TO MYFORM2.PRG
   ```

2. Now open MYFORM2.PRG with the Text Editor.

   ```
   MODI COMM MYFORM2
   ```

3. Remove the following lines of program code:

   ```
   ? TRIM(AForm.FName), AForm.LName
   ? AForm.Street
   ? TRIM(AForm.City)+", "+;
     AForm.State+" "+AForm.Zip
   ```

   (You might want to transfer this code into the Windows Clipboard instead of merely deleting it, since you'll be reproducing it later. To do this, point to the left of the first character, hold down the mouse key, then drag the pointer to a position after the last character. This highlights the code. Press <Ctrl-X>. The code disappears, and now resides in the Clipboard.)

4. Replace the code with the following line:

   ```
   AForm.ListAddr()
   ```

5. Add the following line:

   ```
   this.ListAddr = CLASS::ListOut
   ```

   after this line:

   ```
   this.Zip = "94087"
   ```

```
PROCEDURE ListOut
   ? TRIM(Form.FName), Form.LName
   ? Form.Street
   ? TRIM(AForm.City)+", "+;
     Form.State+" "+AForm.Zip
RETURN
```

Listing 4.2 A Custom Method Declared in a CLASS...ENDCLASS Declaration

6. Add PROCEDURE ListOut, shown in Listing 4.2. Be sure to add it at the end of the CLASS...ENDCLASS declaration, but *before* the ENDCLASS command line.

   (If you transferred the code in Step 3 to the Windows Clipboard, copy it into the procedure automatically. To do this, place the cursor in the position where you want the code to be inserted; then press <Ctrl-V>. However, if you do it this way, you'll have to delete the "A" from all occurrences of "AForm".)

   Your program should now look like the one in Listing 4.3.

```
CLEAR
SET TALK OFF
AForm = NEW NEWFORM()
AForm.Open()
AForm.ListAddr()

CLASS NewForm OF FORM
   this.Height = 20
   this.Width = 30
   this.FName = "Chris"
   this.LName = "Nelson"
   this.Street = "5784 Newlark Dr."
   this.City = "Sunnyvale"
   this.State = "CA"
   this.Zip = "94087"
   this.ListAddr = CLASS::ListOut

   PROCEDURE ListOut
      ? TRIM(form.FName), form.LName
      ? form.Street
      ? TRIM(form.City)+", "+;
        form.State+" "+form.Zip
   RETURN

ENDCLASS
```

Listing 4.3 Five Custom Attribute Properties, One Custom Method Property

7. Save the program with <Ctrl-W>.

8. Run the program.

   DO MYFORM2

   The form opens, and your address is displayed as before.

9. Close the form by double-clicking it in the upper left corner.

The OOP term for the section of code containing PROCEDURE ListOut is not constructor code, but *member functions* code. (Don't be confused by this term; member functions code can contain procedures *and* functions.) Member functions code defines all custom methods for the new class.

At first glance, it may not seem like much was gained by converting the lines of code to a custom method. However, it now takes only one line of code to display your address:

```
AForm.ListAddr()
```

Not having to repeat all four lines of program code is quite a blessing. The subroutine can now be used over and over by other parts of the application, and needn't be repeated anywhere. This blessing is magnified many times when a subroutine is pages long. Making routines into methods is sometimes referred to as *modularization*. This term applies when any chunk of program code is converted into a reusable subroutine, whether that routine is a procedure, a UDF, or a method.

Just as you referenced the class's properties with the *this* keyword, you referenced the form itself with *form* in PROCEDURE ListOut. These two keywords are important language elements, so let's state the rules for their usage explicitly:

- Use *this* in constructor code to reference the custom properties of the new class you are creating.

- Use *form* in member functions code to reference properties of the form.

The custom method ListAddr executes the subroutine PROCEDURE ListOut. This routine was assigned to ListAddr with the following command:

```
this.ListAddr = CLASS::ListOut
```

The CLASS keyword is a bit like the *this* operator. However, while *this* references a property of a class, CLASS references the class itself. Translated into ordinary English, the entire command above says "ListAddr is a custom method of this class, and it executes a subroutine named ListOut." The double colons separating the CLASS keyword from the ListOut function pointer form a symbol that, translated into English, means "ListOut is a subroutine belonging to this custom class."

Containership

When control objects like scroll bars, browse objects, and list boxes are displayed in a form (as shown in Figure 4.2), the control objects are said to be *contained* by the form object. When one object is contained by another, the containing object has a property that holds an object reference pointing to the contained object. You'll see what that means in a moment.

A contained object can't exist independent of its containing object. For example, when a containing object is removed from memory, the contained object is removed from memory automatically. Because of this dependency, the containing object is called the *parent* object, and the contained object is called the *child* object.

Chapter 4 Custom Classes

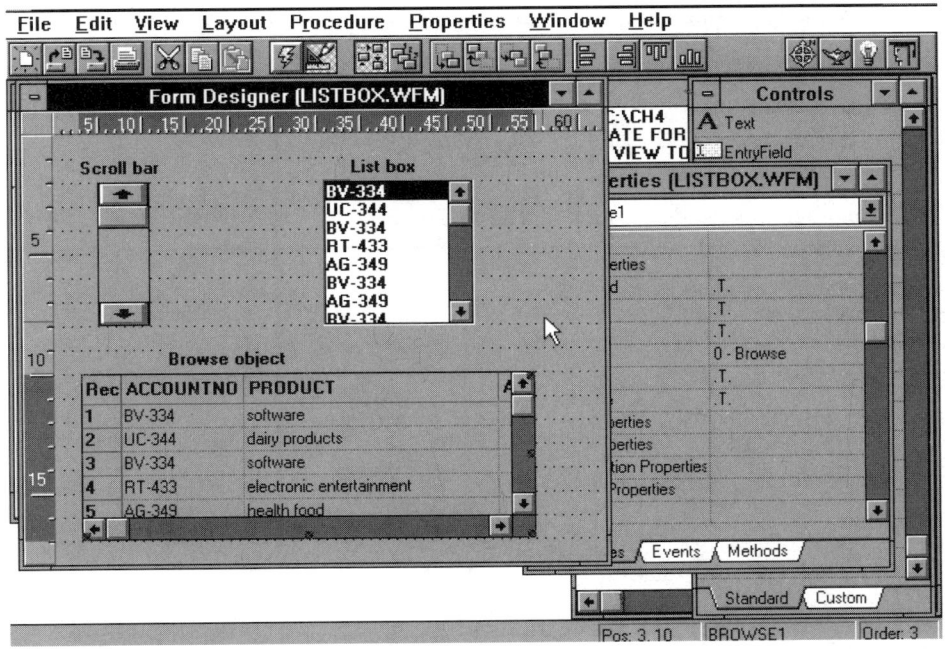

Figure 4.2 A scroll bar, a browse object, and a list box are displayed

Exercise 3

In this exercise you incorporate a browse object definition into the definition of the NewForm object class. Since the browse object definition is contained by the NewForm object class, all objects derived from the NewForm class have a property containing an object reference that points to the browse object.

1. First, make a backup copy of the program you created in Exercise 2.

   ```
   COPY FILE MYFORM2.PRG TO MYFORM3.PRG
   ```

2. Now open MYFORM.PRG with the Text Editor.

   ```
   MODI COMM MYFORM3
   ```

3. Place the following line of program code:

   ```
   this.View = "ACCOUNTS.QBE"
   ```

   under this line:

   ```
   this.ListAddr = CLASS::ListOut
   ```

4. Now enter the following lines of program code under the line you created in Step 3:

```
DEFINE BROWSE NewBrowse OF THIS;
   PROPERTY;
      Height          10,;
      Width           58
```

The program should now look like Listing 4.4.

```
CLEAR
SET TALK OFF
AForm = NEW NEWFORM()
AForm.Open()
AForm.ListAddr()

CLASS NewForm OF FORM
   this.Height = 14
   this.Width = 60
   this.FName = "Chris"
   this.LName = "Nelson"
   this.Street = "5784 Newlark Dr."
   this.City = "Sunnyvale"
   this.State = "CA"
   this.Zip = "94087"
   this.ListAddr = CLASS::ListOut
   this.View = "ACCOUNTS.QBE"

   DEFINE BROWSE NewBrowse OF THIS;
      PROPERTY;
         Height          10,;
         Width           58

   PROCEDURE ListOut
      ? TRIM(form.FName), form.LName
      ? form.Street
      ? TRIM(form.City)+", "+;
        form.State+" "+form.Zip
   RETURN
ENDCLASS
```

Listing 4.4 A Browse Object Contained by the NewForm Object Class

5. Save the program with <Ctrl-W>.

6. Run the program.

   DO MYFORM3

   The form opens, this time with a browse object (see Figure 4.3). The browse object is *contained* by the form object.

Chapter 4 Custom Classes

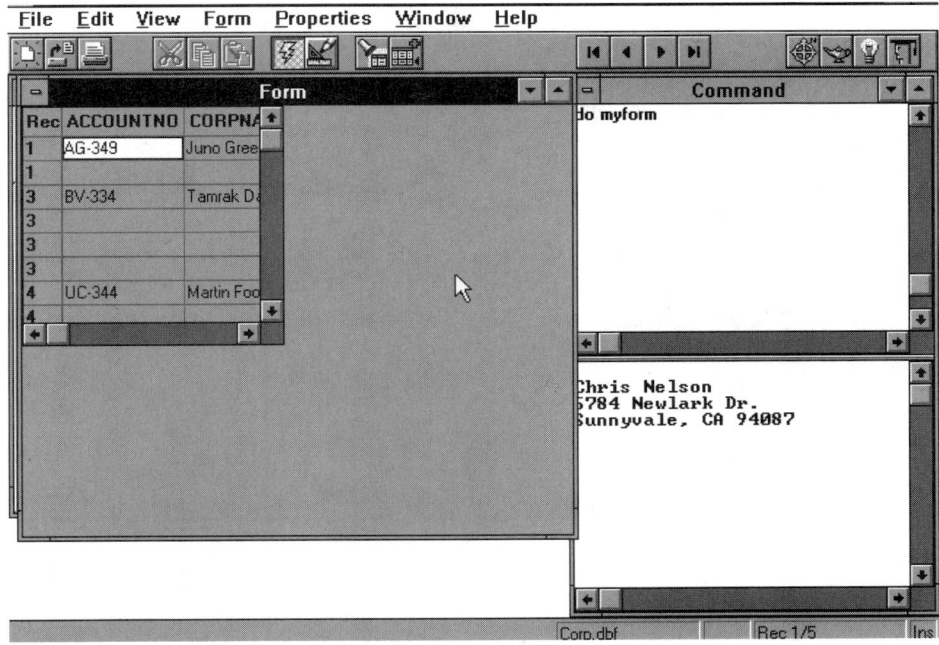

Figure 4.3 The browse object is contained by the form object

7. Close the form by double-clicking it in the upper-left corner.

8. Now open MYFORM3.PRG with the Text Editor.

   MODI COMM MYFORM3

9. Place the following line of program code:

   INSPECT(AForm)

   under this line:

   AForm.ListAddr()

10. Save the program with <Ctrl-W>.

11. Run the program.

    DO MYFORM3

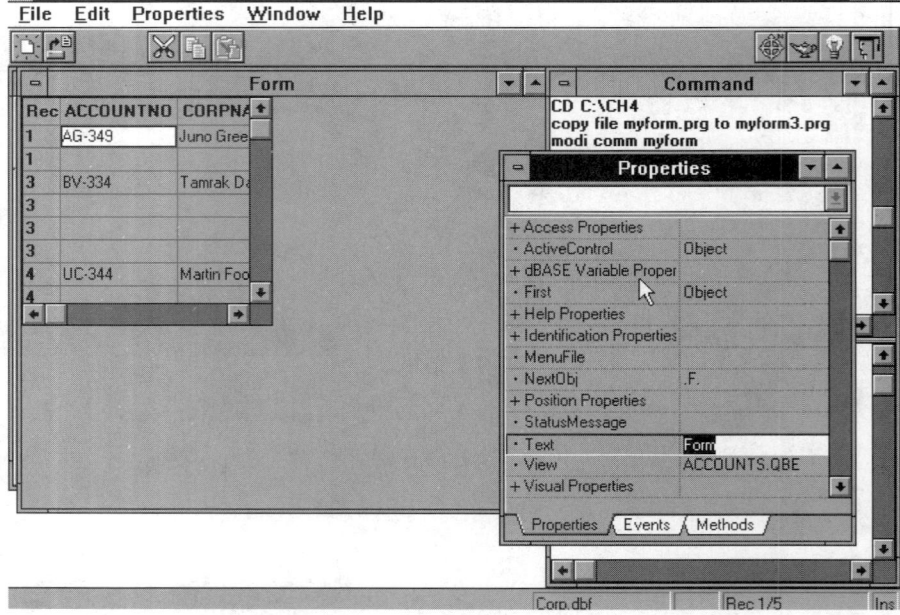

Figure 4.4 The Object Inspector is displayed

The form opens, and the Object Inspector is displayed (see Figure 4.4). Notice that a new entry appears, **dBASE Variable Properties**. This isn't a property *per se*, but a category of properties.

(If the **dBASE Variable Properties** does not appear in the Object Inspector, select the **Properties | Desktop | Application** menu from the dBASE menu bar, then place a check in the **Object Properties Outline** check box. Close the Object Inspector and run the program again.)

Note: If the Object Inspector is hidden behind the Command window, you can access the Object Inspector by minimizing the Command window.

12. Double-click **dBASE Variable Properties** in the Object Inspector.

    A complete list of all custom properties for CLASS NewForm is displayed (see Figure 4.5). Note that one of the properties is NEWBROWSE, which represents the browse object that is now contained by CLASS NewForm. To put it more precisely, NEWBROWSE is a property that contains an object reference pointing to the browse object.

13. Close the Object Inspector by double-clicking it in the upper left corner.

14. Close the form by double-clicking it in the upper left corner.

Chapter 4 Custom Classes

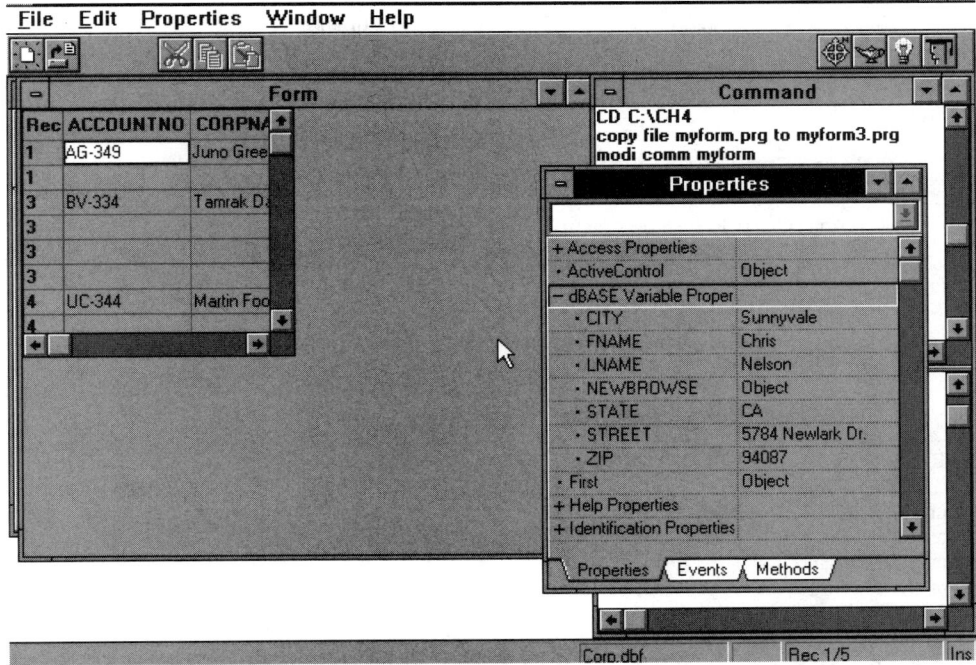

Figure 4.5 Custom properties for CLASS NewForm are displayed

Note that when you closed the form, the browse object disappeared with it. The browse object was contained by the form, and couldn't exist independent of it. In fact, no control object can exist independent of a form.

When one object is contained by another object in dBASE for Windows, the parent object is a usually a form, and the child object is usually a control object. However, any object can contain any other object. The next exercise demonstrates this principle.

Exercise 4

In this exercise you create a form that is contained in another form. In turn, the contained form contains a pushbutton object. You use the Object Inspector to examine the chain of containership. In the process, you encounter an obstacle.

1. First, make a backup copy of the program you created in Exercise 3.

   ```
   COPY FILE MYFORM3.PRG TO MYFORM4.PRG
   ```

2. Now open MYFORM4.PRG with the Text Editor.

   ```
   MODI COMM MYFORM4
   ```

3. Insert the following program code:

```
AForm.ContForm = NEW FORM()
AForm.ContForm.NewBtn =;
     NEW PUSHBUTTON(AForm.ContForm)
AForm.ContForm.NewBtn.OnClick =;
     {; form.Close(); form.Release()}
AForm.ContForm.NewBtn.Left = 17
AForm.ContForm.NewBtn.Top = 6
AForm.ContForm.NewBtn.Text = "Close"
AForm.ContForm.Open()
```

just before this line of program code:

```
INSPECT(AForm)
```

The program should now resemble Listing 4.5.

```
CLEAR
SET TALK OFF
AForm = NEW NEWFORM()
AForm.Open()
AForm.ListAddr()
AForm.ContForm = NEW FORM()
AForm.ContForm.NewBtn =;
     NEW PUSHBUTTON(AForm.ContForm)
AForm.ContForm.NewBtn.OnClick =;
     {; form.Close(); form.Release()}
AForm.ContForm.NewBtn.Left = 17
AForm.ContForm.NewBtn.Top = 6
AForm.ContForm.NewBtn.Text = "Close"
AForm.ContForm.Open()
? inkey(4)
INSPECT(AForm)

CLASS NewForm OF FORM
   this.Height = 14
   this.Width = 60
   this.FName = "Chris"
   this.LName = "Nelson"
   this.Street = "5784 Newlark Dr."
   this.City = "Sunnyvale"
   this.State = "CA"
   this.Zip = "94087"
   this.ListAddr = CLASS::ListOut
*  this.View = "ACCOUNTS.QBE"

   DEFINE BROWSE NewBrowse OF THIS;
   PROPERTY;
     Height         10,;
     Width          58

   PROCEDURE ListOut
     ? TRIM(form.FName), form.LName
```

Chapter 4 Custom Classes

```
    ? form.Street
    ? TRIM(form.City)+", "+;
      form.State+" "+form.Zip
RETURN

ENDCLASS
```

Listing 4.5 A Form Object Contained by the NewForm Object Class

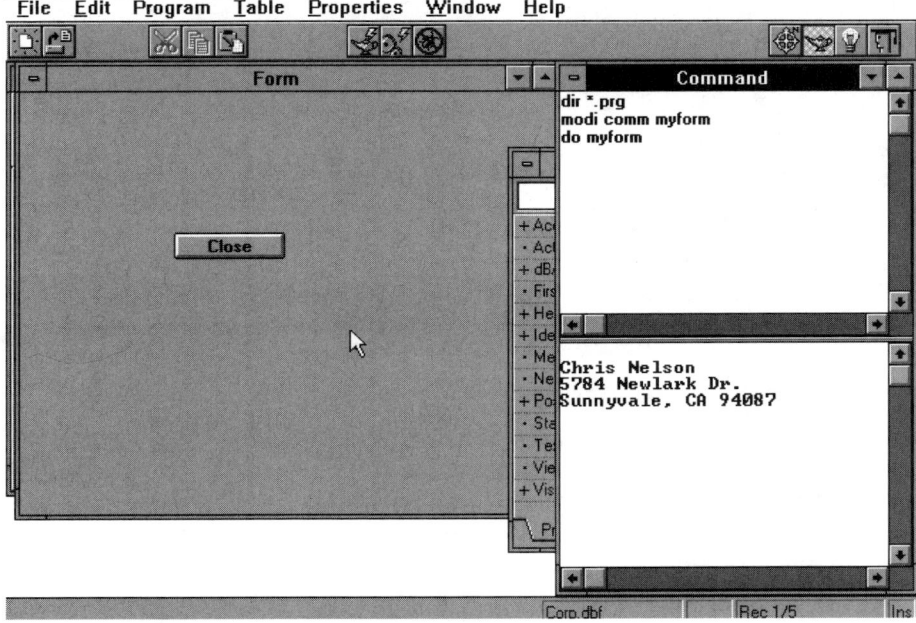

Figure 4.6 A second form opens, displaying a pushbutton

4. Save your work and exit with <Ctrl-W>.

5. Run the program.

   DO MYFORM4

   A second form opens, displaying a pushbutton (see Figure 4.6).

7. Open the **DBASE Variable Properties** list in the Object Inspector by double-clicking it (if it isn't already open).

   Notice that the list now contains **CONTFORM**, an object reference pointing to the contained form object.

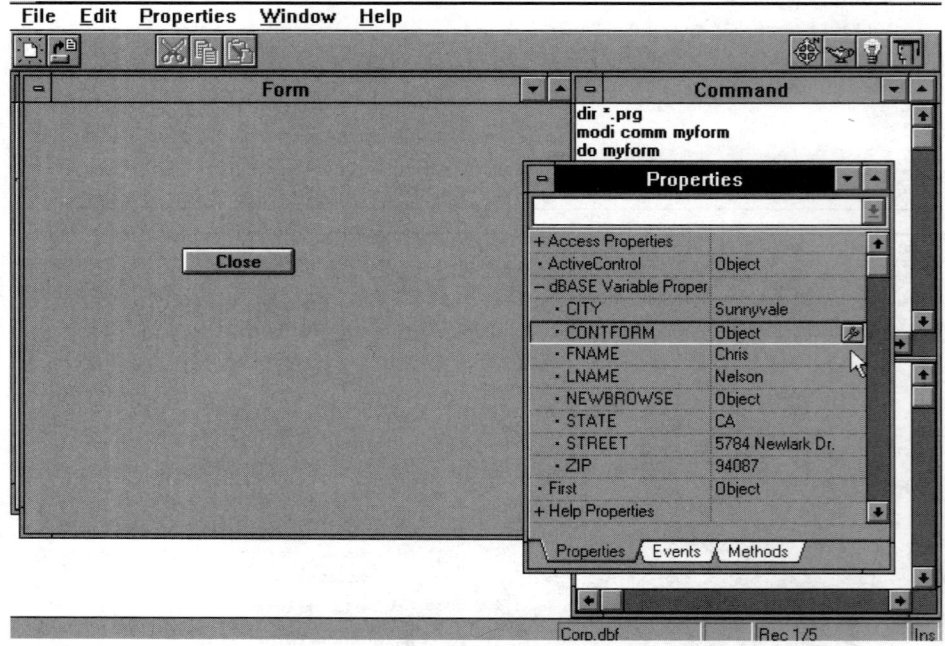

Figure 4.7 A tool button appears to the right of the CONTFORM object

8. Click **CONTFORM** once.

   A tool button appears at the right (see Figure 4.7).

9. Click the tool button.

   Now the Object Inspector displays the properties of the contained form object. For example, NEWBTN, the object reference for the **Close** pushbutton, is listed as a property under **DBASE Variable Properties**.

10. Click **NEWBTN**, then click the tool button that appears at the right.

    Now the Object Inspector displays the properties of the **Close** pushbutton. For example, note that the Text property of the pushbutton is "Close", which matches what you see on the button itself.

    Now let's see how far back we can go.

11. Double-click **Identification Properties**.

    A list of properties is displayed below.

12. Click **Parent**, then the tool button that appears at the right.

Chapter 4 Custom Classes 111

The Object Inspector displays the properties of the contained form object again; you've just gone back one level in the inheritance chain.

13. Double-click **Identification Properties**.

    A list of properties is displayed below. Note that no Parent property is in the list. In fact, the Form object class does not include the Parent property, so we can't return to the contained form object again. (You'll solve this problem in the next exercise.)

14. Click the **Close** pushbutton.

    The contained form and the Object Inspector disappear. The object inspector closes automatically because the object it was evaluating closed.

15. Close the remaining form by double-clicking the upper left corner.

With the help of the Object Inspector, you demonstrated the following:

- The object reference pointing to the contained form object (CONTFORM) was a custom property of the original form (AFORM).
- The object reference pointing to the Close pushbutton (NEWBTN) was a custom property of the contained form object (CONTFORM).

In other words, the AFORM object contained the CONTFORM object, which in turn contained the NEWBTN object. This chainlike relationship is apparent in several of the commands you inserted in Step 3. For example, you used three object references and the dot operator to set the Text property of the **Close** pushbutton:

```
AForm.ContForm.NewBtn.Text = "Close"
```

The relationship can be expressed yet another way. AFORM, the object reference of the parent object, points to the object reference of the child object CONTFORM. In turn, CONTFORM points to the object reference of the child object NEWBTN. Just as the CONTFORM object is contained in the AFORM object, the NEWBTN object is contained in the CONTFORM object. Therefore, it's entirely valid to think of the dot operator as a link in a chain that connects contained and containing objects together. Each successive object reference points to an object that is contained by the previous object.

It's important to note that, although the contained form object (CONTFORM) is referenced by a property of the containing form object (AFORM), the contained form object is *not* part of the NewForm class. This is because the contained form object was declared outside of the CLASS...ENDCLASS definition. In fact, the contained form object was created after the containing form object was created. Consequently, if you create a new object from the NewForm class:

```
NextForm = NEW NEWFORM()
```

the new object does not contain the NewForm property, and no second form is created. In other words, containership in an object doesn't imply membership in the class from which the parent object was derived.

This exercise introduced you to the Parent property. The Parent property contains an object reference that points to its parent object. All control objects have parent properties; however, form objects don't. Consequently, you weren't able to move back one level in the inheritance chain in Step 13. However, there is nothing to keep you from creating a custom Parent property for a form. The next exercise demonstrates this principle.

Exercise 5

In this exercise you give the contained form object a custom property named xParent. This property contains an object reference that points to the containing form object, letting you move backwards in the containership chain.

1. First, make a backup copy of the program you created in Exercise 4.

   ```
   COPY FILE MYFORM4.PRG TO MYFORM5.PRG
   ```

2. Now open **MYFORM5.PRG** with the Text Editor.

   ```
   MODI COMM MYFORM5
   ```

3. Insert the following command:

   ```
   AForm.ContForm.xParent = AForm
   ```

   just before this line of program code:

   ```
   INSPECT(AForm)
   ```

4. Save your work and exit with <Ctrl-W>.

5. Run the program.

   ```
   DO MYFORM5
   ```

   The forms and the Object Inspector appear as before. Note that, as before, the Object Inspector displays the properties of the containing form object.

6. Open the **dBASE Variable Properties** list (if it's not already open).

7. Click the **CONTFORM** property, then click the tool button that appears at the right.

   The Object Inspector displays the properties of the contained form object. Note that the new property, XPARENT, is in the list.

Chapter 4 Custom Classes

8. Click the **XPARENT** property, then click the tool button that appears at the right.

   The Object Inspector displays the properties of the containing form object again.

9. Close both forms and the Object Inspector.

This exercise demonstrates that object references can be duplicated. To understand this concept, examine the command you added to the program:

```
AForm.ContForm.xParent = AForm
```

The command creates a custom property named xParent that holds an object reference pointing to the containing form object. Therefore, the Object Inspector is able to use this reference to move to the containing form object.

Now let's see how the contained form object can be controlled by actions in the containing form.

Exercise 6

In this exercise you place a pushbutton in the containing form object. This pushbutton executes an event handler routine that opens the contained form.

1. First, make a backup copy of the program you created in Exercise 5.

   ```
   COPY FILE MYFORM5.PRG TO MYFORM6.PRG
   ```

2. Now open **MYFORM6.PRG** with the Text Editor

   ```
   MODI COMM MYFORM6
   ```

3. Remove the following line of program code:

   ```
   AForm.ContForm.Open()
   ```

4. Add the following program code just above the definition of the NewBrowse object:

   ```
   DEFINE PUSHBUTTON InBtn OF THIS;
   PROPERTY;
      Top     11,;
      Left    17,;
      Width   20,;
      Text    "Open Window",;
      OnClick {form.ContForm.Open()}
   ```

4. Remove **; form.Release( )** from the following command:

   ```
   AForm.ContForm.NewBtn.OnClick =;
         {; form.Close(); form.Release()}
   ```

The command should now look like this:

```
AForm.ContForm.NewBtn.OnClick =;
     {; form.Close()}
```

The entire program should now resemble Listing 4.6.

```
CLEAR
SET TALK OFF
AForm = NEW NEWFORM()
AForm.Open()
AForm.ListAddr()
AForm.ContForm = NEW FORM()
AForm.ContForm.NewBtn =;
     NEW PUSHBUTTON(AForm.ContForm)
AForm.ContForm.NewBtn.OnClick =;
     {; form.Close()}
AForm.ContForm.NewBtn.Left = 17
AForm.ContForm.NewBtn.Top = 6
AForm.ContForm.NewBtn.Text = "Close"
AForm.ContForm.xParent = AForm
INSPECT(AForm)

CLASS NewForm OF FORM
   this.Height = 14
   this.Width = 60
   this.FName = "Chris"
   this.LName = "Nelson"
   this.Street = "5784 Newlark Dr."
   this.City = "Sunnyvale"
   this.State = "CA"
   this.Zip = "94087"
   this.ListAddr = CLASS::ListOut
   this.View = "ACCOUNTS.QBE"

   DEFINE PUSHBUTTON InBtn OF THIS;
   PROPERTY;
     Top      11,;
     Left     17,;
     Width    20,;
     Text     "Open Window",;
     OnClick  {form.ContForm.Open()}

   DEFINE BROWSE NewBrowse OF THIS;
   PROPERTY;
     Height        10,;
     Width         58

   PROCEDURE ListOut
     ? TRIM(form.FName), form.LName
     ? form.Street
     ? TRIM(form.City)+", "+;
       form.State+" "+form.Zip
```

Chapter 4 Custom Classes

```
RETURN

ENDCLASS
```

Listing 4.6 Opening a Form from a Form

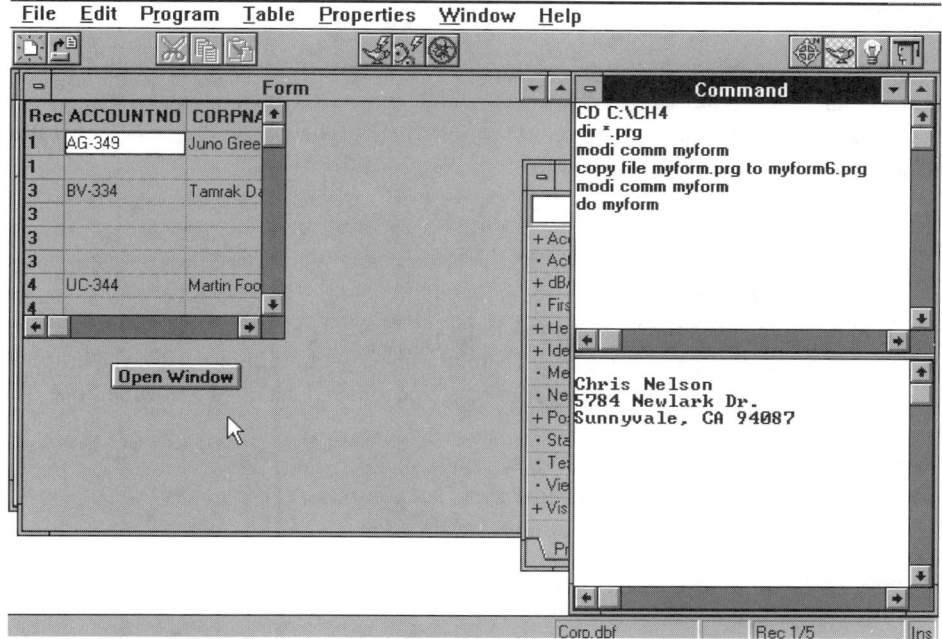

Figure 4.8 A pushbutton labeled Open Window is displayed

5. Save your work and exit with <Ctrl-W>.

6. Run the program.

   `DO MYFORM6`

   A pushbutton labeled **Open Window** appears under the browse object (see Figure 4.8).

7. Click the **Open Window** pushbutton.

   The second form opens.

8. Close the second form by clicking its pushbutton.

9. Repeat Steps 7 and 8 a few times.

10. Close the remaining form and the Object Inspector by double clicking their upper left corners.

This time you opened the form with an event property, OnClick. The command that assigned this action to the property was:

```
OnClick {form.ContForm.Open()}
```

Note that the familiar operator **form** was used to reference the containing form object, while the contained form object was referenced with its object reference, the property ContForm. You can't use the **form** operator twice in an inheritance chain; for example, the following command would generate an error message:

```
OnClick {form.form.Open()}
```

That's due in part to the fact that dBASE interprets any word that follows a dot operator as a property, and requires that it be a property name.

In Step 4 above you removed the form.Release() command from the codeblock. This was necessary, since the Release() method removes an object definition from memory. The contained form would have been unavailable a second time if removed from memory the first time.

So far you've created some custom methods that behave like procedures; that is, they performed actions without returning a value as a function would. The next exercise shows how to make a method behave more like a user-defined function (UDF).

Exercise 7

In this exercise you add a text object definition to the NewForm class definition. (A text object displays a string of characters.) You also create another custom method, which returns a value to display in the text object.

1. First, make a backup copy of the program you created in Exercise 6.

   ```
   COPY FILE MYFORM6.PRG TO MYFORM7.PRG
   ```

2. Now open **MYFORM7.PRG** with the Text Editor.

   ```
   MODI COMM MYFORM7
   ```

3. Enter the following program code:

   ```
   this.TimeDate = CLASS::DateTime
   this.OnOpen =;
      {; form.NewText.Text = form.TimeDate()}
   ```

   under this line:

   ```
   this.View = "ACCOUNTS.QBE"
   ```

Chapter 4 Custom Classes

4. Enter the following program code under the definition of the NewBrowse object:

   ```
   DEFINE TEXT NewText OF THIS;
       PROPERTY;
           Height      1,;
           Width       40,;
           Top         13,;
           Left        16
   ```

5. Enter the following UDF just before the ENDCLASS command:

   ```
   FUNCTION DateTime
      ? DTOC(DATE())+"  "+TIME()
   RETURN DTOC(DATE())+"  "+TIME()
   ```

   The entire program should now look like Listing 4.7.

```
CLEAR
SET TALK OFF
AForm = NEW NEWFORM()
AForm.Open()
AForm.ListAddr()
AForm.ContForm = NEW FORM()
AForm.ContForm.NewBtn =;
      NEW PUSHBUTTON(AForm.ContForm)
AForm.ContForm.NewBtn.OnClick =;
      {; form.Close()}
AForm.ContForm.NewBtn.Left = 17
AForm.ContForm.NewBtn.Top = 6
AForm.ContForm.NewBtn.Text = "Close"
AForm.ContForm.xParent = AForm
INSPECT(AForm)

CLASS NewForm OF FORM
   this.Height = 14
   this.Width = 60
   this.FName = "Chris"
   this.LName = "Nelson"
   this.Street = "5784 Newlark Dr."
   this.City = "Sunnyvale"
   this.State = "CA"
   this.Zip = "94087"
   this.ListAddr = CLASS::ListOut
   this.View = "ACCOUNTS.QBE"
   this.TimeDate = CLASS::DateTime
   this.OnOpen =;
      {; form.NewText.Text = form.TimeDate()}

   DEFINE PUSHBUTTON InBtn OF THIS;
   PROPERTY;
      Top     11,;
```

```
     Left    17,;
     Width   20,;
     Text    "Open Window",;
     OnClick {form.ContForm.Open()}

  DEFINE BROWSE NewBrowse OF THIS;
  PROPERTY;
     Height          10,;
     Width           58

  DEFINE TEXT NewText OF THIS;
     PROPERTY;
        Height       1,;
        Width        40,;
        Top          13,;
        Left         16

  PROCEDURE ListOut
     ? TRIM(form.LName), form.FName
     ? form.Street
     ? TRIM(form.City)+", "+;
       form.State+" "+form.Zip
  RETURN

  FUNCTION DateTime
     ? DTOC(DATE())+"   "+TIME()
  RETURN DTOC(DATE())+"   "+TIME()

ENDCLASS
```

Listing 4.7 A Text Object Contained by the NewForm Object Class

6. Save the program with <Ctrl-W>.

7. Run the program.

    DO MYFORM7

    The date and time appear under the browse object, as shown in Figure 4.9.

8. Double-click **dBASE Variable Properties**.

    NEWTEXT now appears in the list of custom properties.

9. Close the Object Inspector by double clicking the upper left corner.

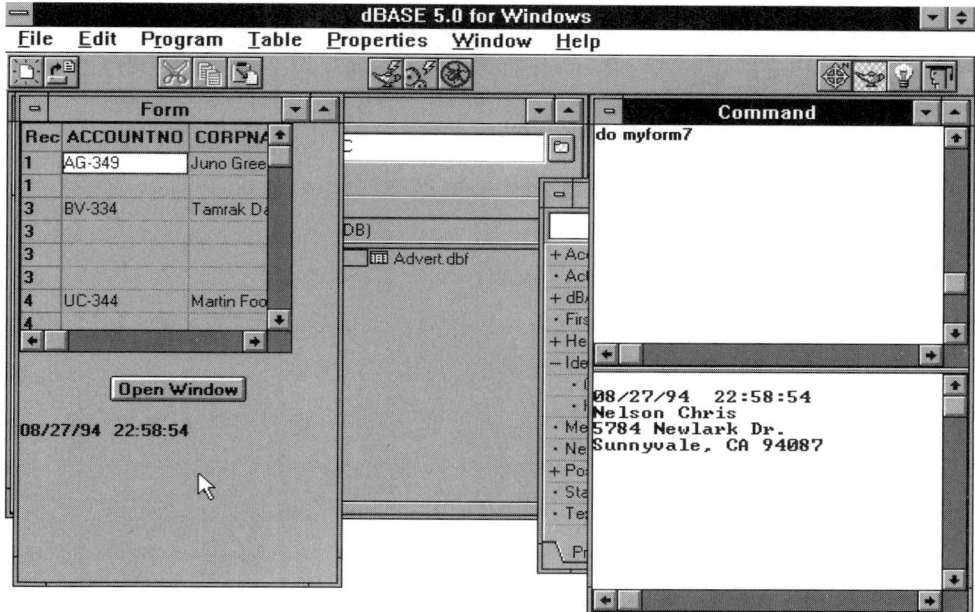

Figure 4.9   The date and time appear under the browse object

10. Close the form by double clicking in the upper left corner.

Text objects usually serve as labels, prompts, or explanatory messages. Each text object contains a property that is also named Text, which determines the content of the label, prompt, or message. (The Text property can contain character data only.)

Because the NewForm object class was derived from the Form object class, the NewForm class inherited all the properties of the Form object class. One of these properties is OnOpen, an event property that executes a subroutine immediately after a form is opened. In this case, the OnOpen property executed a codeblock:

```
{; form.NewText.Text = form.TimeDate()}
```

Custom Classes for Control Objects

You should now be familiar with the concept of deriving a custom class from the Form class. However, you can also create custom classes from other stock classes like Text, Browse, and Pushbutton.

Exercise 8

In this exercise you write a program that uses the Browse object class to create a new object class called NewBrowse. You include an instance of this class in the class declaration of another class.

1. Start a new program file.

   ```
   MODI COMM BFORM
   ```

2. Enter the program code shown in Listing 4.8.

   Note that this time there are two class declarations, one for a form object and one for a browse object.

```
PUBLIC f
f = NEW FineForm()
f.Open()

CLASS FineForm OF FORM
   this.Text          = "Form"
   this.Width         = 60.00
   this.Height        = 20.00
   this.Top           = 2.00
   this.Left          = 2.00
   this.Minimize      = .F.
   this.Maximize      = .F.
*  this.View = "ACCOUNTS.QBE"
   DEFINE NewBrowse MyBrowse OF THIS
ENDCLASS

CLASS NewBrowse(form) OF BROWSE(form)
   this.Width         = 54.00
   this.Height        = 13.00
   this.Top           = 1.00
   this.Left          = 2.00
   this.ColorNormal   = "W+/B"
   this.Append        = .T.
ENDCLASS
```

Listing 4.8 A Custom Class Derived from the Browse Object Class

3. Save your work and exit.

4. Run the program.

   ```
   DO BFORM
   ```

   A form is displayed containing a browse object, as shown in Figure 4.10. The browse object is blue with white lettering inside.

Chapter 4   Custom Classes

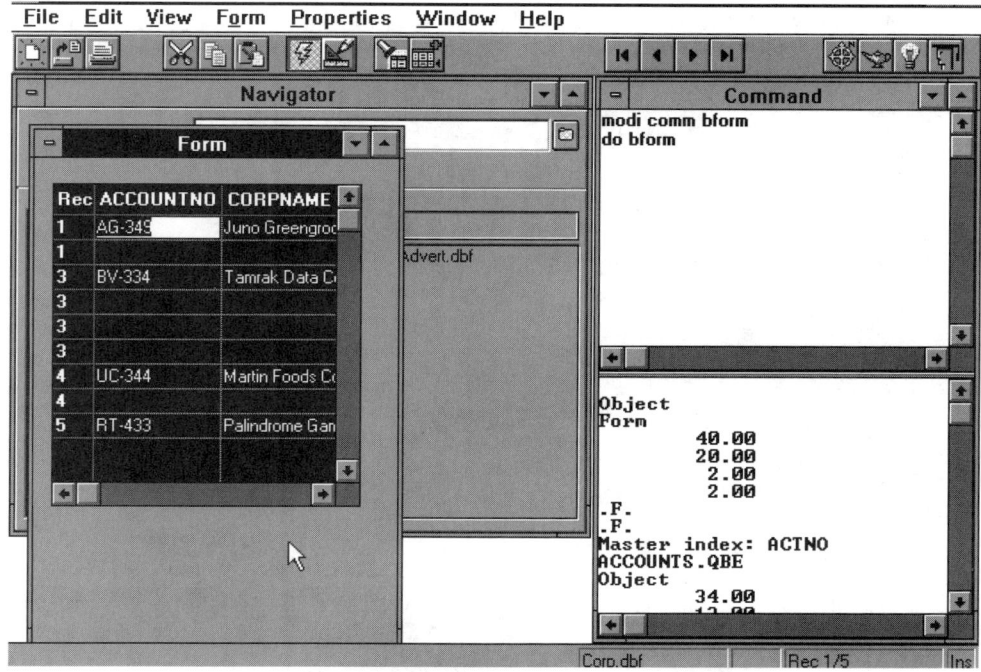

Figure 4.10   The form contains a browse object

5. Close the form by double-clicking the upper left corner.

Note that the CLASS...ENDCLASS command you used to create the NewBrowse class differed slightly from the CLASS...ENDCLASS command you used to create the FineForm class. The former uses parameters:

```
CLASS NewBrowse(form) OF BROWSE(form)
```

while the latter did not:

```
CLASS FineForm OF FORM
```

Why the difference? Recall that a browse object is a control object. Control objects are *always* contained in another object (usually a form object); that is, a control object always has a *parent object*. Therefore, when you declare a custom control object, you are required to specify the parent object with a parameter. In this case, the parent is (as usual) a form object.

Let's look at another example.

Exercise 9

In this exercise you declare a custom class that is based on the Pushbutton object class. When clicked, a pushbutton derived from this class opens a form displaying the address of the corporation in the current record.

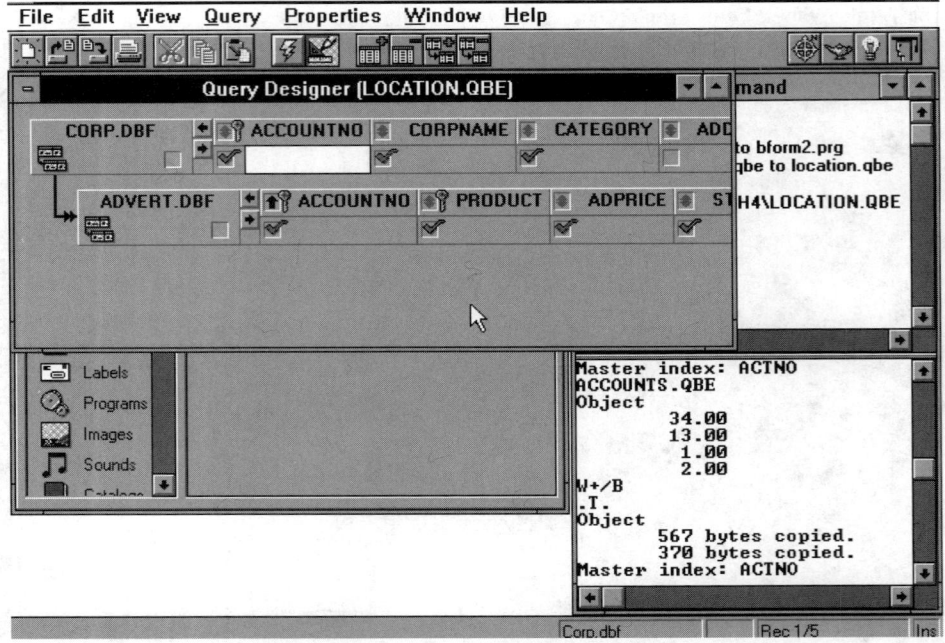

Figure 4.11 The Query Designer is presented

First, you create a new query to make the right fields available.

1. First, make a backup copy of the program you created in Exercise 8.

    ```
    COPY FILE BFORM.PRG TO BFORM2.PRG
    ```

2. Make a duplicate of the QBE file ACCOUNTS.QBE.

    ```
    COPY FILE ACCOUNTS.QBE TO LOCATION.QBE
    ```

3. Open the Query Designer with the following command:

    ```
    MODIFY VIEW LOCATION
    ```

    The Query Designer opens, as shown in Figure 4.11.

4. First, let's deactivate the fields we don't need. Click on the green check marks in the following fields: ACCOUNTNO (in both skeletons), CATEGORY, PRODUCT, ADPRICE, and STARTDATE.

    The query should now resemble Figure 4.12.

Chapter 4 Custom Classes 123

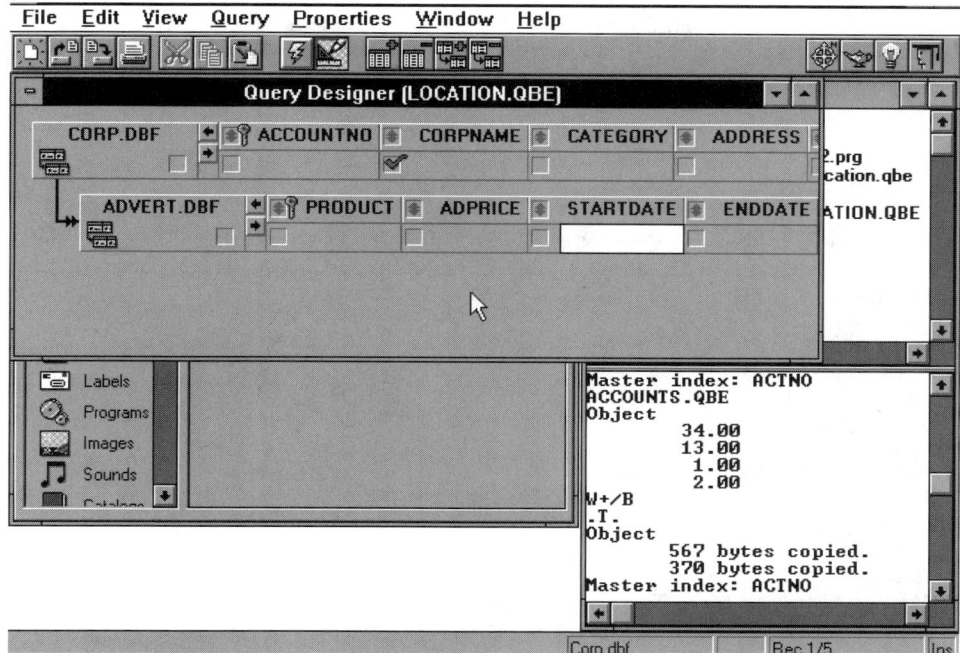

Figure 4.12 The query design screen after deactivating fields

5. Now give green check marks to the following fields: CITY, ADDRESS, STATE, and ZIP.

   (If necessary, use the black arrow keys near the left edge of the skeleton to scroll the skeleton to the left.)

6. Double-click the upper left corner of the Query Designer window.

   A confirmation prompt appears.

7. Click the **Yes** pushbutton.

   Control returns to the input pane of the Command window.

8. Now open BFORM2.PRG with the Text Editor.

   MODI COMM BFORM2

9. Change the following line of program code:

   this.View = "ACCOUNTS.QBE"

   to:

```
            this.View = "LOCATION.QBE"
```

10. Add the following line of program code:

    ```
    DEFINE NewBtn MyButton OF THIS
    ```

    after this line:

    ```
    DEFINE NewBrowse MyBrowse OF THIS
    ```

```
f.xMessage = NEW FORM("The Company Address")
f.xMessage.Left = 50
f.xMessage.Height = 10
f.xMessage.Width = 60
f.xMessage.T1 = NEW TEXT(f.xMessage)
f.xMessage.T1.Width = 40
f.xMessage.T1.Top = 2
f.xMessage.T1.Left = 4
f.xMessage.T2 = NEW TEXT(f.xMessage)
f.xMessage.T2.Width = 40
f.xMessage.T2.Top = 4
f.xMessage.T2.Left = 4
f.xMessage.T3 = NEW TEXT(f.xMessage)
f.xMessage.T3.Width = 40
f.xMessage.T3.Top = 6
f.xMessage.T3.Left = 4
```

Listing 4.9 Code that Creates a New Form

```
CLASS NewBtn(form) OF PUSHBUTTON(form)
    this.Width   = 18.00
    this.Height  = 1.5
    this.Top     = 16.00
    this.Left    = 20.00
    this.Text    = "Display Info"
    this.OnClick = CLASS::ShowBox

    PROCEDURE ShowBox
      form.xMessage.Open()
      form.xMessage.T1.Text = CORP->CORPNAME
      form.xMessage.T2.Text = CORP->ADDRESS
      form.xMessage.T3.Text = TRIM(CORP->CITY)+", "+;
                              CORP->STATE+" "+;
                              CORP->ZIP
    RETURN
ENDCLASS
```

Listing 4.10 Code that Declares a Custom Class and an Event Handler

11. Add the program code shown in Listing 4.9 after this line of code:

Chapter 4 Custom Classes

```
        f.Open()
```

12. Add the procedure declaration shown in Listing 4.10 at the end of the program.

    The program should now look like the one in Listing 4.11.

```
PUBLIC f
f = NEW FineForm()
f.Open()
f.xMessage = NEW FORM("The Company Address")
f.xMessage.Left = 50
f.xMessage.Height = 10
f.xMessage.Width = 60
f.xMessage.T1 = NEW TEXT(f.xMessage)
f.xMessage.T1.Width = 40
f.xMessage.T1.Top = 2
f.xMessage.T1.Left = 4
f.xMessage.T2 = NEW TEXT(f.xMessage)
f.xMessage.T2.Width = 40
f.xMessage.T2.Top = 4
f.xMessage.T2.Left = 4
f.xMessage.T3 = NEW TEXT(f.xMessage)
f.xMessage.T3.Width = 40
f.xMessage.T3.Top = 6
f.xMessage.T3.Left = 4

CLASS FineForm OF FORM
    this.Text         = "Form"
    this.Width        = 60.00
    this.Height       = 20.00
    this.Top          = 2.00
    this.Left         = 2.00
    this.Minimize     = .F.
    this.Maximize     = .F.
    this.HelpFile     = ""
    this.HelpId       = ""
    this.MousePointer = 1
    this.View = "LOCATION.QBE"
    DEFINE NewBrowse MyBrowse OF THIS
    DEFINE NewBtn MyButton OF THIS
ENDCLASS

CLASS NewBrowse(form) OF BROWSE(form)
    this.Width       = 54.00
    this.Height      = 13.00
    this.Top         = 1.00
    this.Left        = 2.00
    this.ColorNormal = "W+/B"
    this.Append = .T.
ENDCLASS

CLASS NewBtn(form) OF PUSHBUTTON(form)
    this.Width    = 18.00
```

```
       this.Height = 1.5
       this.Top    = 16.00
       this.Left   = 20.00
       this.Text   = "Display Info"
       this.OnClick = CLASS::ShowBox

       PROCEDURE ShowBox
         form.xMessage.Open()
         form.xMessage.T1.Text = CORP->CORPNAME
         form.xMessage.T2.Text = CORP->ADDRESS
         form.xMessage.T3.Text = TRIM(CORP->CITY)+", "+;
                                 CORP->STATE+" "+;
                                 CORP->ZIP
       RETURN
ENDCLASS
```

Listing 4.11 A Program that Displays Data in a Window and a Browse Object

13. Save your work and exit.

14. Run the program.

    ```
    DO BFORM2
    ```

    The form opens, this time with a pushbutton labeled **Display Info**, as shown in Figure 4.13.

15. Click the **Display Info** pushbutton.

    Another form appears, displaying the address of the corporation in the current record (see Figure 4.14).

16. Click on another record in the browse object.

    The highlight moves to that record.

17. Click the **Display Info** pushbutton again.

    The information in the display form now shows data from the record to which you moved.

18. Close both forms by double-clicking the upper left corner.

Chapter 4   Custom Classes   127

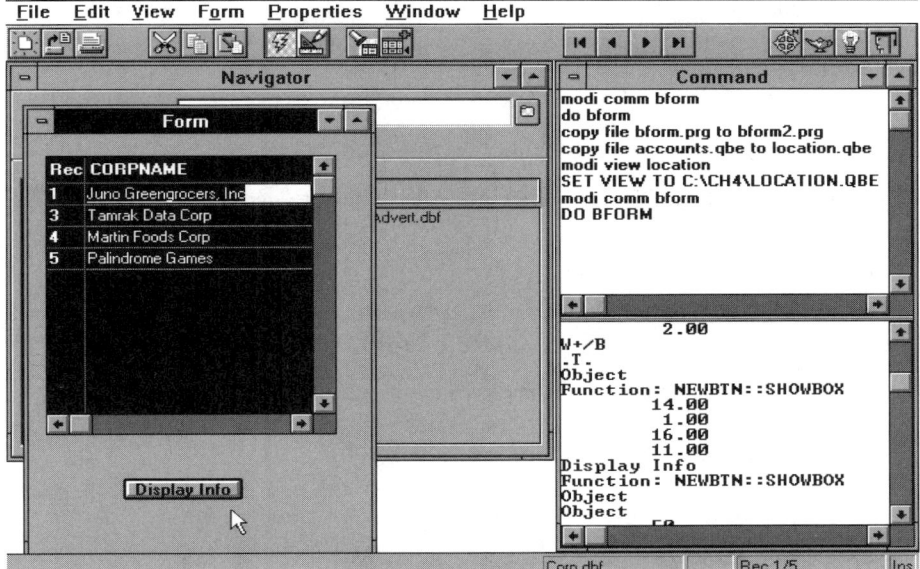

Figure 4.13   The form opens with pushbutton Display Info

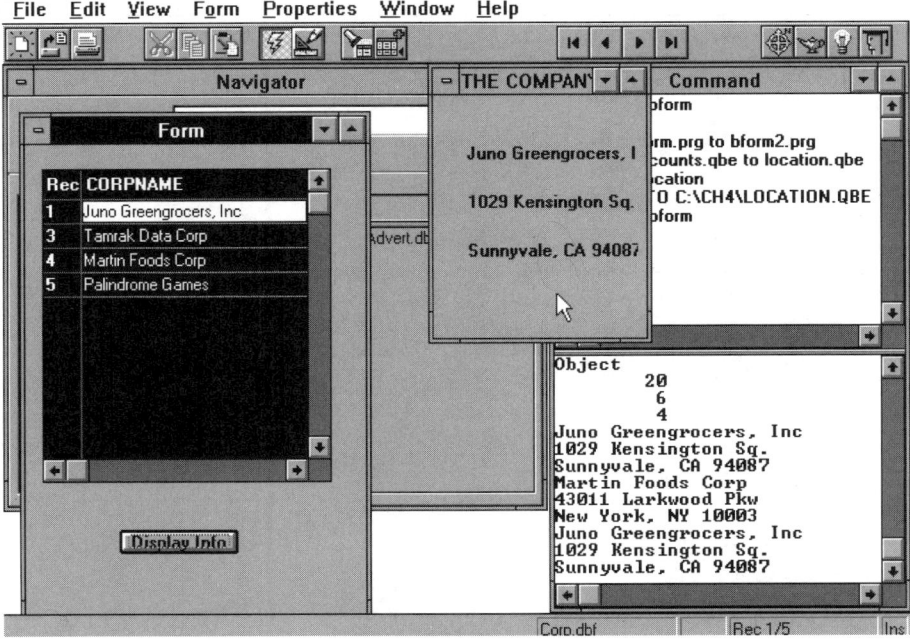

Figure 4.14   Corporate address of the current record is displayed

In this exercise, the xMessage window is an instance of the Form object class. It was created after an instance of the custom class FineForm was created and opened:

```
f = NEW FineForm()
f.Open()
f.xMessage = NEW FORM("The Company Address")
```

However, for reasons discussed earlier, it's often better to declare a new class. The next exercise alters the code to do that.

Exercise 10

In this exercise you alter the code to make a custom class named xMess. Like the custom class FineForm, the xMess class is derived from the Form object class.

1. First, make a backup copy of the program you created in Exercise 9.

   ```
   COPY FILE BFORM2.PRG TO BFORM3.PRG
   ```

2. Now open BFORM3.PRG with the Text Editor.

   ```
   MODI COMM BFORM3
   ```

3. Remove the program code shown in Listing 4.12.

```
f.xMessage = NEW FORM("The Company Address")
f.xMessage.Left = 50
f.xMessage.Height = 10
f.xMessage.Width = 60
f.xMessage.T1 = NEW TEXT(f.xMessage)
f.xMessage.T1.Width = 40
f.xMessage.T1.Top = 2
f.xMessage.T1.Left = 4
f.xMessage.T2 = NEW TEXT(f.xMessage)
f.xMessage.T2.Width = 40
f.xMessage.T2.Top = 4
f.xMessage.T2.Left = 4
f.xMessage.T3 = NEW TEXT(f.xMessage)
f.xMessage.T3.Width = 40
f.xMessage.T3.Top = 6
f.xMessage.T3.Left = 4
```

Listing 4.12 Remove This Code

```
CLASS xMess OF FORM
   Left   = 50
   Height = 10
   Width  = 50

   DEFINE TEXT T1 OF THIS;
      PROPERTY;
```

Chapter 4 Custom Classes

```
            Width   40,;
            Top     2,;
            Left    4

      DEFINE TEXT T2 OF THIS;
         PROPERTY;
            Width   40,;
            Top     4,;
            Left    4

      DEFINE TEXT T3 OF THIS;
         PROPERTY;
            Width   40,;
            Top     6,;
            Left    4

ENDCLASS
```

Listing 4.13 Add This Code

    4.   Add the code shown in Listing 4.13 to the end of the program.

        The program should now look like Listing 4.14.

```
PUBLIC f
f = NEW FineForm()
f.xMessage = NEW xMess(f)
f.Open()

CLASS FineForm OF FORM
    this.Text           = "Form"
    this.Width          = 60.00
    this.Height         = 20.00
    this.Top            = 2.00
    this.Left           = 2.00
    this.Minimize       = .F.
    this.Maximize       = .F.
    this.HelpFile       = ""
    this.HelpId         = ""
    this.MousePointer   = 1
    this.View = "LOCATION.QBE"
    DEFINE NewBrowse MyBrowse OF THIS
    DEFINE NewBtn MyButton OF THIS
ENDCLASS

CLASS NewBrowse(form) OF BROWSE(form)
    this.Width         = 54.00
    this.Height        = 13.00
    this.Top           = 1.00
    this.Left          = 2.00
    this.ColorNormal   = "W+/B"
    this.Append = .T.
ENDCLASS
```

```
CLASS NewBtn(form) OF PUSHBUTTON(form)
   this.Width  = 18.00
   this.Height = 1.5
   this.Top    = 16.00
   this.Left   = 20.00
   this.Text   = "Display Info"
   this.OnClick = CLASS::ShowBox

   PROCEDURE ShowBox
      form.xMessage.Open()
      form.xMessage.T1.Text = CORP->CORPNAME
      form.xMessage.T2.Text = CORP->ADDRESS
      form.xMessage.T3.Text = TRIM(CORP->CITY)+", "+;
                              CORP->STATE+" "+;
                              CORP->ZIP
   RETURN
ENDCLASS

CLASS xMess OF FORM
   Left   = 50
   Height = 10
   Width  = 50

   DEFINE TEXT T1 OF THIS;
      PROPERTY;
         Width 40,,;
         Top    2,;
         Left   4

   DEFINE TEXT T2 OF THIS;
      PROPERTY;
         Width 40,,;
         Top    4,;
         Left   4

   DEFINE TEXT T3 OF THIS;
      PROPERTY;
         Width 40,,;
         Top    6,;
         Left   4

ENDCLASS
```

Listing 4.14 Form Now Derived from a Custom Class

5. Add the following command:

    `f.xMessage = NEW xMess(f)`

    After this command:

```
        f = NEW FineForm()
```

6. Run the program.

   ```
   DO BFORM
   ```

   The form opens as before.

7. Confirm that the program works as before.

8. Close both forms.

What Next?

This completes your introduction to custom classes. Now you're ready to use the Form Designer, a tool that generates program code for you and lets you create applications easily and quickly. Because you've actually written programs from scratch, you have the knowledge to interpret that code--an indispensible asset to any serious application developer.

Chapter 5
The Form Designer

The previous chapters showed how to develop object-oriented programs with the MODIFY COMMAND editor. However, dBASE for Windows offers a tool called the *Form Designer* that automates the development process. With the Form Designer you can develop sophisticated applications in a fraction of the time it takes to develop them with the editor.

Using the Form Designer

The Form Designer was designed to shorten the development process. It lets you construct and design forms in a natural, intuitive way. At the end of each Form Designer session, dBASE generates program code that exactly replicates the form you design. This code is stored in a file with an extension of .WFM.

Exercise 1

This exercise introduces you to the Form Designer.

1. First be sure that the current default directory contains ADVERT.DBF, CORP.DBF, and all associated files that you created in the previous chapters. If these files do not currently exist, make them now.

2. Start a Form Designer session.

   ```
   CREATE FORM XFORM
   ```

   Four windows appear, as shown in Figure 5.1. (If any of these windows are missing, you can invoke them by selecting **View | Controls**, **View | Object Properties**, or **View | Procedures**.)

   - The window labeled **Form Designer [XFORM.WFM]** is known as the *design surface window*. The design surface is a replica of the form you design. (In the steps and exercises that follow, we usually refer to the design surface as the form.)
   - The window labeled **Properties [XFORM.WFM]** is the now-familiar Object Inspector.
   - The window labeled **Controls** is known as the *Object Pallette*. The Object Pallette offers the choice of any control object for placement on the design surface.

Chapter 5 The Form Designer 133

- The horizontal window labeled **Procedures [XFORM.WFM]** (mostly obscured by the other windows) is known as the *Procedure Editor*. The procedure editor is the medium in which you write subroutines for event properties.

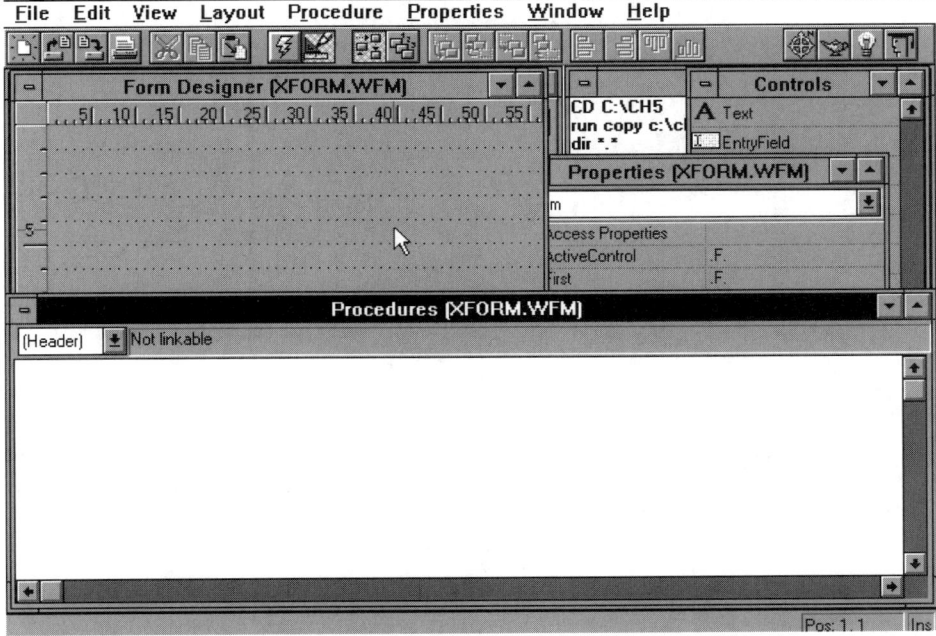

Figure 5.1 The Form Designer

3. Move the mouse pointer to the right edge of the design surface window.

   The pointer changes to a double arrow (see Figure 5.2).

4. Hold down the left mouse key, drag the right edge of the design surface window to the right about one inch, then release the mouse key.

   The window is now one inch wider.

5. Now move the mouse pointer to the caption bar at the top of the design surface window and drag the window down about a half inch.

   The caption bar is the only place on the design surface window from which you can drag the entire window without resizing it.

6. Using the techniques demonstrated in Steps 3 through 5, resize the design surface window to resemble the one shown in Figure 5.3.

   The top ruler in the design surface should read from 0 to 80, and the left ruler should read from 0 to 16 or thereabouts.

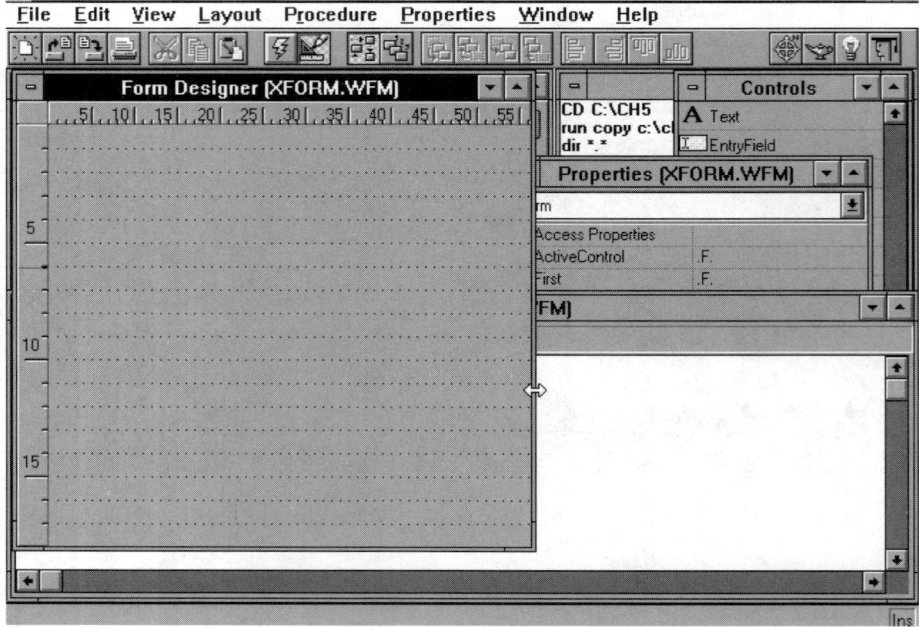

Figure 5.2   The pointer changes to a double arrow

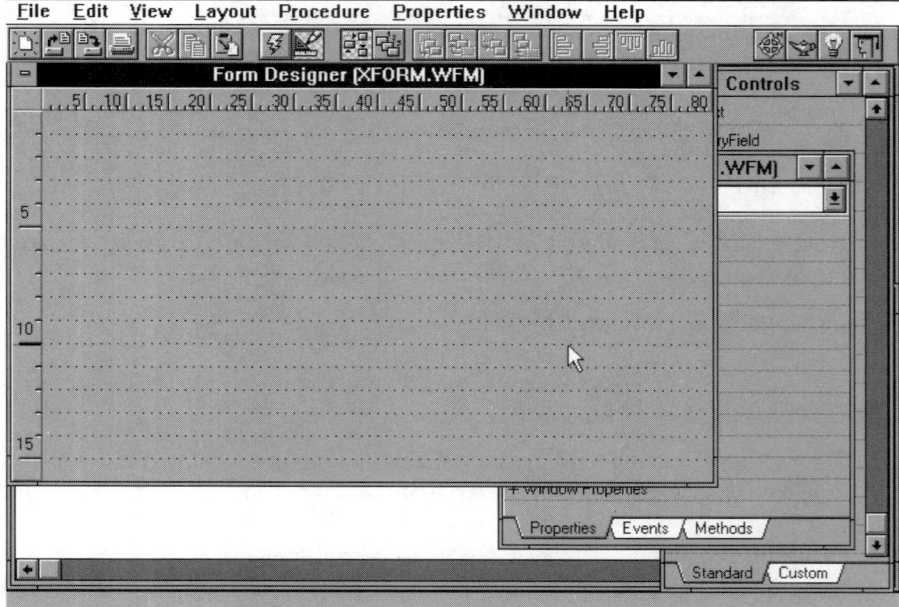

Figure 5.3   Resized design surface window

Chapter 5 The Form Designer

7. Now click anywhere on the Object Inspector (the window titled **Properties (XFORM.WFM)**).

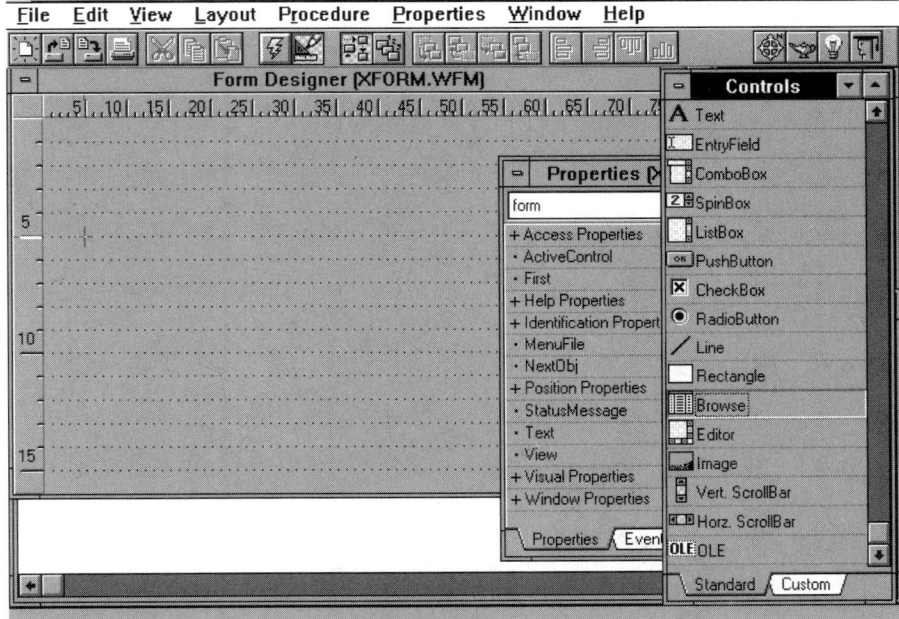

Figure 5.4 Pointer is positioned on the 5 mark for both lines

The Object Inspector comes to the foreground, and may now partially obscure the design surface window. Note that part of the Object Pallette is still visible at the far right.

8. Click anywhere on the Object Pallette.

The Object Pallette comes to the foreground, and may now partially obscure the Object Inspector.

9. Click on **Browse** in the Object Pallette.

10. Now move the mouse pointer to the design surface, near the upper left corner (but don't press the mouse key yet).

Note that lines appear in the rulers to the left and above, indicating where the pointer is located.

11. Adjust the position of the pointer so both lines are on the 5 mark (see Figure 5.4).

12. Hold down the left mouse key, then drag down and to the right until the position of the pointer is at 15 (on the left ruler) and 75 (on the top ruler).

13. Release the mouse key.

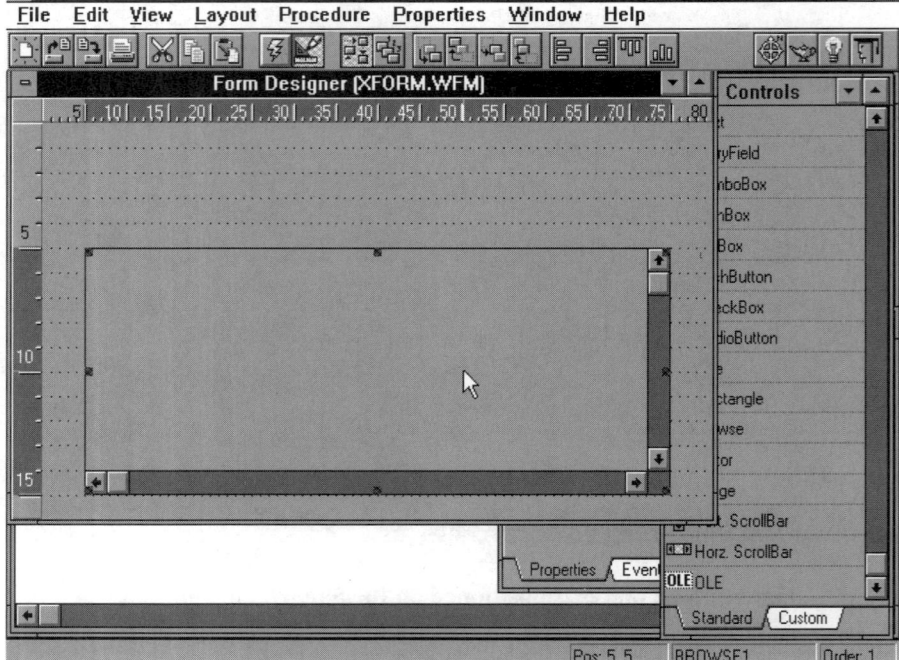

Figure 5.5 A large box with scrollbars appears in the form

A large box with scrollbars appears in the form, as shown in Figure 5.5. This is a browse object.

14. That's enough for now. Close the Form Designer by double-clicking the control box at the upper left corner of the design surface window.

A confirmation dialog box appears.

16. Click the **Yes** button.

Control returns to the Command pane.

The form you just created contains a browse object. This browse object doesn't access or display any data yet; recall from Exercise 4 of Chapter 3 that you make data available to a form by *basing* it on QBE with the View property of the containing form. Control objects, such as browse objects, which are contained by the form access data from the QBE (or individual table file) upon which the form is based.

The next exercise demonstrates this principle. In the process, the concept of the two-way tool is introduced.

Two-Way Tools

When you used the Form Designer to create the form and the browse object contained by the form, dBASE generated a program that, when executed, reproduces the form and opens it. You'll view this program in the next exercise.

The program can be modified in two ways:

- You can go back into the Form Designer and modify the form in the design surface window.

- You can open the program in the MODIFY COMMAND editor and alter it manually.

If you modify the program with the MODIFY COMMAND editor and then examine the form in the Form Designer, the Form Designer recognizes the changes you made; the changes are reflected in the design surface window and the Object Inspector. Conversely, if you make a change from the Form Designer and then examine the program with an editor, the changes are visible in the program code. The Form Designer is therefore said to be a *two-way tool*. In fact, any tool that generates program code and recognizes changes you make with an editor is a two-way tool. As you'll see in Exercise 3, the Query Designer is also a two-way tool. Another feature of dBASE for Windows, the Menu Designer, is a two-way tool as well.

Exercise 2

In this exercise you base the form on two QBEs: first ACCOUNTS.QBE, then LOCATION.QBE. (If you haven't created these QBEs yet, create them now. Instructions for creating ACCOUNTS.QBE are in Chapter 1, and instructions for creating LOCATION.QBE are in Chapter 4.)

1. Open the program file you created in the previous exercise with the editor:

   MODI COMM XFORM.WFM

   The program shown in Listing 5.1 is displayed (see below).

```
** END HEADER -- do not remove this line*
* Generated on 99/99/99
*
LOCAL f
f = NEW XFORMFORM()
f.Open()

CLASS XFORMFORM OF FORM
   Set Procedure To C:\DBASEWIN\SAMPLES\BUTTONS.CC additive
   this.Height =         15.9404
   this.Left =           10.5
   this.Top =            1.1758
```

```
this.Text = "Form"
this.Width =           80
this.HelpId = ""
this.HelpFile = ""

DEFINE BROWSE BROWSE1 OF THIS;
    PROPERTY;
      FontBold    .F.,;
      Height          10,;
      Left             5,;
      Top              5,;
      Width           70,;
      ColorNormal "N/W"

ENDCLASS
```

Listing 5.1 Program Code Generated by the Form Designer

2. Add the following line of program code:

    `this.View = "ACCOUNTS.QBE"`

    below this line of code:

    `this.HelpId = ""`

3. Save and exit with <Ctrl-W>.

4. Now open the form in the Form Designer:

    `MODIFY FORM XFORM`

    Notice that this time, the data from ACCOUNTS.QBE is displayed in the form, as shown in Figure 5.6. Since the Form Designer is a two-way tool, it recognized your changes and displayed the form accordingly.

    Now let's look at the two-way tool from another perspective.

5. Click the Object Inspector.

    The Object Inspector window moves to the foreground.

6. Click the View property in the Object Inspector.

    A tool button appears at the right.

7. Click the tool button.

    A dialog box appears, as shown in Figure 5.7. The **Choose View** check box is currently selected. This is what we want.

Chapter 5   The Form Designer   139

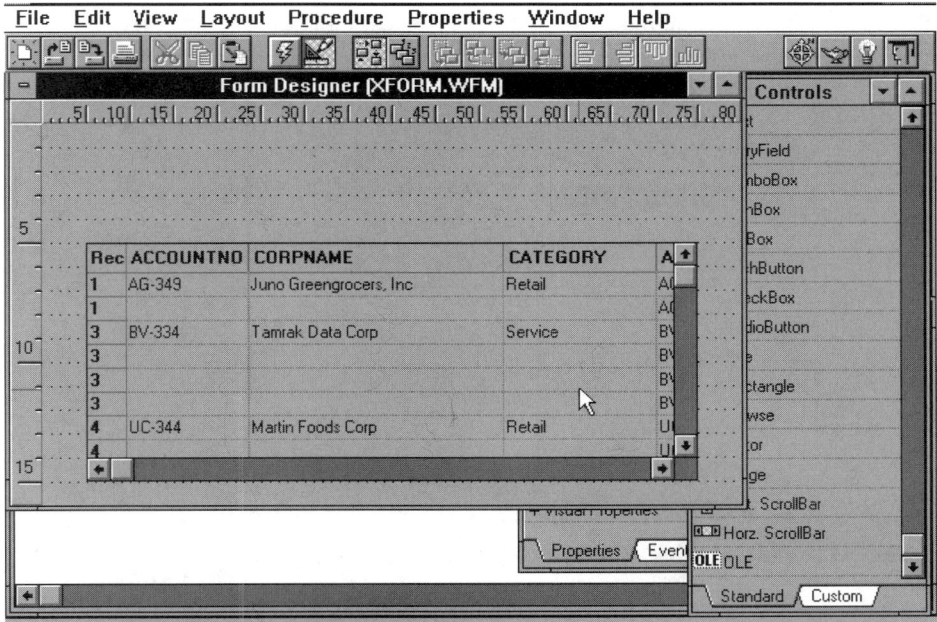

Figure 5.6   Data from ACCOUNTS.QBE is displayed in the form

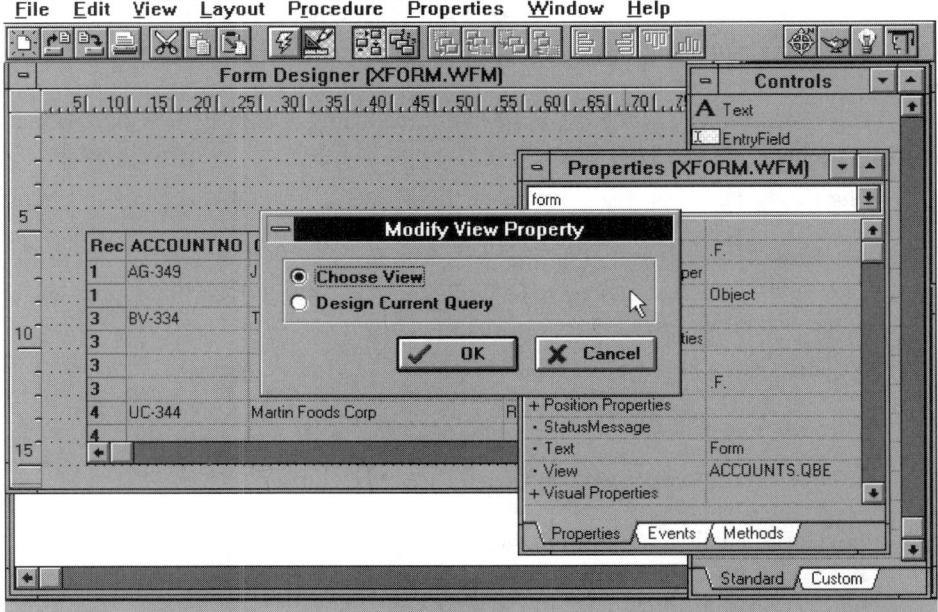

Figure 5.7   Modify View Property dialog box appears

8. Click the **OK** button.

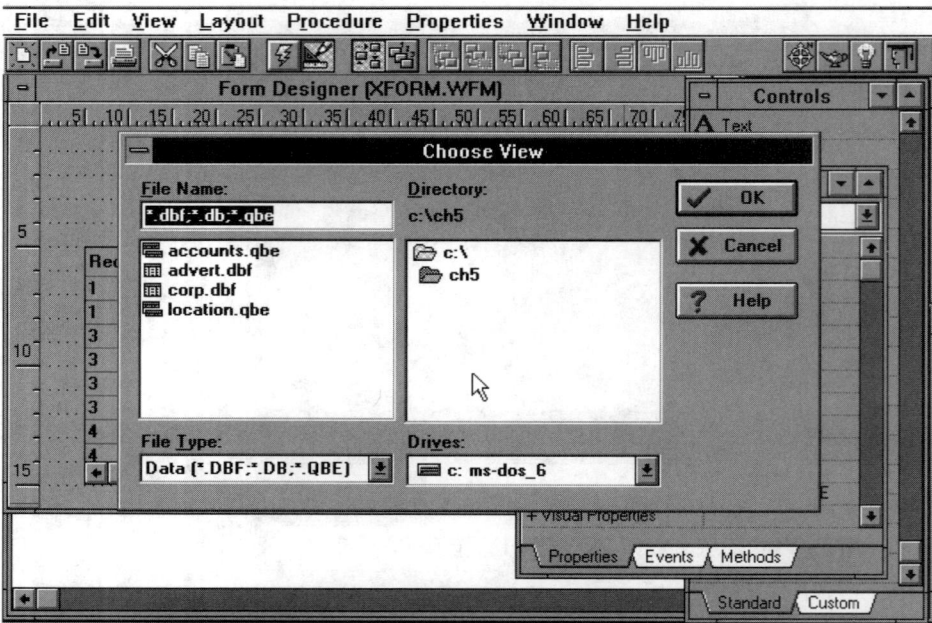

Figure 5.8 The Choose View dialog box appears

Another dialog box appears, as shown in Figure 5.8.

9. Click **location.qbe** in the list at the left of the dialog box, then click the **OK** button at the right.

   The dialog box disappears, and data from LOCATION.QBE appears in the browse object.

10. Close the Form Designer by double-clicking the control box at the upper left corner of the design surface window.

    A confirmation dialog box appears.

11. Click the **Yes** button.

    Control returns to the Command pane.

12. Now examine the program with the editor.

    ```
    MODI COMM XFORM.WFM
    ```

    Note that the following line now appears in the program code:

Chapter 5 The Form Designer

> this.View = "LOCATION.QBE"

The entire program now looks like the one in Listing 5.2.

```
** END HEADER -- do not remove this line*
* Generated on 99/99/99
*
LOCAL f
f = NEW XFORMFORM()
f.Open()

CLASS XFORMFORM OF FORM
   Set Procedure To C:\DBASEWIN\SAMPLES\BUTTONS.CC additive
   this.Height =          15.9404
   this.Left   =          10.5
   this.Top    =           1.1758
   this.Text = "Form"
   this.Width  =          79.666
   this.HelpId = ""
   this.HelpFile = ""
   this.View = "ACCOUNTS.QBE"

   DEFINE BROWSE BROWSE1 OF THIS;
      PROPERTY;
        FontBold .F.,;
        Height          10,;
        Left             5,;
        Top              5,;
        Width           70,;
        ColorNormal "N/W"

ENDCLASS
```

Listing 5.2 The View Property Set by the Form Designer

Declare object reference	`LOCAL f`
Create an instance of the form	`f = NEW XFORMFORM()`
Open the form	`f.Open()`
Custom form class declaration	`CLASS XFORMFORM OF FORM`
Constructor code	`this.Top = 1.06`
	`this.Width = 80.60`

	`this.HelpId = ""`
	`this.View = LOCATION.QBE"`
	`this.Text = "Form"`
	`this.HelpFile = ""`
	`this.Height = 16.47`
	`this.Left = 3.00`
Control object definitions	`DEFINE BROWSE BROWSE1 OF THIS;`
	`  PROPERTY;`
	`    Top         1.00,;`
	`    Width      72.00,;`
	`    FontBold   .F.,;`
	`    ColorNormal "N/W",;`
	`    Height     14.00,;`
	`    Left        4.00`
Member functions code	`<None yet>`
End declaration	`ENDCLASS`

Listing 5.3 Layout of Code Generated by the Form Designer

13. Quit the editor and return to the Command pane.

Let's take a closer look at the program code generated by the Form Designer. The code creates a custom class named XFORMFORM. (dBASE created this name by simply attaching the character string "FORM" to the end of the program's file name, XFORM). The default size and dimensions of the form created from this custom class (determined by the Top, Width, Height, and Left properties) conform to the size and dimensions of the design surface window when you saved your work and exited from the Form Designer. The same is true of the browse object (BROWSE1) declared with the DEFINE BROWSE command.

All programs that are generated by the Form Designer follow the general format of the one in Listing 5.2. Listing 5.3 shows an outline of this format. The first active line of program code declares an object reference (f) that will point to the form object. The next line creates an instance of the form--the form itself. The third line opens the form. The remaining lines are the declaration of the custom form class and the objects contained by each instance of that class.

Note that there is currently no program code in the member functions section. The next exercise uses the Procedure Editor to create such code.

Reacting to Mouse Events

The mouse is one of the most important tools for working in the Windows environment. Its point-and-shoot capabilities make interaction with Windows applications (and Windows itself) easy and intuitive.

Each time you click with the mouse (or even move the mouse pointer), you generate a *mouse event*. A mouse event is any mouse-related occurrence that can be detected and interpreted by Windows or a Windows application. dBASE for Windows provides about a dozen event properties that detect such occurrences and execute subroutines in response. The next exercise introduces one of these properties.

Exercise 3

In this exercise you write a subroutine that delivers statistics on the data accessed by a browse object. This subroutine is assigned to an event property named OnLeftDblClick, which is activated each time the user double-clicks the browse object with the Left mouse button.

1. Open the form in the Form Designer:

   MODIFY FORM XFORM

2. Click the browse object in the design surface window.

   The browse object is surrounded with small black marks, as shown in Figure 5.9. These marks are called *selection boxes*. When a control object is surrounded by selection boxes, the Object Inspector displays the properties of that object.

3. Click the Object Inspector.

   The Object Inspector moves to the foreground.

4. Click the **Events** tab at the bottom of the Object Inspector.

   The event properties are displayed.

5. Click the OnLeftDblClick property, then click the Tool Button that appears at the right.

   The Procedure Editor appears in the foreground. Note that the first line of program code is already written for you:

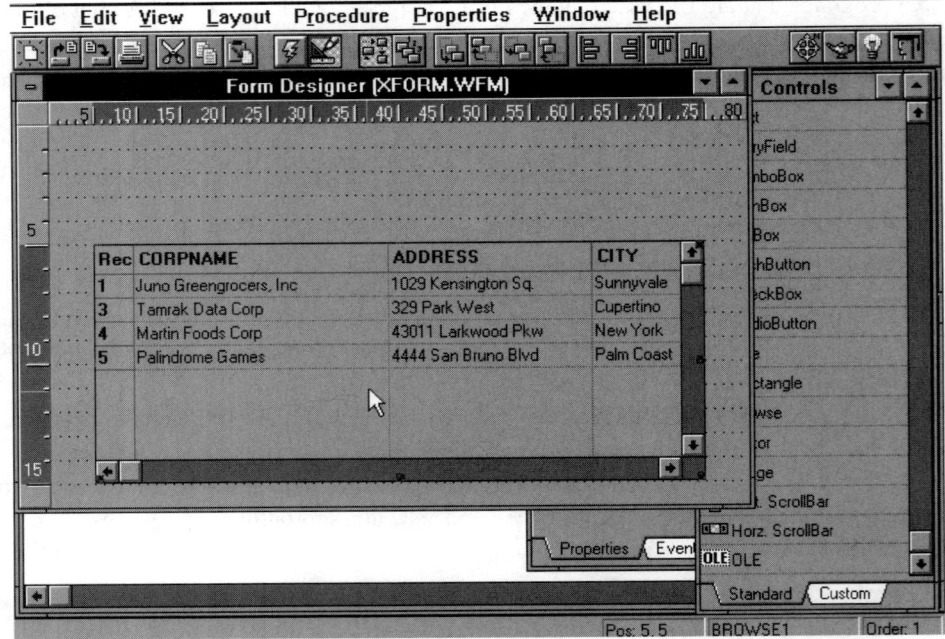

Figure 5.9 The browse object is surrounded by small black marks

```
Procedure BROWSE1_OnLeftDblClick(flags, col, row)
```

6. Below this line of program code, enter the routine shown in Listing 5.4.

```
xDialog.tCount.Text =;
   "Record count: "+LTRIM(STR(RECCOUNT()))
  xDialog.tRecno.Text = ;
   "Current record: "+LTRIM(STR(RECNO()))
  xDialog.ReadModal()
RETURN
```

Listing 5.4 Code for the OnLeftDblClick Property of a Pushbutton

7. Save your work by double-clicking the Control box at the upper left corner of the Procedure Editor.

    The Procedure Editor disappears.

8. Now click on the design surface window, somewhere outside the browse object.

    The selection boxes on the browse object disappear. This means that the form is now selected, and the form's properties are now displayed in the Object Inspector.

9. Click the Object Inspector.

Chapter 5 The Form Designer

The Object Inspector moves to the foreground.

10. Click the OnOpen property in the Object Inspector; then click the Tool Button that appears on the right.

    The Procedure Editor appears again.

11. Enter the program code shown in Listing 5.5.

```
PUBLIC xDialog
xDialog = NEW FORM("STATS")
xDialog.Height = 7
xDialog.Width = 25
xDialog.Top = 6
xDialog.Left = 80
xDialog.MDI = .F.
xDialog.tCount = NEW TEXT(xDialog)
xDialog.tCount.Top = 1
xDialog.tCount.Left = 2
xDialog.tCount.Width = 25
xDialog.tRecno = NEW TEXT(xDialog)
xDialog.tRecno.Top = 3
xDialog.tRecno.Left = 2
xDialog.tRecno.Width = 25
xDialog.OKBtn = NEW PUSHBUTTON(xDialog)
xDialog.OKBtn.Text = "OK"
xDialog.OKBtn.Top = 5
xDialog.OKBtn.Left = 6
xDialog.OKBtn.Width = 12
xDialog.OKBtn.OnClick = {;xDialog.Close()}
```

Listing 5.5 Code for the OnOpen Property of a Form

12. Save your work by double-clicking the Control box at the upper left corner of the Procedure Editor.

    The Procedure Editor disappears.

13. Now click the **Run** SpeedButton (the one with a lightning bolt in it).

    In a few seconds, all Form Designer windows disappear, and the form is displayed in place of the design surface window, as shown in Figure 5.10. Note that the first field in the first record is highlighted.

14. Double-click the first field.

    A window containing table statistics and an **OK** pushbutton appears (see Figure 5.11).

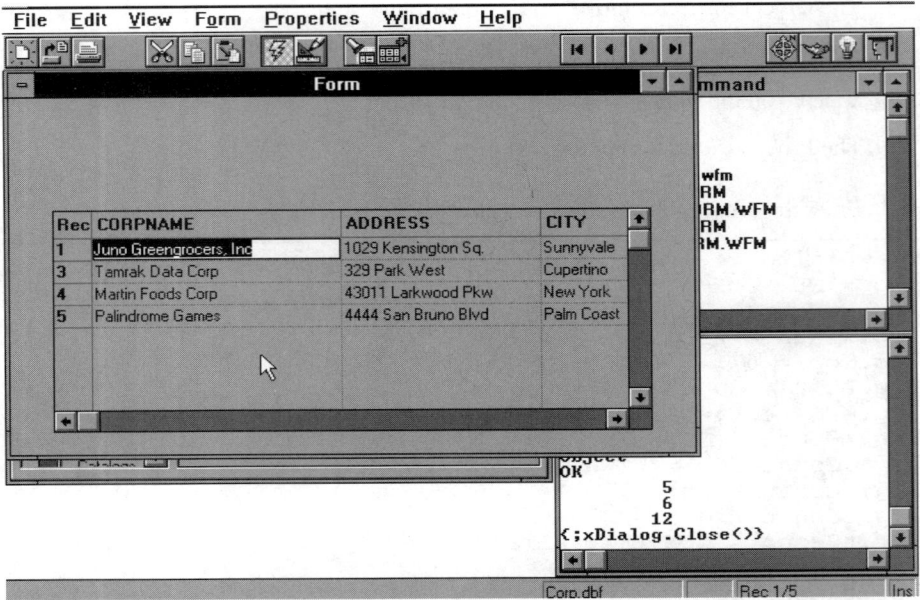

Figure 5.10 First field in the first record is highlighted

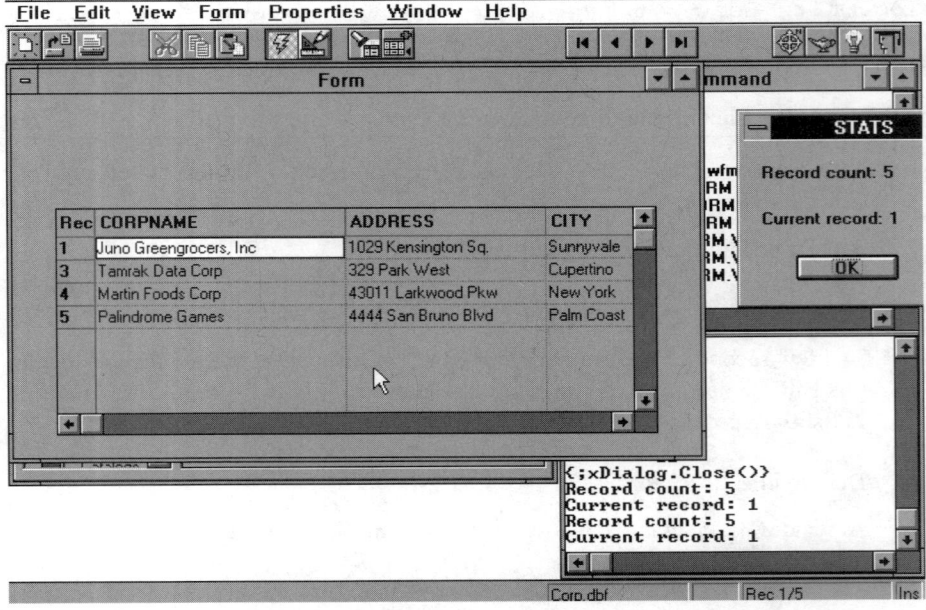

Figure 5.11 A window containing table statistics appears on the right

Chapter 5 The Form Designer

15. Click the **OK** pushbutton.

16. Close the form by double-clicking the Control box at the upper left corner.

    Control returns to the Command pane. Now let's look at the program you just produced with the Form Designer.

17. Open the program with the Text Editor.

    MODI COMM XFORM.WFM

    The program should look like the one in Listing 5.6 (shown below). Note that the member functions code section now contains two procedures (one named Form_OnOpen and the other named BROWSE1_OnLeftDblClick1).

```
** END HEADER -- do not remove this line*
* Generated on 99/99/99
*
LOCAL f
f = NEW XFORMFORM()
f.Open()

CLASS XFORMFORM OF FORM
   Set Procedure To C:\DBASEWIN\SAMPLES\BUTTONS.CC additive
   this.OnLeftDblClick = CLASS::FORM_ONLEFTDBLCLICK
   this.Height =          15.9404
   this.Left   =          10.5
   this.Top    =           1.1758
   this.Text = "Form"
   this.Width  =          79.666
   this.View = "ACCOUNTS.QBE"
   this.OnOpen = CLASS::FORM_ONOPEN
   this.HelpId = ""
   this.HelpFile = ""

   DEFINE BROWSE BROWSE1 OF THIS;
       PROPERTY;
         FontBold .F.,;
         Height          10,;
         Left             5,;
         Top              5,;
         Width           70,;
         ColorNormal "N/W"

   Procedure Form_OnLeftDblClick(flags, col, row)
      xDialog.tCount.Text =;
        "Record count: "+LTRIM(STR(RECCOUNT()))
      xDialog.tRecno.Text = ;
        "Current record: "+LTRIM(STR(RECNO()))
      xDialog.ReadModal()
   RETURN
```

```
Procedure Form_OnOpen
PUBLIC xDialog
xDialog = NEW FORM("STATS")
xDialog.Height = 7
xDialog.Width = 25
xDialog.Top = 6
xDialog.Left = 80
xDialog.MDI = .F.
xDialog.tCount = NEW TEXT(xDialog)
xDialog.tCount.Top = 1
xDialog.tCount.Left = 2
xDialog.tCount.Width = 25
xDialog.tRecno = NEW TEXT(xDialog)
xDialog.tRecno.Top = 3
xDialog.tRecno.Left = 2
xDialog.tRecno.Width = 25
xDialog.OKBtn = NEW PUSHBUTTON(xDialog)
xDialog.OKBtn.Text = "OK"
xDialog.OKBtn.Top = 5
xDialog.OKBtn.Left = 6
xDialog.OKBtn.Width = 12
xDialog.OKBtn.OnClick = {;xDialog.Close()}

ENDCLASS
```

Listing 5.6 Two Procedures in the Member Functions Section

The code you wrote for the OnOpen property of the form (Listing 5.6) performed the following tasks:

- Declared an object reference variable (xDialog) as PUBLIC. Declaring a variable public makes it available to other routines.

- Created a second form from the stock class Form, specified its dimensions, and set its MDI property to false (.F.). Among other things, setting MDI to false lets you use other windows while the second window is open.

- Created two text objects for displaying information on the current record.

- Created a pushbutton for closing the second form.

- Assigned a codeblock to the OnClick property of the pushbutton. This codeblock closes the second form.

The code you wrote for the OnLeftDblClick property performed the following tasks:

- Set the Text property of the first text object (tCount) to display the total number of records

- Set the Text property of the second text object (tRecno) to display the number of the current record

- Open the second form, which contains the text objects

Note that the name of each procedure consists mostly of the object class to which it is assigned and the name of the event property that triggers it, separated by an underscore character. For example, the subroutine you assigned to the browse object is named BROWSE1_OnLeftDblClick1. dBASE generates these names automatically. However, there is nothing special about them; any unique names would have worked just as well. You can edit the program and change the names to less unwieldy ones if you like.

Object Refreshing

It is extremely important that control objects reflect the current values of the field to which they are linked. However, this is not always so; for example, when two or more objects are linked to the same field and one of the objects makes a change in the field, the other object may not reflect the change automatically. Fortunately, the language of dBASE for Windows has a command (SHOW OBJECT) that forces objects to reflect the current values of their fields. This is known as *refreshing*.

Exercise 4

In this exercise you create three objects: an entry field, a spin box, and a scroll bar. Each object is linked to the same value, the numeric field ADPRICE of ADVERT.DBF. Each object can change the value in ADPRICE, so it's important that the change be reflected in all objects when one object changes the field. You use the SHOW OBJECT command to do this.

1. Start a new form with the Form Designer.

   CREATE FORM EXC4

   The Form Designer windows appear.

2. Resize the design surface window so its dimensions are roughly 15 (by the left ruler) by 65 (by the top ruler).

   The form should look like the one in Figure 5.12.

3. Go to the Object Inspector and click the View property.

   As before, a Tool button appears at the right.

4. Click the Tool button.

   The Choose View dialog box appears.

5. Double-click **Accounts.qbe**.

150   Easy dBASE for Windows Object-Oriented Programming

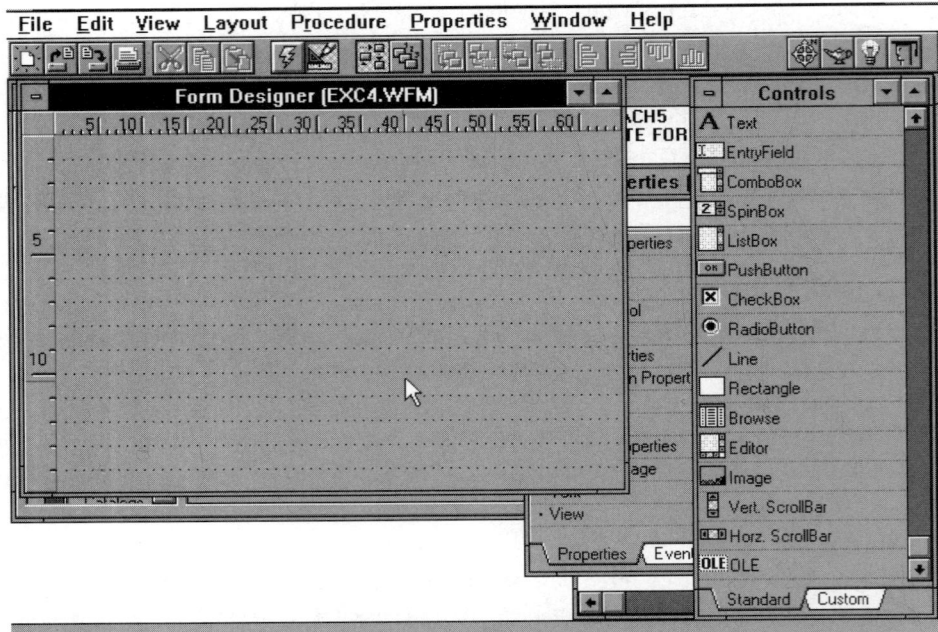

Figure 5.12 Resized design surface

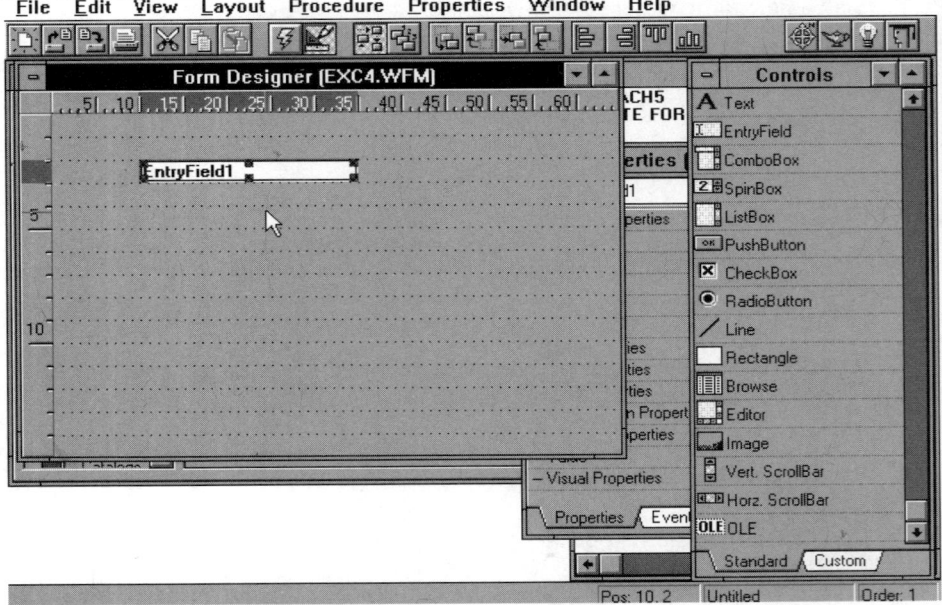

Figure 5.13 An entry field is created

Chapter 5 The Form Designer   151

The dialog box disappears, and **ACCOUNTS.QBE** is displayed in the View property of the Object Inspector.

6. Click **EntryField** in the Object Pallette.

7. Place the mouse pointer at row 2 (indicated by the left ruler), column 10 (indicated by the top ruler), and hold down the mouse button. Drag the pointer to row 3, column 35, then release the mouse button.

   An entry field is created, as shown in Figure 5.13.

8. Click **SpinBox** in the Object Pallette.

9. Using the technique described in Step 7, create a spin box from row 4, column 10 to row 6, column 26.

10. Click **Vertical ScrollBar** in the Object Pallette, then create a scroll bar from row 1, column 40 to row 11, column 45.

    The form should now resemble Figure 5.14.

    Now you must link these objects with the data retrieved by ACCOUNTS.QBE.

11. Click the entry field.

    The entry field is surrounded by selection boxes. (We refer to this as *selection* in all subsequent steps.)

12. Click **DataLink** in the Object Inspector, then on the Tool button that appears at the right.

    The Choose Field dialog box is displayed.

13. Click on **ADVERT** in the list at the left.

    This specifies that you want to select a field from ADVERT.DBF.

14. Click on **ADPRICE**, then click the **OK** button.

15. Repeat Steps 11 through 14 for the spin box and the scroll bar.

    In each case, the object should be linked to the ADPRICE field of ADVERT.DBF.

16. Select the spinbox you created, then double-click **Edit Properties** in the Object Inspector.

    A list of properties appear, one of which is RangeMax (currently set to 100).

17. Change the value in RangeMax to 32766.

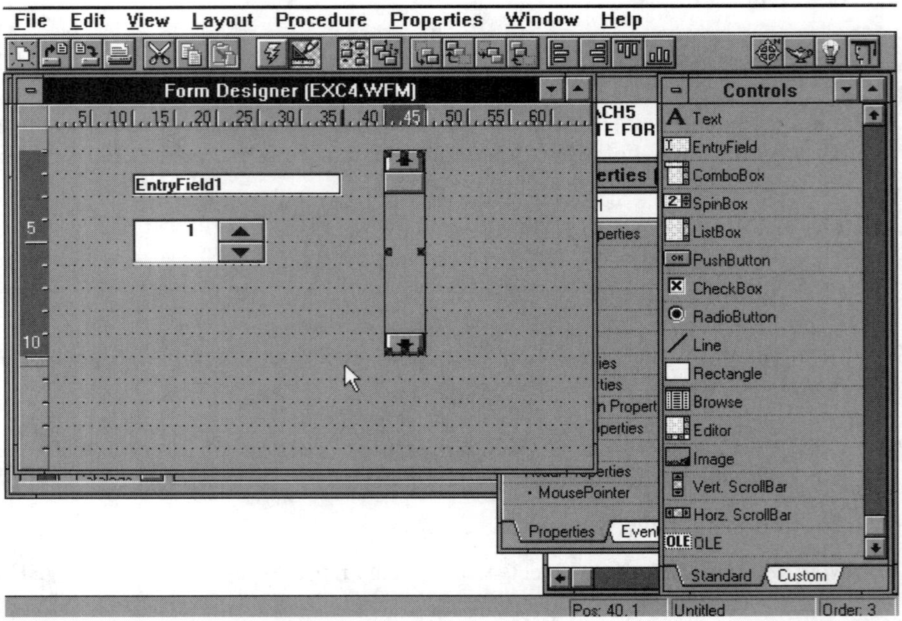

Figure 5.14 The form with an EntryField, SpinBox, and a ScrollBar

18. Repeat Steps 16 and 17 with the scroll bar.

19. Select the entry field, click **OnChange** in the **Events** page of the Object Inspector, then click the Tool button at the right.

    The Procedure editor appears.

20. Enter the following program code, then quit by double-clicking the Control box at the upper left corner:

    ```
    SHOW OBJECT form.SCROLLBAR1
    SHOW OBJECT form.SPINBOX1
    ```

21. Select the spin box, click **OnChange** in the Object Inspector, then click the Tool button at the right.

    The Procedure editor appears.

22. Enter the following program code, then quit by double-clicking the Control box at the upper left corner:

```
SHOW OBJECT form.ENTRYFIELD1
SHOW OBJECT form.SCROLLBAR1
```

21. Select the scroll bar, click **OnChange** in the Object Inspector, then click the Tool button at the right.

    The Procedure editor appears.

22. Enter the following program code, then quit by double-clicking the Control box at the upper-left corner:

    ```
    SHOW OBJECT form.ENTRYFIELD1
    SHOW OBJECT form.SPINBOX1
    ```

    Now you're ready to run the program.

23. Click the **Run** SpeedButton.

    All Form Designer windows disappear, and the form is ready to use.

24. Move the slider button on the scroll bar all the way down.

    The number 32766.00 appears in the entry field and the spin box.

25. Click in the left of the spin box, delete the number that appears there, enter the number 15000 manually, then press <Enter>.

    Note that the change is reflected in the scroll bar and the entry field.

26. Continue performing experiments like these until you feel you understand the way the objects work. When you are finished, close the Form Designer.

This exercise illustrates the importance of refreshing. When an object is refreshed, it reflects the current value of the data to which it is linked. In the example above, three objects were linked to the same field (ADPRICE, a numeric value). Refreshing ensured that each change made to ADPRICE by one object was instantly reflected in the other objects. For example, when the number in the spin box is changed, the OnChange property of that object uses the SHOW OBJECT command to refresh the entry field and the scroll bar, making them reflect the change.

Refreshing is not always necessary; in many cases, objects refresh even without the SHOW OBJECT command. For example, when you change the value in a scroll bar, it is reflected in an entry field automatically (if both objects are linked to the same field). However, there are situations where this can't be counted on, so it is best to make sure by explicitly telling dBASE to refresh. In fact, there's even a term for this; a program that is designed to work every time and in all situations is said to be *robust*.

Incidentally, there is another dBASE command named REFRESH that refreshes the objects in a form. The difference between REFRESH and SHOW OBJECT is that SHOW

OBJECT refreshes individual objects, while REFRESH always refreshes every object in the form.

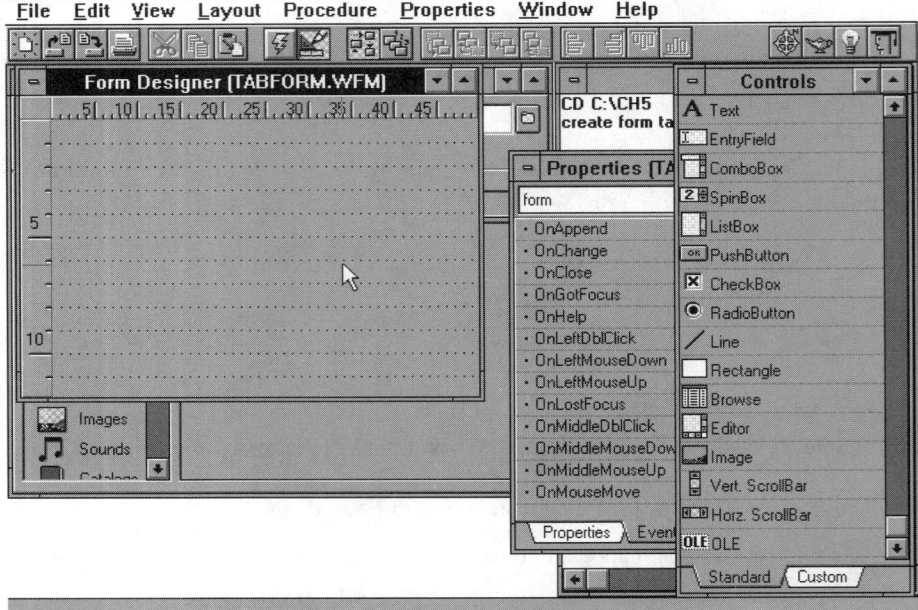

Figure 5.15   Resized design surface window

In Step 17 you set the RangeMax property of the spin box and the scroll bar to 32766, the highest number you can set it to. RangeMax sets an upper limit on the value that can be contained in the object. A related property, RangeMin, sets the lower limit.

Object Grouping

When an object is selected by the user at runtime, it is said to have *focus*. Only one object can have focus at a time, and that object is the only one that can be used to add or change the data to which it is linked.

There are two ways to move focus from object to object in a form at runtime. The obvious way is to click it with the mouse; the less obvious way is to press <Tab> (which moves "forward" through the objects) or <Shift-Tab> (which moves "backward" through the objects). The order in which focus is given to objects when <Tab> or <Shift-Tab> is pressed is known as the form's *tabbing order*.

Exercise 5

In this exercise you create a form with a list box and three pushbuttons. You experiment with the natural (that is, the default) tabbing order of the form. In the next exercise, you alter this tabbing order.

1. Start a new form with the Form Designer.

    CREATE FORM TABFORM

    The Form Designer appears.

2. Resize the design surface window to be 12 rows high and 50 columns wide, as shown in Figure 5.15.

3. Click the **View** property in the Object Inspector, then click the Tool button that appears at the right.

    The Choose View dialog box appears. This time, you base the form on a table file (.DBF) instead of a query (.QBE).

4. Click **advert.dbf** in the list offered by the dialog box, then click the **OK** pushbutton.

    The dialog box disappears, and the **ADVERT.DBF** is displayed by the **View** property in the Object Inspector.

5. Using what you now know about the Object pallette and the design surface window, create the following items:

    - A list box from row 2, column 5 to row 9, column 20
    - A pushbutton from row 2 column 22, to row 3, column 38
    - A pushbutton from row 4 column 22, to row 5, column 38
    - A pushbutton from row 6 column 22, to row 7, column 38

6. Using the Text property of each pushbutton, create the following lables:

    - **Top Button** in the top pushbutton
    - **Mid Button** in the middle pushbutton
    - **Last Button** in the last pushbutton

7. Select the list box, then double-click **Data Linkage Properties** in the Object Inspector.

    Among others, the **DataSource** property appears.

8. Click the **DataSource** property, then click the Tool button that appears at the right.

    The Choose Data Source dialog box appears.

9. Click the down arrow button, select **Field**, then click the tool button.

    The Choose Field dialog box appears.

10. Double-click the ACCOUNTNO field. When the Choose Field dialog box disappears, click the **OK** button.

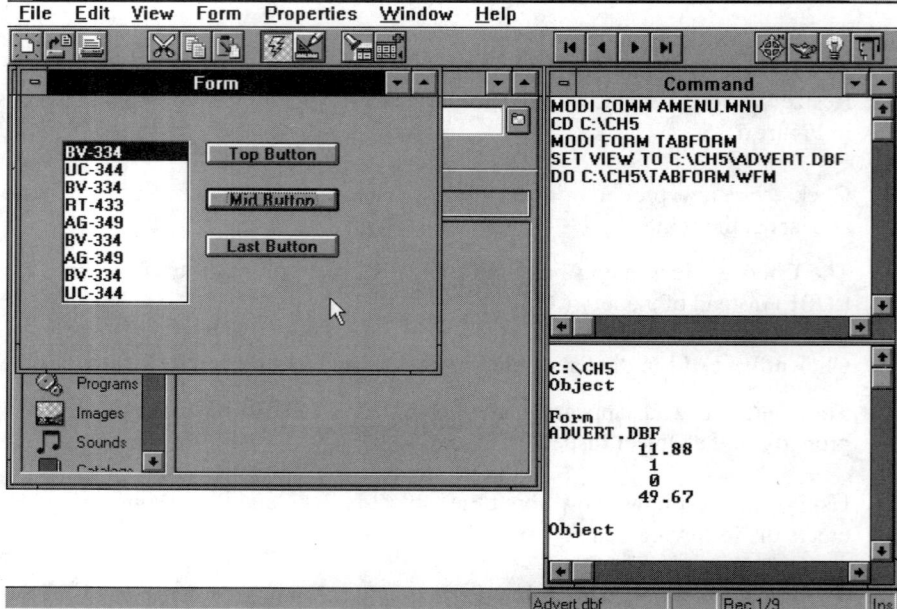

Figure 5.16   Result of running the form

The Choose Data Source dialog box disappears.

11. Now run the form by clicking the Run speedbutton (the one with the lightning bolt).

    In a few seconds, the form is displayed in Run mode, as shown in Figure 5.16.

12. Press <Tab>.

    Note that focus moves from the list box to the top pushbutton.

13. Press <Tab> again.

    Focus moves from the top pushbutton to the next one down.

14. Press <Shift-Tab>.

    Focus moves back to the top pushbutton.

15. Keep pushing <Tab> and <Shift-Tab> until you feel you understand the default tabbing order of the form.

16. Close the form.

As is apparent, the default tabbing order of a form is usually left to right, top to bottom. But what if you want focus to move in a different order? For example, what if you want the middle pushbutton to receive initial focus instead of the list box? The next exercise shows how the Form Designer handles this issue.

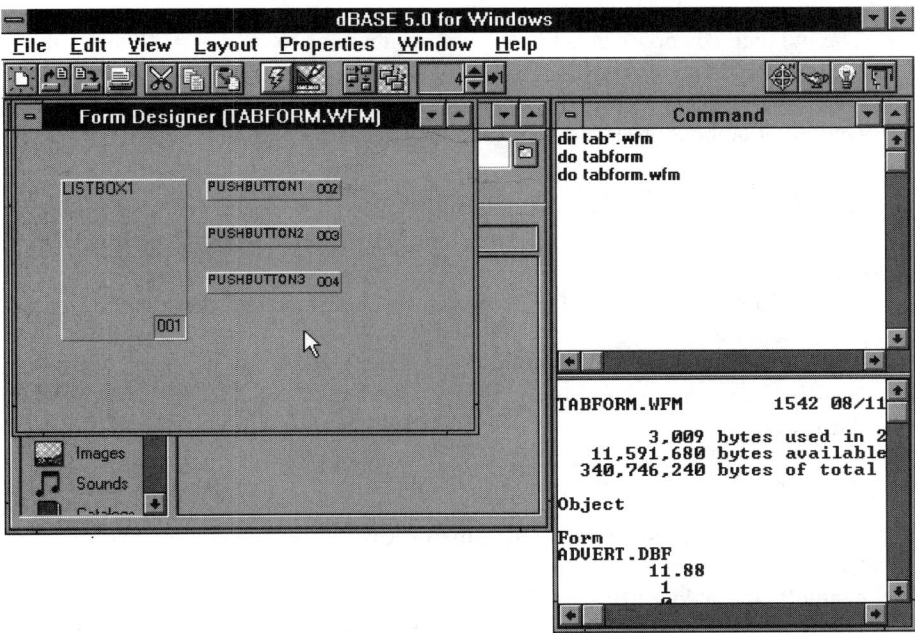

Figure 5.17   Each object is numbered

Exercise 6

In this exercise you change the tabbing order of the form you created in Exercise 5.

1. Open the form in the Form Designer.

   ```
   MODIFY FORM TABFORM
   ```

2. Click **View | Order View** from the dBASE menu.

   The form takes on a somewhat flat appearance, and each object is numbered (see Figure 5.17). Each number represents its object's place in the tabbing order of the form. The list box is first in the tabbing order, the top pushbutton is the second, and so on.

   Note also that a spin box appears in the SpeedBar. This spin box contains the tabbing order number to insert in each object you select; that is, each time you click on an object, that number is given as the tabbing order number of that object. Currently, the number is 1.

3. Click the middle pushbutton.

   Note that the number 1 is now placed in the middle pushbutton. Note also that the number in the spin box is incremented to 2.

4. Click the top pushbutton.

   The number 2 is now placed in the top pushbutton. Note also that the number in the list box is incremented to 3.

5. Get out of tabbing order mode by clicking **View | Layout View**.

6. Run the form by clicking the Run SpeedButton.

   Note that the middle pushbutton has focus.

7. Press <Tab> and <Shift-Tab> until you've confirmed the new tabbing order, then close the form.

8. Now let's see what code changes were made by the Form Designer. Open the form in the Text Editor.

   ```
   MODI COMM TABFORM.WFM
   ```

   The program code should resemble that in Listing 5.7 (shown below). Note that the tabbing order matches the order in which the objects are declared in the program. For example, the **Mid Button** pushbutton was declared first, then the list box. Whether you write code yourself or generate it with the Form Designer, the tabbing order of a form conforms to the order of declaration.

```
** END HEADER -- do not remove this line*
* Generated on 08/27/94
*
LOCAL f
f = NEW TABFORMFORM()
f.Open()

CLASS TABFORMFORM OF FORM
   Set Procedure To C:\DBASEWIN\SAMPLES\BUTTONS.CC additive
   this.Height =          12
   this.Left =            1
   this.Top =             0
   this.Text = "Form"
   this.Width =           49.666
   this.View = "ADVERT.DBF"
   this.HelpId = ""
   this.HelpFile = ""

   DEFINE PUSHBUTTON PUSHBUTTON2 OF THIS;
      PROPERTY;
```

```
            Height          1,;
            Left           22,;
            Top             4,;
            Group .T.,;
            Text "Mid Button",;
            Width          16,;
            ColorNormal "N/W"

    DEFINE PUSHBUTTON PUSHBUTTON1 OF THIS;
        PROPERTY;
            Default .T.,;
            Height          1,;
            Left           22,;
            Top             2,;
            Group .T.,;
            Text "Top Button",;
            Width          16,;
            ColorNormal "N/W"

    DEFINE LISTBOX LISTBOX1 OF THIS;
        PROPERTY;
            Height          7,;
            ID            100,;
            Left            5,;
            Top             2,;
            Width          15,;
            ColorNormal "N/W*",;
            ColorHighLight "W+/B",;
            DataSource "FIELD ADVERT->ACCOUNTNO"

    DEFINE PUSHBUTTON PUSHBUTTON3 OF THIS;
        PROPERTY;
            Height          1,;
            Left           22,;
            Top             6,;
            Group .T.,;
            Text "Last Button",;
            Width          16,;
            ColorNormal "N/W"

ENDCLASS
```

Listing 5.7 Tabbing Order Determined by Order of Declaration

9. Close the editor.

Configuring the Form Designer

It should already be obvious that the Form Designer is a highly flexible tool. Not only can you create a form and the objects contained by it, but you can adjust their sizes and properties easily and quickly. However, the Form Designer is even more flexible than that. dBASE for Windows offers the Form Designer Properties window, which lets you adjust the properties of the Form Designer itself.

Exercise 7

In this exercise you become acquainted with the Form Designer Properties window, which lets you adjust the way the Form Designer creates forms.

1. Open the form you created in the previous exercise with the Form Designer.

   ```
   MODIFY FORM EXC4
   ```

   The Form Designer windows appear.

2. Click **Properties | Form Designer...**.

   The Form Designer Properties window appears, as shown in Figure 5.18. Note that the **Show Grid**, **Snap To Grid**, and **Show Ruler** check boxes are checked, indicating that these settings are in an ON condition.

3. Click the **Show Grid** check box.

   The check disappears.

4. Click the **OK** button.

   The design surface window now has no grid lines, as shown in Figure 5.19. This feature is useful when you want to see how the form will look when it is active, without actually running the form.

5. Click **Properties | Form Designer...** again.

6. Click the **Show Grid** check box again, restoring the check in the check box.

7. Click the **Snap To Grid** check box.

   The check disappears.

8. Click the **OK** button.

9. Place the mouse pointer on the spin box, hold down the left mouse button, and drag the spin box to row 5 1/2 through 6 1/2 (on the left ruler) and any column position.

Chapter 5 The Form Designer 161

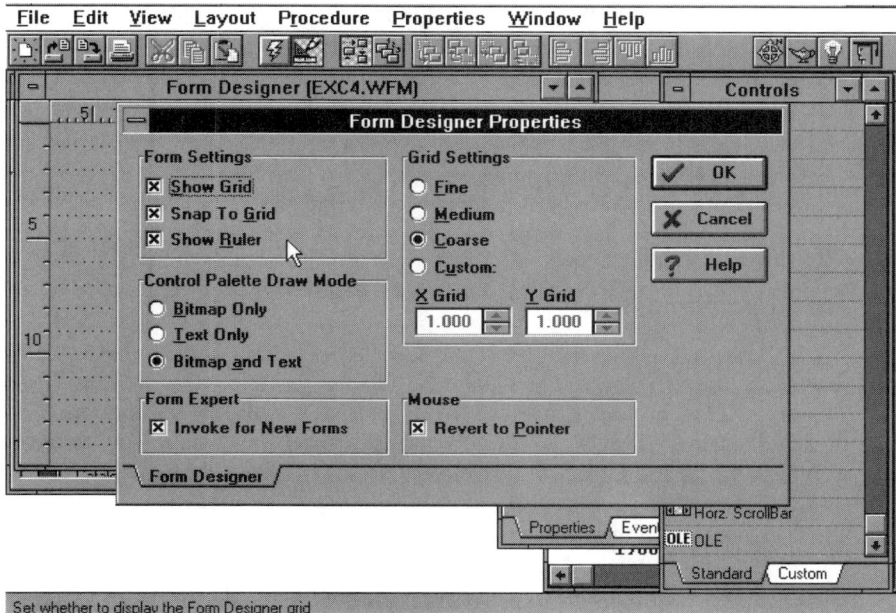

Figure 5.18 The Form Designer Properties window appears

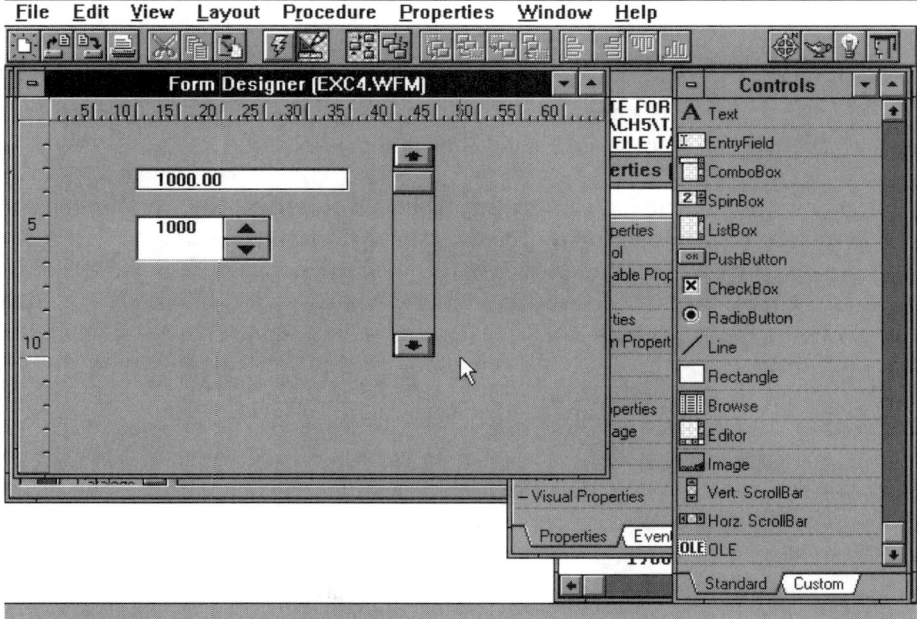

Figure 5.19 The design surface without grid lines

Note that it is now possible to place the object in fractional coordinates; the object no longer "snaps" to integer coordinates. This feature is useful when you want to place objects in precise locations.

10. Click **Properties | Form Designer...** again.

11. Click the **Snap To Grid** check box again, restoring the check in the check box.

12. Click the **Show Ruler** check box.

    The check disappears.

13. Click the **OK** button.

    The top and left rulers are now removed. As with the **Show Grid** option, this feature is useful when you want to see how the form will look when it is active, without actually running the form.

14. Click **Properties | Form Designer...** again.

15. Click the **Show Ruler** check box again, restoring the check in the check box.

16. Click the **OK** button.

17. Close the Form Designer.

When you turn the **Snap To Grid** option off, you allow the maximum flexibility for object placement; thereafter, the grid serves as a passive guide only, and does not influence object placement. The price you pay for this flexiblity is twofold:

- It's more difficult to line objects up with one another, since the grid no longer positions objects in standard row or column coordinates. For example, you might want to neatly align a column of pushbuttons in (the classic example is the **OK**, **NO**, and **CANCEL** pushbutton trio seen in so many Windows applications). When **Snap To Grid** is set off, you have to do the alignment by hand--sometimes a painful task.

- It's more difficult to size similar objects (like pushbutton groups) identically. The grid serves as a very handy sizing tool, and the **Snap To Grid** option makes each object conform to standard proportions.

The settings you make in the Form Designer Properties window remain until you change them explicitly. Even if you terminate the current dBASE session and start a new one, the settings you specify remain until you change them again.

Now let's see how to configure the grid of the design surface window.

Exercise 8

In this exercise you adjust the height of each row in the design surface window.

Chapter 5   The Form Designer   163

1. Open the form with the Form Designer.

   ```
   MODIFY FORM EXC4
   ```

   The Form Designer windows appear.

2. Examine the grid lines in the design surface window, and note their distance from one another.

3. Click **Properties | Form Designer...**.

   Note that the **Coarse** radio button in the **Grid Settings** section of the Form Designer Properties window is selected.

4. Click the **Medium** radio button, then click the **OK** button.

   Note that the grid lines are closer together. This allows you to place objects with more precision, even when the **Snap To Grid** check box is checked.

5. Click **Properties | Form Designer...** again.

6. Click the **Custom** radio button.

   Note that two spin boxes are now active just beneath the radio button.

7. Click the downward arrow of the **X Grid** radio button until the number 0.375 appears there.

8. Click the **OK** pushbutton.

   Note that the lines are closer together.

9. Continue experimenting with settings in the **X Grid** and **Y Grid** spin boxes until you feel you understand each.

10. Set the grid setting back to **Coarse**.

11. Close the Form Designer.

The grid on a form helps you line up objects on a form without having to do it manually. Because of the adjustability of the grid, you can specify for yourself how wide the units of placement are and to what degree of precision you place each object. If you pack a form with many objects and space is at a premium, you'll likely want the grid to have narrower rows and columns, so objects can be placed closer together. (This also holds true if you want to create especially small objects on the form.) Conversely, if a form is sparsely populated with objects, you'll likely want wider rows and columns.

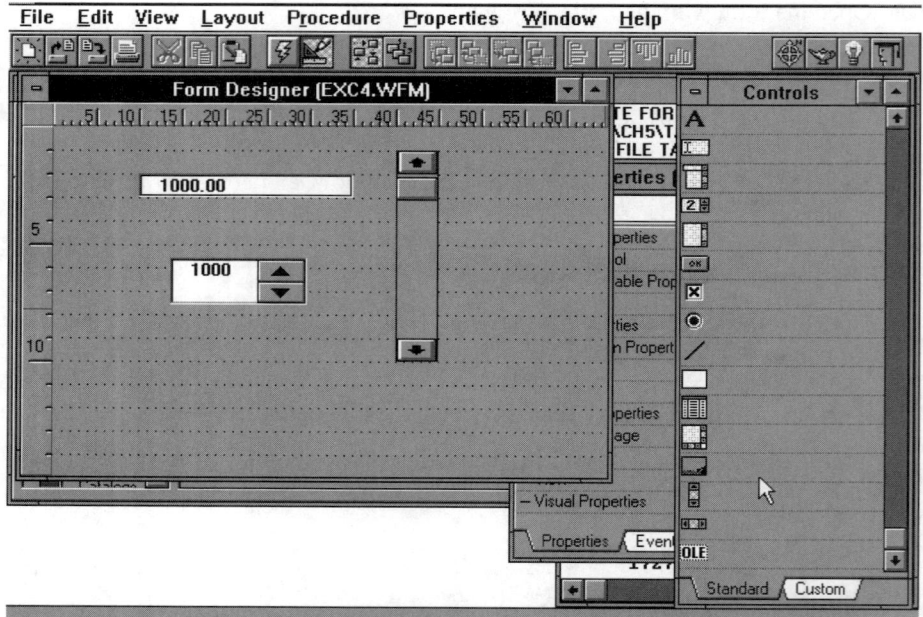

Figure 5.20 The Object Pallette displays only the bitmap icons

So far you've seen how to configure the design surface window; now let's see how to configure the Object Pallette.

Exercise 9

In this exercise you determine how items are displayed in the Object Pallette.

1. Open the form with the Form Designer.

    ```
    MODIFY FORM EXC4
    ```

    The Form Designer windows appear.

2. Examine the Object Pallette.

    Note that each control object option contains a bitmap icon and a name. Some programmers prefer one or the other, but not both.

3. Click **Properties | Form Designer...**

    Note that the **Object Pallette Draw Mode** section of the Form Designer Properties window contains radio buttons. The **Bitmap and Text** radio button is selected by default.

4. Click the **Bitmap Only** radio button.

Chapter 5 The Form Designer 165

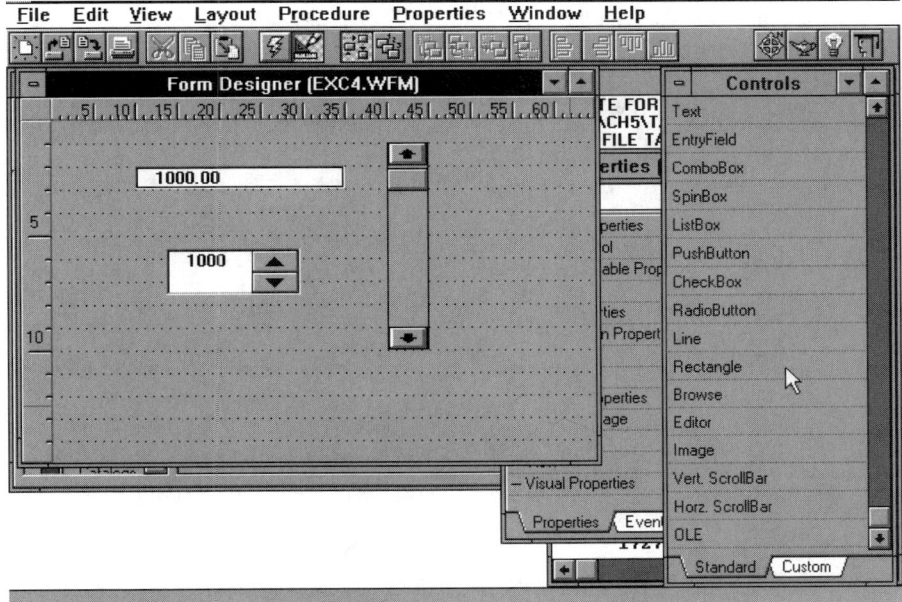

Figure 5.21 This time, the bitmap icons are not displayed

The button is now selected.

5. Click the **OK** button.

   Note that now the Object Pallette displays only the bitmap icons; the names of the control objects are not displayed (see Figure 5.20).

6. Click **Properties | Form Designer...**

7. This time, click the **Text Only** radio button, then click the **OK** pushbutton.

   Now the Object Pallette displays only the names of the control objects; the bitmap icons are not displayed (see Figure 5.21).

8. If you wish, change the Object Pallette back to its original condition, then close the Form Designer.

Now let's look at one more feature of the Form Designer you can configure: the behavior of the mouse pointer.

Exercise 10

In this exercise you make it possible to create multiple copies of an object by changing the way the mouse pointer responds to your actions.

1. Open the form with the Form Designer.

166 Easy dBASE for Windows Object-Oriented Programming

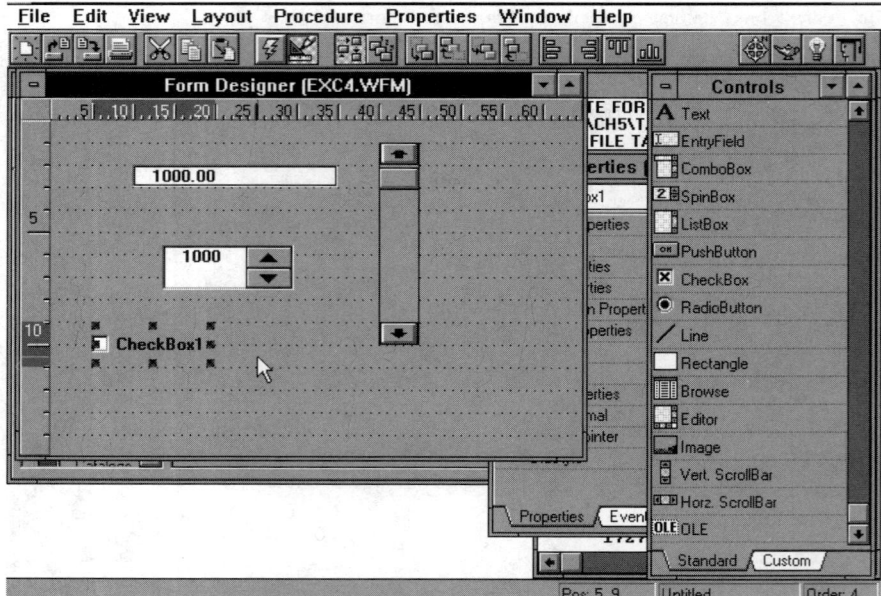

Figure 5.22 A CheckBox appears

```
MODIFY FORM EXC4
```

The Form Designer windows appear.

2. Click **Checkbox** in the Object Pallette.

3. Place the mouse pointer at row 9, Column 5, then click the left mouse button once.

   A check box is automatically placed at that location (see Figure 5.22).

4. Now place the mouse pointer at row 3, column 48, and click the left mouse button once.

   No new object is created this time. Note that the selection boxed disappeared from the first check box; this is because you selected the form. But what if you want to create multiple check boxes without using the Object Pallette?

5. Remove the check box by selecting it, then pressing <Del>.

6. Click **Properties | Form Designer....**

   Note that the **Revert To Pointer** check box under the **Mouse** heading is checked.

7. Remove this check by clicking the check box, then click the **OK** pushbutton.

8. Click the **Pushbutton** option in the Object Palette.

9. Place the mouse pointer at row 7, column 10, and click the left mouse button once.

   As before, a new check box is created.

10. Without using the Object Pallette, place the mouse pointer at row 10, column 10 and click the left mouse button once.

    This time, another check box is created.

11. Click **Properties | Form Designer...**, then replace the check in **Revert To Pointer** by clicking it once.

12. Click the **OK** pushbutton.

13. Close the Form Designer.

As you get to know the Form Designer and evaluate your particular needs and preferences, use the settings demonstrated here to make application development as quick and easy as possible.

What Next?

Forms, and the control objects you place in them, make data access and modification easy for your users. However, there is also a vital class of object called Menu that lets you create standard Windows menus. Menus play a crucial role in most serious Windows applications, so much so that dBASE for Windows has a two-way tool called the Menu Designer that creates and modifies them. That is the subject of the next chapter.

Chapter 6
Working with Menus

Menus have been an important medium of communication between human and computer for decades, and their significance is not diminished by the Windows environment. Not only does Windows itself use menus, but users have come to expect a menu system in Windows applications. Many users (including employers and clients) are uncomfortable without menus, and often insist on having them. Consequently, many of your applications are likely to be judged (rightly or wrongly) on the quality and utility of the menu systems you design.

Fortunately, dBASE for Windows has an object class named Menu from which you can create sophisticated and powerful menu systems. In addition, there is a two-way tool known as the *Menu Designer* that generates program code for creating and activating menu systems. Let's look at the Menu object class first.

The Menu Object Class

Figure 6.1 (see page 170) shows a typical menu system. Each menu (**File**, **Edit**, **View**, and **Help**) is an instance of the Menu class, and each option offered by each menu (for example, **Open**, **Close**, **Create/Modify**, and **Delete** of the **File** menu) is also an instance of the class. Let's do an example.

The program code that generates a menu system usually resides in a *menu file* (extension .MNU). You assign a menu file to a form with the form's MenuFile property.

Exercise 1

In this exercise you create a simple menu system. In the process, you use the MDI property of forms to determine where the menu is displayed. The menu system you create offers no menu options; you'll add these in the next exercise.

1. Start a menu file with the Text Editor.

   MODI COMM AMENU.MNU

2. Write the program shown in Listing 6.1 (shown below), then save and exit.

```
Parameter FormObj
NEW AMENUMENU(FormObj,"Root")
CLASS AMENUMENU(FormObj,Name) OF MENU(FormObj,Name)
   this.Text = ""

   DEFINE MENU FILE OF THIS;
       PROPERTY;
         Text "File"
```

```
    DEFINE MENU EDIT OF THIS;
        PROPERTY;
           Text "Edit"

    DEFINE MENU VIEW OF THIS;
        PROPERTY;
           Text "View"

    DEFINE MENU HELP OF THIS;
        PROPERTY;
           Text "Help"

ENDCLASS
```

Listing 6.1 Creating Five Menus

3. Start a program file with the Text Editor.

   ```
   MODI COMM GOMENU
   ```

4. Write the program shown in Listing 6.2, then save and exit.

```
CLEAR ALL
X = NEW FORM()
X.MDI = .F.
x.Left = 30
x.Top = 9
x.Width = 60
x.MenuFile = "AMENU.MNU"
x.Text = "A Typical Menu System"
x.Open()
```

Listing 6.2 Creating a New Form and Specifying the Menu File

5. Run the program.

   ```
   DO GOMENU
   ```

   The form shown in Figure 6.1 appears. Each item on the top of the form is a *menu*, and the region of the form in which the menus appear is known as the *menu bar*. Menu bars are standard features common to most Windows applications. For example, the dBASE menus at the top of the screen (**File**, **Edit**, **Program**, **Table**, **Properties**, **Window**, and **Help**) are displayed in the *dBASE menu bar*, which is part of the *dBASE application window*--the window that opens when you start a dBASE session.

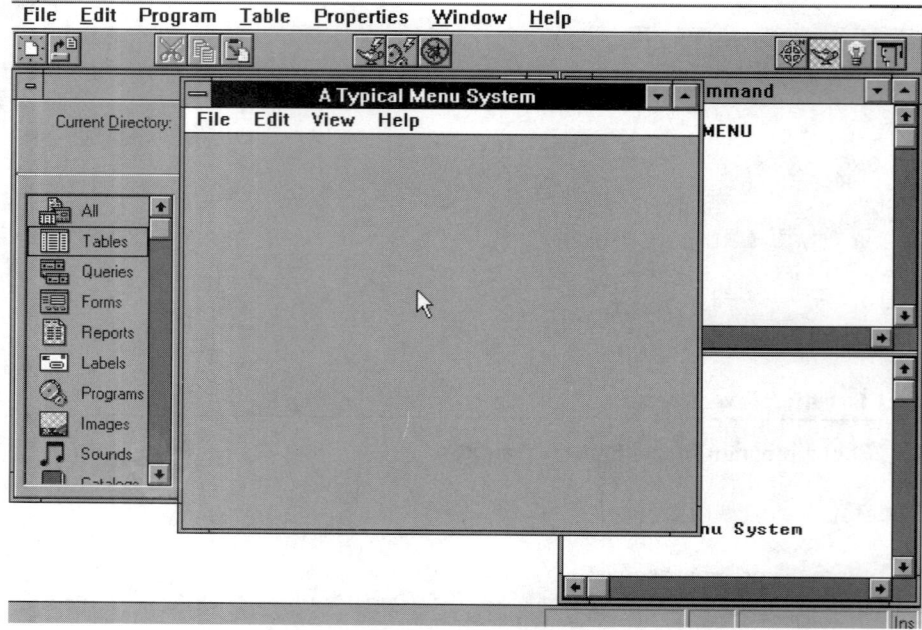

Figure 6.1   A typical menu

Any time you create a menu with the Menu object class, it appears in a menu bar, in either a form or in the dBASE application window.

6. Click on several of the menus.

   Notice that no options appear under them.

7. Press <Alt-Tab>.

   The form disappears. This is because the MDI property of the form is set to false (see Listing 6.2).

8. Press <Alt-Tab> again.

   The form reappears.

9. Close the form.

10. Open the program file again.

    ```
    MODI COMM GOMENU
    ```

11. Change the following line of program code:

Chapter 6 Working with Menus 171

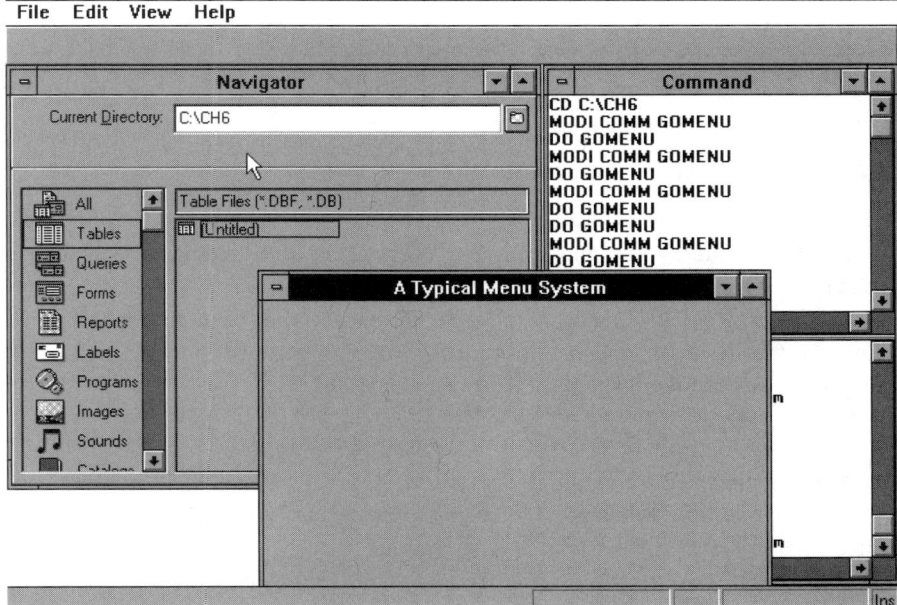

Figure 6.2 Menus appear at the upper left portion of the screen

```
X.MDI = .F.
```

to:

```
X.MDI = .T.
```

12. Save and exit.

13. Run the program.

    ```
    DO GOMENU
    ```

    Note that this time, no menus appear in the form. Instead, they're at the upper-left portion of the screen, where they replace the dBASE menus in the dBASE menu bar (see Figure 6.2).

14. Press <Alt-Tab>.

    This time, the entire dBASE application frame window disappears, taking the form with it. This is also due to the fact that the MDI property of the form is set to true.

15. Press <Alt-Tab> again.

    The form and the dBASE application frame window reappear.

16. Close the form.

Examine the program in Listing 6.1. This program uses the CLASS...ENDCLASS command to create a custom class named AMENUMENU and creates a menu object (that is, an *instance* of the Menu class) with the following command:

```
NEW AMENUMENU(FormObj,"Root")
```

The FormObj parameter is an object reference that points to the parent form. This object reference is automatically stored in the Parent property of the menu object that is created, allowing the menu object to know in which form it's contained.

The parameter "Root" is stored in the Name property of the menu object, and serves as an object reference that points to the menu object. For example, the following command would change the prompt of the **File** menu object from **File** to **Hello**:

```
form.Root.File.Text = "Hello"
```

Note that the form is the containing object and the Root menu object the contained object. In turn, the Root menu object contains the other menu objects (**File**, **Edit**, **View**, and **Help**). In other words, Root is the top-level menu object, and the other menu objects are subsidiary menu objects that branch out from it, rather like an inverted tree. The Root menu object is not visible to the user, since it doesn't have a Text prompt like **File** or **View**. It actually serves as the "root" for all others; hence the name.

When you set the MDI property of a form to true (.T.), the form conforms to a standard known as Multiple Document Interface. MDI forms have several characteristics that set them apart from non-MDI forms. The most immediately obvious of these characteristics is the fact that an MDI form's menu system appears in the dBASE menu bar instead of the form's menu bar.

Another characteristic, which you demonstrated in Steps 14 and 15, is that an MDI form is a *child* of the dBASE application frame window. The child window (in this case, the form) can only be displayed inside its parent window (in this case, the dBASE application frame window). When a form is non-MDI, it said to be a *peer* of the dBASE application frame window. When one window is a peer of another, Windows interprets an <Alt-Tab> key press as a directive to switch from one to another. When one window is the child of another, Windows interprets the key press as a directive to switch to another window entirely.

Now let's give some options to one of the menus.

Exercise 2

In this exercise you add menu options to the **Edit** menu. These options, known as *menu items*, are menu objects in their own right. In fact, all selectable elements that appear in a menu system are menu objects, each with its own property settings and each with an object reference that points to it.

1. Open the menu file with the Text Editor.

```
MODI COMM AMENU.MNU
```

2. Add the program code shown in Listing 6.3 under the following command:

```
DEFINE MENU FILE OF THIS;
    PROPERTY;
        Text "File"
```

```
    DEFINE MENU OPEN OF THIS.FILE;
        PROPERTY;
            Text "Open"

    DEFINE MENU CLOSE OF THIS.FILE;
        PROPERTY;
            Text "Close"

    DEFINE MENU CREATE OF THIS.FILE;
        PROPERTY;
            Text "Create/Modify"

    DEFINE MENU DELETE OF THIS.FILE;
        PROPERTY;
            Text "Delete"

    DEFINE MENU EXECUTE OF THIS.FILE;
        PROPERTY;
            Text "Execute"
```

Listing 6.3 Code that Creates Menu Options

3. Save and exit.

4. Run the program.

   DO GOMENU

   As before, the menu appears in the dBASE menu bar.

5. Click the **File** menu.

   The **File** menu's new options are displayed, as shown in Figure 6.3. Menus like this are sometimes called *dropdown menus*. Each option in a dropdown menu (such as **Open, Close, Create/Modify, Delete** or **Execute**) is called a *menu item*.

6. Click any of the menu items in the dropdown menu.

   The dropdown menu disappears, and nothing else happens. This is because you haven't assigned a subroutine to any of the options. You'll fix that in the next exercise.

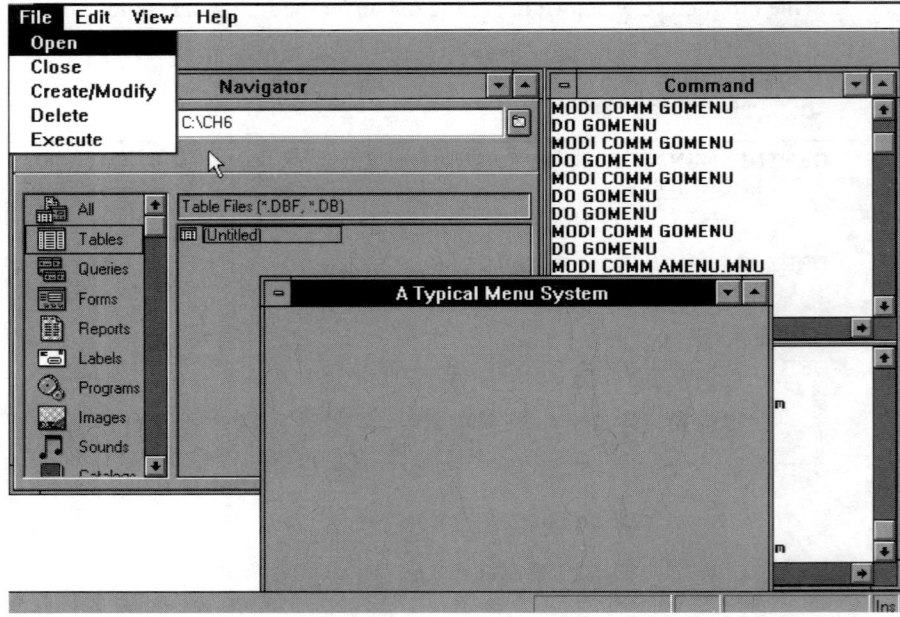

Figure 6.3 File menu's new options are displayed

7. Close the form.

Let's examine one of the commands that created menu items for the **File** menu.

```
DEFINE MENU OPEN OF THIS.FILE;
    PROPERTY;
        Text "Open"
```

Note that the OF clause uses the THIS keyword to reference (with the Dot Operator) the File menu object. The **Open** menu is said to be a *child* of the **File** menu, and can be referenced in the same way as any child object. For example, the following command would replace the Text property of the **Open** child menu with the word "Invoke":

```
this.File.Open.Text = "Invoke"
```

The **this** keyword represents the Root menu (which is unseen). All subsequent references lead to the Text property through a chain of containership as follows:

- The **File** menu object is contained by the Root menu object.
- The **Open** menu object is contained by the **File** menu object.
- The **Text** property is contained by the **Open** menu object.

Now let's attach an action to one of the menu items in the **File** menu.

Chapter 6 Working with Menus

Exercise 3

In this exercise you attach an action--that is, a subroutine--to the **Open** menu item of the **File** menu. The subroutine is a codeblock that opens the **Open File** dialog box, from which files are selected. In this example, only query files (.QBE) will be available in the dialog box.

1. Open the menu file with the Text Editor.

   ```
   MODI COMM AMENU.MNU
   ```

2. Add a comma and a semicolon at the end of the following command:

   ```
   DEFINE MENU OPEN OF THIS.FILE;
       PROPERTY;
         Text "Open"
   ```

   The command should now look like:

   ```
   DEFINE MENU OPEN OF THIS.FILE;
       PROPERTY;
         Text "Open",;
   ```

3. Add the following program code under the command:

   ```
   OnClick {; Form.View = GETFILE("*.QBE")}
   ```

   This line is the new end of the command, so don't put a comma or semicolon after it.

   The program now resembles the one in listing 6.4 (shown below).

```
Parameter FormObj
NEW AMENUMENU(FormObj,"Root")
CLASS AMENUMENU(FormObj,Name) OF MENU(FormObj,Name)
  this.Text = ""
  DEFINE MENU FILE OF THIS;
      PROPERTY;
        Text "File"

      DEFINE MENU OPEN OF THIS.FILE;
        PROPERTY;
        Text "Open",;
        OnClick {; Form.View = GETFILE("*.QBE")}

      DEFINE MENU CLOSE OF THIS.FILE;
        PROPERTY;
        Text "Close",;
        OnClick {; Form.View = ""; CLEAR ALL}

      DEFINE MENU CREATE OF THIS.FILE;
        PROPERTY;
        Text "Create/Modify",;
```

```
        OnClick {; CREATE VIEW}

    DEFINE MENU DELETE OF THIS.FILE;
        PROPERTY;
        Text "Delete"

DEFINE MENU EDIT OF THIS;
    PROPERTY;
    Text "Edit"

DEFINE MENU VIEW OF THIS;
    PROPERTY;
    Text "View"

DEFINE MENU HELP OF THIS;
    PROPERTY;
    Text "Help"

ENDCLASS
```

Listing 6.4 Actions Attached to Several Menu Items

4. Save and exit.

   Now let's add a browse object to show the results of invoking different queries.

5. Open the main program file with the Text Editor.

   MODI COMM GOMENU

6. Add the following lines of program code:

   ```
   x.ABrowse = NEW BROWSE(x)
   x.ABrowse.Top = 1
   x.ABrowse.Left = 1
   x.ABrowse.Width = 58
   ```

   under this line:

   ```
   x.Text = "A Typical Menu System"
   ```

7. Save and exit.

Chapter 6 Working with Menus

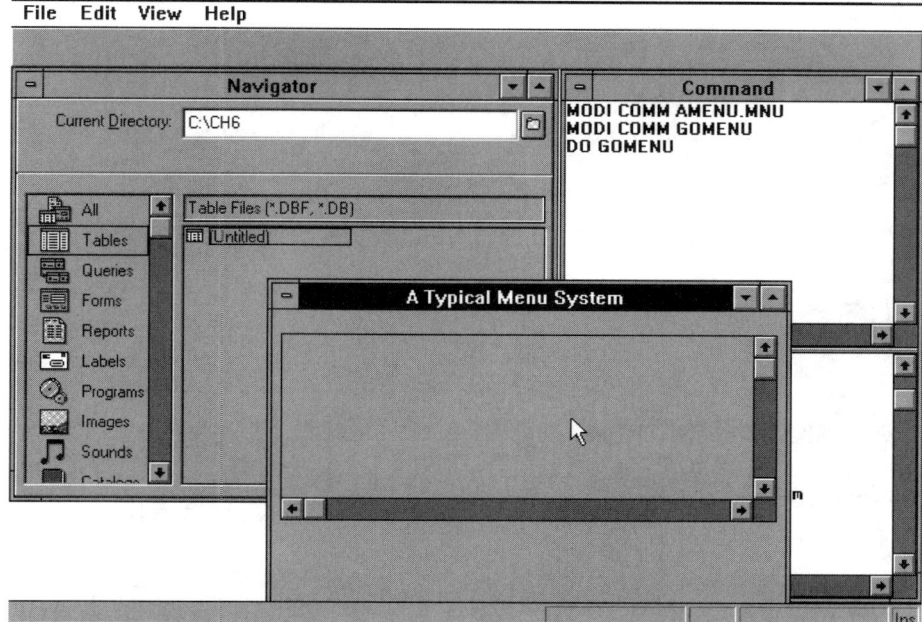

Figure 6.4 The form is displayed with a blank browse object

8. Run the program.

   DO GOMENU

   The form is displayed with a blank browse object (see Figure 6.4). Note that, since the form's MDI property is still set at true (.T.), the form's menu system appears in the dBASE menu bar near the top left of the screen.

9. Click the **File** menu.

   The dropdown list appears.

10. Click the **Open** menu item.

    The Open File dialog box is displayed, as shown in Figure 6.5. Note that only QBE files are listed; this is due to the "*.QBE" parameter you placed between the parentheses of the GETFILE() function.

11. Click **accounts.qbe**, then click the **OK** pushbutton.

    The dialog box disappears, and in a few seconds the data from ACCOUNTS.QBE appears in the browse object.

    Let's try it again.

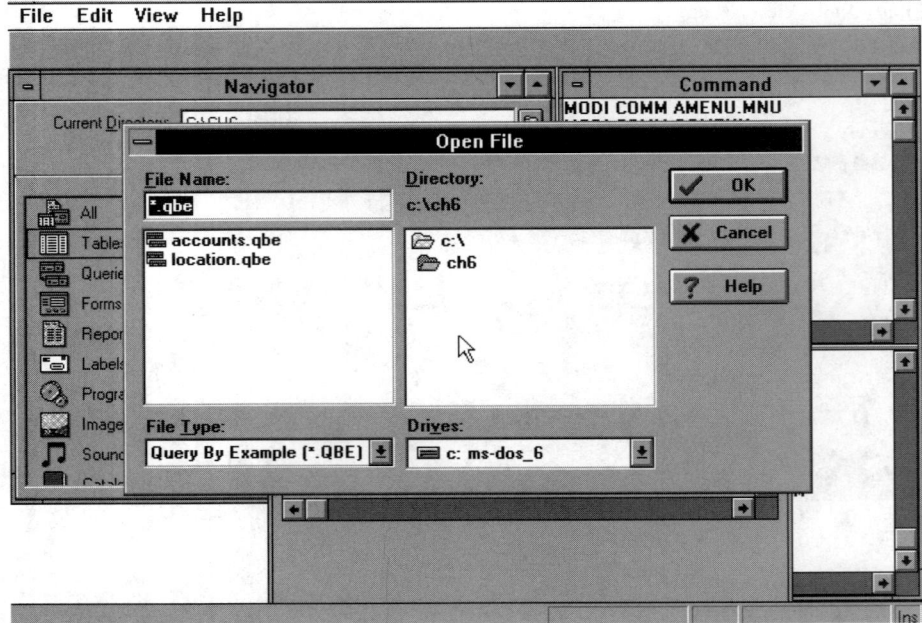

Figure 6.5 The Open File dialog box is displayed

12. Click **File | Open** again.

13. Double-click **location.qbe**.

    In a few seconds, data from LOCATION.QBE appears. Note that double-clicking the file name accomplished the same thing as clicking the **OK** button, as you did in Step 11.

14. Close the form.

Let's examine the codeblock a little more closely:

```
OnClick {; Form.View = GETFILE("*.QBE")}
```

Like the pushbutton object class, the Menu object class has the OnClick event property. This property responds whenever the user clicks while the mouse pointer is over the object. OnClick is arguably the most important property of the Menu class, since clicking menu items is the most common and natural user action when menu objects are used.

The GETFILE() function opens the **Open File** dialog box, which lets the user select a file. When the user selects a file, the dialog box closes automatically and the file name is returned to the calling program. In this case, the file name was inserted directly into the View property of the containing form.

Now let's add some more actions to the **File** menu.

Chapter 6 Working with Menus 179

Exercise 4

In this exercise you assign actions to the **Close** and **Create/Modify** menu items of the **File** menu. The **Close** action closes the current QBE (if any) and clears memory of all variables. The **Create/Modify** action opens the Query Designer, letting the user modify the currently open query. If no query is currently active, the user can create a new one.

1. Open the menu file with the Text Editor.

   ```
   MODI COMM AMENU.MNU
   ```

2. Add a comma and a semicolon at the end of the following command:

   ```
   DEFINE MENU CLOSE OF THIS.FILE;
       PROPERTY;
         Text "Close"
   ```

3. Add the following line after the command in Step 2:

   ```
   OnClick {; Form.View = ""; CLEAR ALL}
   ```

4. Add a comma and a semicolon at the end of the following command:

   ```
   DEFINE MENU CREATE OF THIS.FILE;
       PROPERTY;
         Text "Create/Modify"
   ```

5. Add the following command after the command in Step 4:

   ```
   OnClick {; CREATE VIEW}
   ```

6. Save and exit.

7. Run the program.

   ```
   DO GOMENU
   ```

   As before, the form is displayed, and nothing appears in the browse object.

8. Click **File | Open**.

   The Open File dialog box appears.

9. Open any query you like.

10. Now click **File | Create/Modify**.

The Query Designer is activated, with the query settings ready to be altered. However, don't alter them (unless you have backup copies).

11. Close the Query Designer and the form.

    Note that closing the Query Designer also closed the query; no data is displayed in the browse object.

12. Start the program again.

    ```
    DO GOMENU
    ```

13. Click **File | Create/Modify** again.

    The Open Table Required dialog box is displayed.

14. Using the knowledge you have gained about creating and modifying queries, create a QBE. Give it any characteristics you like.

15. Close the Query Designer.

16. Close the form.

The subroutine (codeblock or procedure) you assign to the OnClick property executes in either of two circumstances:

- When the user clicks the menu item, as demonstrated in the previous exercises
- When the user highlights the menu item with the arrow keys and presses <Enter>, as demonstrated in the next exercise

It may seem a bit confusing that the *OnClick* subroutine executes when the user uses the keyboard only; shouldn't it only respond to a click event? However, seen in the general Windows context, it makes sense. Among the well-established Windows customs regarding menus and menu items is the rule that highlighting a menu or a menu item and pressing <Return> is equivalent to clicking it with the mouse. Had the OnClick property been designed differently, it would have violated a generally recognized Windows standard.

Now let's add one final action to the **File** menu.

Exercise 5

In this exercise you create a subroutine and assign it to the **Delete** menu item. When you run the program, you demonstrate the keyboard technique for selecting menu items and executing an OnClick subroutine.

1. First, make an expendable copy of a QBE file.

    ```
    COPY FILE ACCOUNTS.QBE TO REMOVE.QBE
    ```

Chapter 6 Working with Menus 181

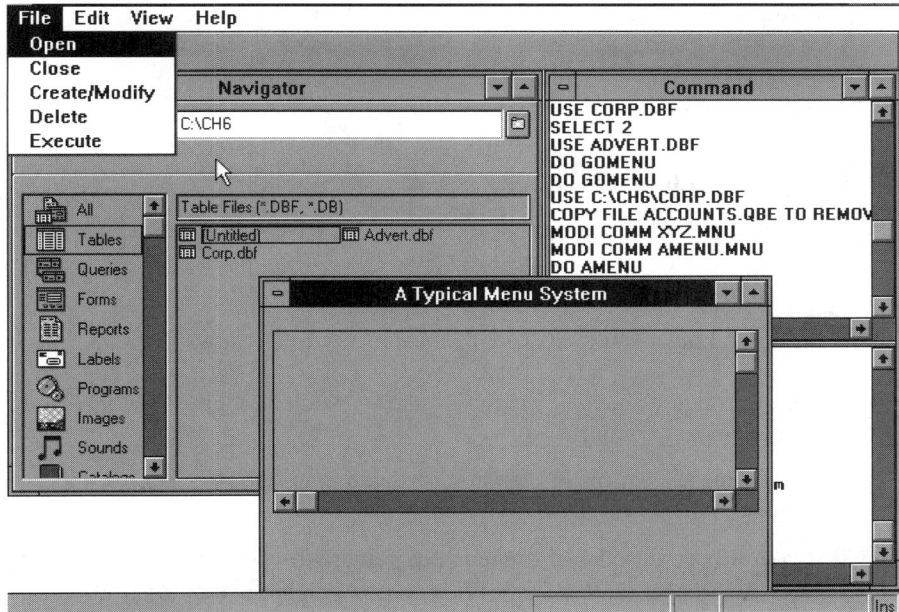

Figure 6.6 The dropdown menu appears

2. Open the menu file with the Text Editor.

   MODI COMM AMENU.MNU

3. Add a comma and a semicolon at the end of the following command:

   DEFINE MENU DELETE OF THIS.FILE;
     PROPERTY;
     Text "Delete"

4. Add the following line after the command in Step 3:

   OnClick {; DELETE FILE (GETFILE("*.QBE"))}

5. Save and exit.

6. Run the program.

   DO GOMENU

7. Instead of using the mouse, press <Alt-F>.

The dropdown menu appears, as shown in Figure 6.6.

8. Press **D**.

   The Open File dialog box appears.

9. Click **remove.qbe**, then click the OK button.

   The Open File dialog box disappears. REMOVE.QBE is deleted.

10. Close the form.

The rules for invoking menu items with the keyboard are as follows:

- To open a dropdown menu (as in Step 7 above), you press the <Alt> key, then the first letter of the menu prompt.
- To select a menu item (as in Step 8 above) you press the first letter of the menu item without the <Alt> key.

Now that you've been introduced to menu programming, you're ready to use the two-way tool that generates such code automatically. This tool is known as the *Menu Designer*, and it saves you much time and effort.

Using the Menu Designer

The Menu Designer is a tool that lets you build a menu system in a rational and intuitive way. As you build the menu system, you can see what it looks like even as you create and modify it. As with the Form Designer, the Menu Designer is a two-way tool that automatically generates the program code needed to reproduce the menu you create. Since it is a two-way tool, you can alter the program code with the Text Editor, and the Menu Designer will interpret and accept the changes.

Exercise 6

In this exercise (and several that follow), you use the Menu Designer to recreate the menus you created in the previous exercises. You'll probably finish these exercises in a fraction of the time it took to complete the others, even though you may not be familiar with the Menu Designer at all. This is due to the ease and intuitive feel of the Menu Designer itself, and the simplicity of the design process.

1. First, clear memory and close all open files.

   ```
   CLEAR ALL
   ```

2. Start a new menu file with the Menu Designer.

   ```
   CREATE MENU ABC
   ```

Chapter 6   Working with Menus   183

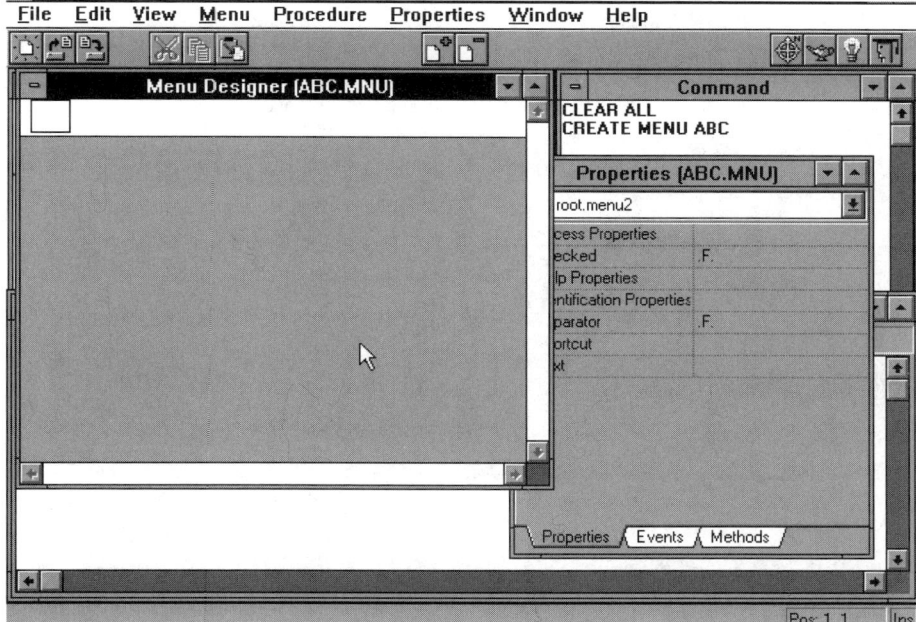

Figure 6.7   The Menu Designer

The Menu Designer is displayed, as shown in Figure 6.7. Three windows were opened:

- The design surface window, labeled **Menu Designer (ABC.MNU)**
- The Object Inspector
- The Procedure Editor (displayed horizontally and partially obscured by the design surface window and the Object Inspector)

(If any of these windows are missing, you can activate them from the **View** menu.)

Note that the cursor appears in a small box at the upper left corner of the design surface window. That's where your work begins.

3. Type the word **File** in the box.

   You just created a menu. **File** is the top-level menu, since it is the one from which all dropdown menus are accessed. (However, don't confuse the top-level menu with the Root menu; recall that the Root menu can't be seen.)

4. Press the <DownArrow> key.

   The box moves below the **File** menu (see Figure 6.8).

5. Enter the word **Open** in the box, then press the <DownArrow> key again.

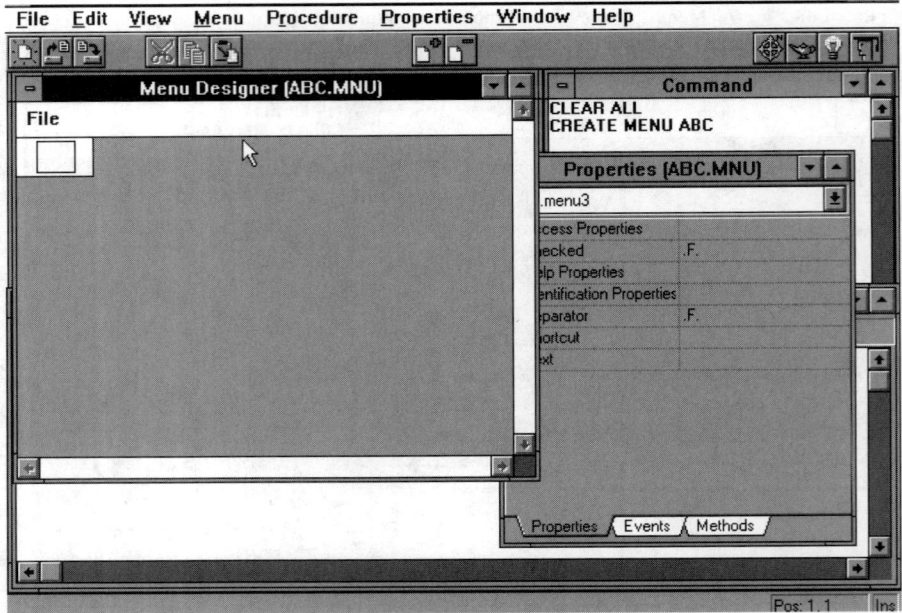

Figure 6.8 The box moves below the File menu

6. Enter the word **Close** in the box, then press the <DownArrow> key again.

7. Enter the words **Create/Modify** in the box, then press the <DownArrow> key again.

8. Enter the word **Delete** in the box, then press the <DownArrow> key again.

9. Enter the word **Execute** in the box.

10. Press <UpArrow> five times (or as many times as it takes to move the box to the **File** menu).

11. Press <Tab>.

    The box moves to the right.

12. Enter the word **Edit**, then press <Tab> again.

    The box moves to the right again.

13. Enter the word **View**, then press <Tab> again.

    The box moves to the right again.

Chapter 6 Working with Menus

14. Enter the word **Help**.

15. Close the Menu Designer by double-clicking the Control box at the upper left corner of the design surface window. When the confirmation prompt appears, click the **Yes** button.

16. Now let's look at the menu system you created. Open GOMENU.PRG in the Text Editor.

    MODI COMM GOMENU

17. Change the following line of program code:

    x.MenuFile = "AMENU.MNU"

    to:

    x.MenuFile = "ABC.MNU"

18. Run the program.

    DO GOMENU

    The same menu as before appears in the dBASE menu bar.

19. Click the **File** menu to confirm that the same menu items are presented.

20. Close the form.

21. Use the Text Editor to examine the program you generated with the Menu Designer.

    MODI COMM ABC.MNU

    The program should look like the one in Listing 6.5 (shown below). Note the similarity to previous menu files you created yourself in previous exercises.

```
Parameter FormObj
NEW ABCMENU(FormObj,"Root")
CLASS ABCMENU(FormObj,Name) OF MENU(FormObj,Name)
   this.Text = ""

   DEFINE MENU FILE OF THIS;
        PROPERTY;
          Text "File"

          DEFINE MENU OPEN OF THIS.FILE;
              PROPERTY;
                Text "Open"
```

```
            DEFINE MENU CLOSE OF THIS.FILE;
                PROPERTY;
                    Text "Close"

            DEFINE MENU CREATE OF THIS.FILE;
                PROPERTY;
                    Text "Create"

            DEFINE MENU DELETE OF THIS.FILE;
                PROPERTY;
                    Text "Delete"

            DEFINE MENU EXECUTE OF THIS.FILE;
                PROPERTY;
                    Text "Execute"

        DEFINE MENU EDIT OF THIS;
            PROPERTY;
                Text "Edit"

        DEFINE MENU VIEW OF THIS;
            PROPERTY;
                Text "View"

        DEFINE MENU HELP OF THIS;
            PROPERTY;
                Text "Help"

ENDCLASS
```

Listing 6.5 Code Generated by the Menu Designer

22. Exit the Text Editor when you're finished examining the generated code.

As you can see, the Menu Designer is an incredible labor-saving tool. And since it's a two-way tool, you can make changes easily with the Text Editor, which we demonstrate in the next exercise.

Exercise 7

In this exercise you demonstrate the two-way tool capability of the Menu Designer. You use the Text Editor to place a codeblock in the **Open** menu option of the **File** menu, then use the Menu Designer to place another codeblock in the **Close** menu option. When you run the form, both changes are recognized. When you reopen the menu file in the Menu Designer, both changes remain.

1. Open the menu file with the Text Editor.

   ```
   MODI COMM ABC.MNU
   ```

Chapter 6 Working with Menus

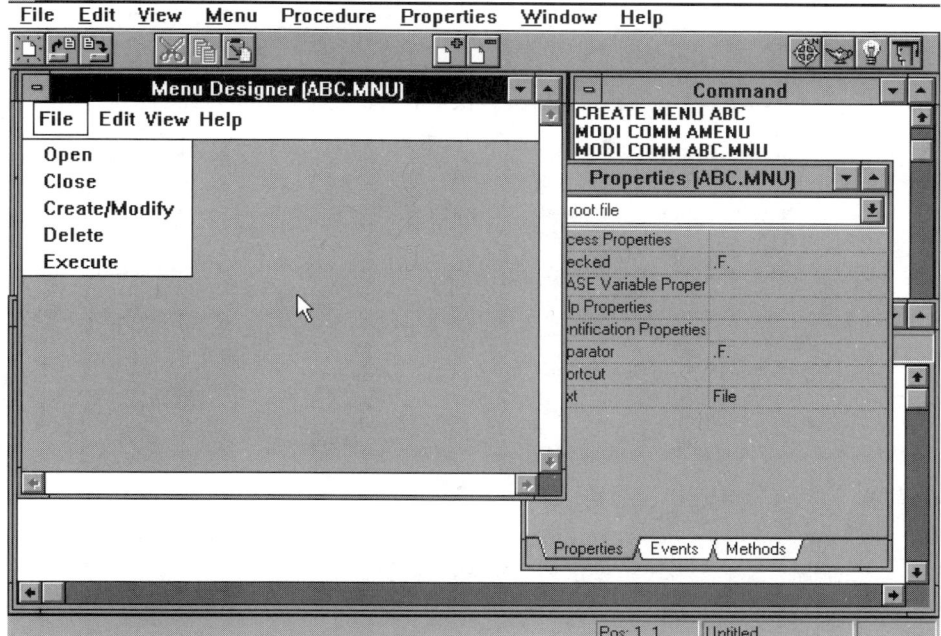

Figure 6.9 The File menu is open by default

2. As you did in Exercise 3, add a comma and a semicolon at the end of the following command:

```
DEFINE MENU OPEN OF THIS.FILE;
    PROPERTY;
       Text "Open"
```

3. As you did in Exercise 3, add the following program code under the command.

```
OnClick {; Form.View = GETFILE("*.QBE")}
```

4. Save and exit.

5. Now open the menu file with the Menu Designer.

    MODI MENU ABC

    The **File** menu is open by default, as shown in Figure 6.9.

6. Click the **Open** menu item in the design surface window.

7. Click the Events tab at the bottom of the Object Inspector.

The event properties of the menu object appear in the foreground of the Object Inspector.

8. Click the OnClick property. (Avoid clicking the Tool button at the right.)

    Note that the codeblock you specified in ABC.MNU is displayed.

9. Click the **Close** menu item in the design surface window.

10. Click the OnClick property in the Object Inspector. (As before, avoid clicking the Tool button at the right.)

11. Enter the following codeblock:

    {; Form.View = ""; CLEAR ALL}

12. Press <DownArrow> once.

    The highlight moves down to the OnHelp property. (Moving to another property after adding a codeblock to a property is sometimes necessary to be sure the Object Inspector saves the change.)

13. Close the Menu Designer by double-clicking the Control box at the upper left corner of the design surface window. When the confirmation prompt appears, click the **Yes** button.

14. Run the program.

    DO GOMENU

    The menu appears in the dBASE menu bar as before.

15. Test the **File | Open** and **File | Close** options to confirm that they work as before, then close the form.

16. Open the menu file with the Text Editor.

    MODI COMM ABC.MNU

    Note the similarities to previous versions of the menu file.

17. Exit the Text Editor when you're finished examining the generated code.

As with the Form Designer, the fact that the Menu Designer is a two-way tool makes it easy to create and modify applications. The only difference is that the application generated by the Menu Designer is a menu system, not a form.

Chapter 6 Working with Menus 189

So far you've recreated half of the **File** menu. In the next exercise, you complete the job. In exercises that follow, you create a cascading menu.

Exercise 8

In this exercise you assign actions to the **Create/Modify** and **Delete** items of the **File** menu.

1. First, make an expendable copy of a QBE file.

   ```
   COPY FILE ACCOUNTS.QBE TO REMOVE.QBE
   ```

2. Open the menu file with the Menu Designer.

   ```
   MODI MENU ABC
   ```

3. Press the <DownArrow> key three times.

   The box now surrounds the **Create/Modify** menu item.

4. Click the **OnClick** property in the Object Inspector. Be careful not to click the Tool button that appears at the right.

5. Enter the following code block:

   ```
   {; CREATE VIEW}
   ```

6. Click the OnHelp property.

7. Now click the **Delete** menu item in the design surface window.

   The box now surrounds this item.

8. Click the **OnClick** property in the Object Inspector. Be careful not to click the Tool button that appears at the right.

9. Enter the following code block:

   ```
   {; DELETE FILE (GETFILE("*.QBE"))}
   ```

10. Click the OnHelp property.

11. Close the Menu Designer by double-clicking the Control box at the upper left corner of the design surface window. When the confirmation prompt appears, click the **Yes** button.

12. Run the program.

```
    DO GOMENU
```

The menu appears in the dBASE menu bar as before.

13. Test the **File | Create/Modify** and **File | Delete** options to confirm that they work as before, then close the form.

14. Open the menu file with the Text Editor.

    ```
    MODI COMM ABC.MNU
    ```

    Note the similarities to previous versions of the menu file.

15. Exit the Text Editor when you're finished examining the generated code.

Now your menu system is exactly as it was before. In the next exercise you add another menu to the menu system.

Exercise 9

In this exercise you use the Menu Designer to create a three-level menu system. A three-level menu system consists of at least three objects:

- The top-level menu object (Root, the invisible menu object that contains all other menu objects)
- A dropdown menu that appears under the Root menu (like the **File** menu you've already created)
- A dropdown menu that is opened from one of the menu items in the first dropdown menu

When a dropdown menu is activated from a menu item in another dropdown menu, the menus are said to be *cascading*.

1. Open the menu file with the Menu Designer.

   ```
   MODI MENU ABC
   ```

2. Press the <DownArrow> key five times.

   The box is now placed below the **Delete** menu item.

3. Replace **Execute** with the character string **Export**.

4. Now press <Tab>.

   The box moves to the right, as shown in Figure 6.10. You've just begun a cascading menu.

Chapter 6   Working with Menus   191

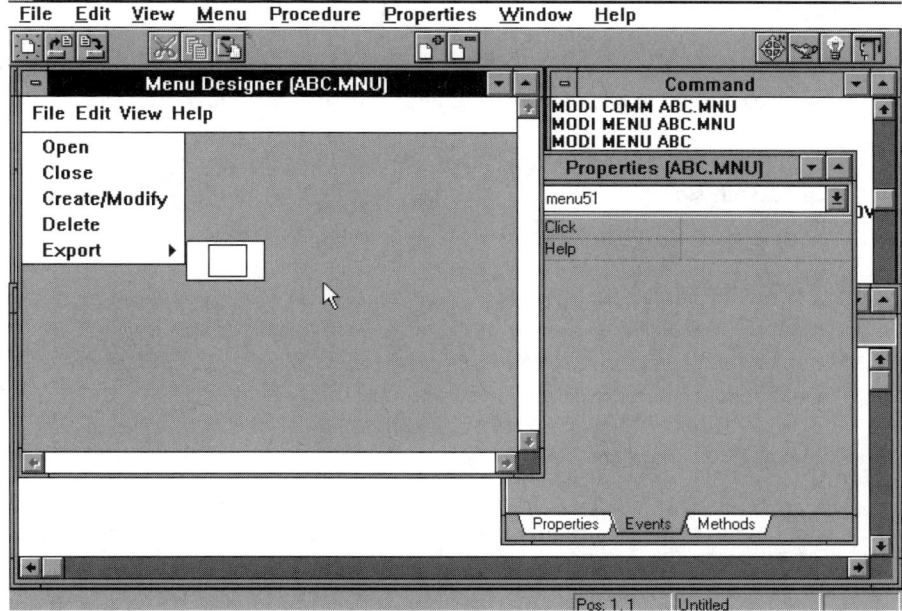

Figure 6.10   The box moves to the right

5. Enter the character string **SDF**.

   The SDF acronym stands for System Data Format, a type of text file to which data is often sent when it must be imported into other systems like mid-range and mainframe computer systems. In an SDF file, data is arranged in neatly arranged rows and columns. Each row contains data from one record, and each column corresponds to a field.

6. Press the <DownArrow> key once.

   The box is placed below the **SDF** menu item.

7. Enter the character string **Paradox**.

   Paradox is a database management system developed by Borland, the same company that makes the dBASE line of products. Tables used by Paradox have a different format and configuration than dBASE tables, so translation is required to transfer data between the systems.

8. Press the <DownArrow> key once.

   The box is placed below the **Paradox** menu item.

9. Enter the character string **Delimited**.

Like an SDF file, a delimited file is a text file to which data is often sent when it must be imported into other systems. As with an SDF file, each row contains the data from a single record. However, unlike an SDF file, fields are not arranged in neat columns; instead, each field in each record is separated (that is, *delimited*) with a comma.

10. Close the Menu Designer by double-clicking the Control box at the upper left corner of the design surface window. When the confirmation prompt appears, click the **Yes** button.

11. Run the program.

    ```
    DO GOMENU
    ```

    The menu appears in the dBASE menu bar as before.

12. Click the **File** menu once.

    The menu items of the **File** menu appear, as shown in Figure 6.11. Note that the new **Export** menu item has a triangle to the right of it. This symbol indicates that selecting the item opens a cascading menu.

13. Click the **Export** menu item once.

    The cascading menu appears, as shown in Figure 6.12. However, none of the options is useful, since you've assigned no actions to them yet. You'll do that in the next exercise.

14. Close the form.

As with other menus, cascading menus must be assigned actions (that is, procedures, functions, or codeblocks) before they are useful. So far, you've only assigned codeblocks to menu items. Let's try some procedures this time.

Exercise 10

In this exercise you assign some procedures (instead of codeblocks) to the menu items in the cascading menu you created in the previous exercise. This time, you use a tool that resembles the dBASE Text Editor to write the procedures.

1. Open the menu file with the Menu Designer.

    ```
    MODI MENU ABC
    ```

2. Press the <DownArrow> key five times, then press <Tab>.

    The box should now surround the **SDF** menu item in the cascading menu.

3. Click the OnClick property, then click the Tool button at the right.

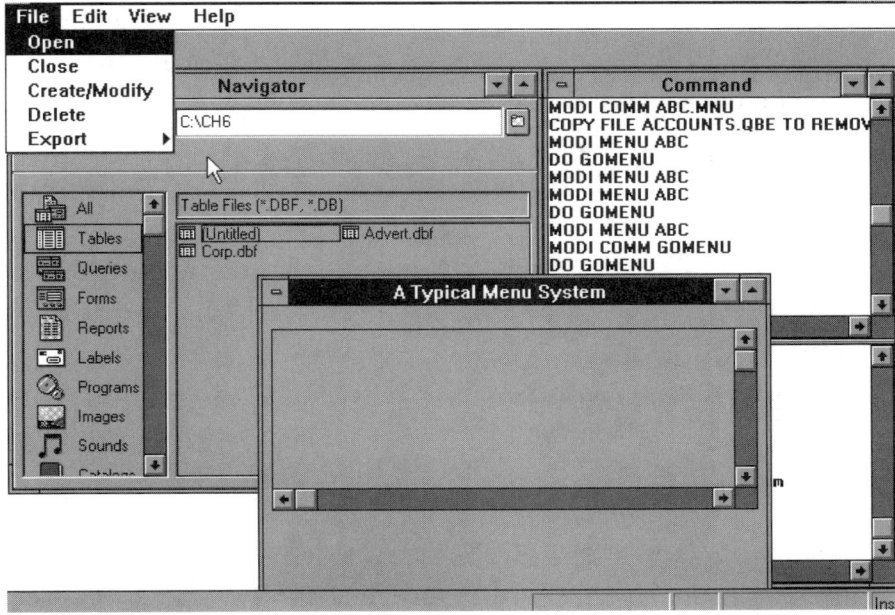

Figure 6.11 The menu items of the File menu appear

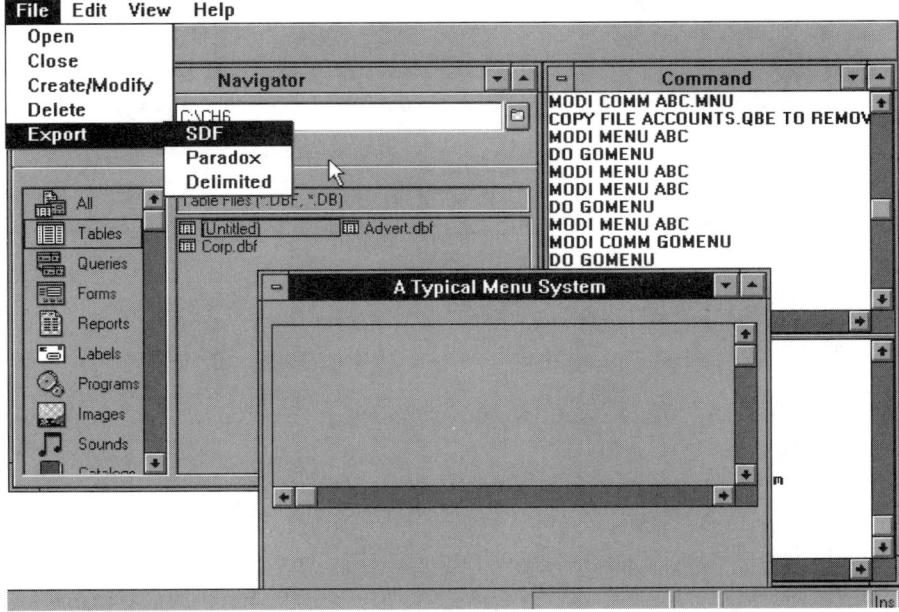

Figure 6.12 The cascading menu appears

The Procedure Editor is displayed. Note that the following line is already written for you:

```
Procedure SDF_OnClick
```

4. Under that line of program code, enter the following lines:

   ```
   FileName = ALIAS()+".SDF"
   COPY TO (FileName) SDF
   RETURN
   ```

   The entire procedure should now look like:

   ```
   Procedure SDF_OnClick
     FileName = ALIAS()+".SDF"
     COPY TO (FileName) SDF
   RETURN
   ```

5. Close the Procedure Editor by double-clicking the Control box at its upper left corner.

6. Now click the **Paradox** menu item in the cascading menu.

   The box now surrounds this menu item.

7. Click the OnClick property, then click the Tool button at the right.

   The Procedure Editor appears. Note that the following line is already written for you:

   ```
   Procedure PARADOX_OnClick
   ```

8. Under that line of program code, enter the following lines:

   ```
   FileName = ALIAS()+".DB"
   COPY TO (FileName) TYPE PARADOX
   RETURN
   ```

9. Close the Procedure Editor by double-clicking the Control box at its upper left corner.

10. Now click the **Delimited** menu item in the cascading menu.

    The box now surrounds this menu item.

11. Click the OnClick property, then click the Tool button at the right.

    The Procedure Editor appears. Note that the following line is already written for you:

Chapter 6 Working with Menus

```
Procedure DELIMITED_OnClick
```

12. Under that line of program code, enter the following lines:

    ```
    FileName = ALIAS()+".TXT"
    COPY TO (FileName) TYPE DELIMITED
    RETURN
    ```

13. Close the Procedure Editor and the Menu Deswigner by double-clicking the Control box at their upper-left corners.

14. Now run the program.

    ```
    DO GOMENU
    ```

    The menu appears in the dBASE menu bar as before.

15. Open a query from the **File | Open** menu item.

16. Click **File | Export | SDF**.

    You just sent all data output by the current QBE to an SDF file. This file has an extension of .SDF.

17. Click **File | Export | Paradox**.

    You just sent all data output by the current QBE to a Paradox table file. This file has an extension of .DB

18. Click **File | Export | Delimited**.

    You just sent all data output by the current QBE to a delimited file. This file has an extension of .TXT.

19. Close the form.

20. Check for the existence of the files you created.

    ```
    DIR *.SDF
    DIR *.DB
    DIR *.TXT
    ```

When you created the cascading menu and saved your work, the Menu Designer added the program code shown in Listing 6.6. Let's examine the first two commands in this program code.

```
DEFINE MENU EXPORT OF THIS.FILE;
    PROPERTY;
      Text "Export"
```

```
    DEFINE MENU SDF OF THIS.FILE.EXPORT;
        PROPERTY;
          OnClick CLASS::SDF_ONCLICK,;
          Text "SDF"

    DEFINE MENU PARADOX OF THIS.FILE.EXPORT;
        PROPERTY;
          OnClick CLASS::PARADOX_ONCLICK,;
          Text "Paradox"

    DEFINE MENU DELIMITED OF THIS.FILE.EXPORT;
        PROPERTY;
          OnClick CLASS::DELIMITED_ONCLICK,;
          Text "Delimited"
```

Listing 6.6 Cascading Menus

The first command creates the cascading menu:

```
DEFINE MENU EXPORT OF THIS.FILE;
    PROPERTY;
      Text "Export"
```

The prompt of this menu is displayed as **Export**, the last menu item in the **File** menu. The **File** menu is denoted by the OF THIS.FILE clause of the DEFINE MENU command. (Recall that THIS is the object reference of the entire menu system--the Root menu, which is not visible to the user--and that FILE is the object reference of the **File** menu, which is contained by the Root menu.)

The following command creates the **SDF** menu item of the **Export** menu:

```
DEFINE MENU SDF OF THIS.FILE.EXPORT;
    PROPERTY;
      OnClick CLASS::SDF_ONCLICK,;
      Text "SDF"
```

The OF THIS.FILE.EXPORT clause of the DEFINE command typifies the chain of object references used to create menus and menu items. The chain goes as follows:

- THIS references the Root menu--the invisible, top-level menu object.
- FILE references the **File** menu, which is contained by the Root menu. An alternate way of saying this is that the **File** menu is the *child* of the Root menu.
- EXPORT references the **Export** menu, which is contained by the **File** menu; that is, the **Export** menu is the child of the **File** menu.

In other words, the **Export** menu is contained by the **File** menu, and the **File** menu is contained by the Root menu (which ultimately contains all menus).

```
Procedure SDF_OnClick
   FileName = ALIAS()+".SDF"
   COPY TO (FileName) SDF
RETURN

Procedure PARADOX_OnClick
   FileName = ALIAS()+".DB"
   COPY TO (FileName) TYPE PARADOX
RETURN

Procedure DELIMITED_OnClick
   FileName = ALIAS()+".TXT"
   COPY TO (FileName) TYPE DELIMITED
RETURN
```

Listing 6.7 Code Added by Menu Designer

The Menu Designer also added the program code shown in Listing 6.7. These are the procedures you created with the Procedure Editor in Steps 3 through 13. Each of these subroutines is assigned to the OnClick property of an **Export** menu item. For example, note that the following line is part of the DEFINE command for the **SDF** menu item:

```
OnClick CLASS::SDF_ONCLICK,;
```

Recall from Chapter 3 that, although the CLASS keyword is a bit like the THIS keyword, THIS is used for referencing the properties of a class, while CLASS references the class itself. Translated into ordinary English, the entire command above says "OnClick, an event property of this class, is assigned a subroutine named SDF_ONCLICK." The double colons separating the CLASS keyword from the SDF_ONCLICK function pointer form a symbol that, translated into English, means "SDF_ONCLICK is a subroutine belonging to this custom class."

Let's look at procedure SDF_ONCLICK. The first command:

```
FileName = ALIAS()+".SDF"
```

stores the name and extension of the new SDF file to a variable named FileName. The ALIAS() function returns the name of the currently active table file or, if a QBE is active, the name of the parent table. For example, if you use ACCOUNTS.QBE, the name returned is CORP, since CORP.DBF is the parent table in that query. The character string ".SDF" is concatenated to the end of the value returned by ALIAS, so the full file name of the generated file is "CORP.SDF."

The second and last command in procedure SDF_ONCLICK tells dBASE to copy the data from the QBE to a .SDF file, translating it to the SDF format in the process:

```
COPY TO (FileName) SDF
```

The parentheses tell dBASE to treat the contents of FileName as a file name, not just a character string.

What Next?

You now have the knowledge you need to create and modify forms, menus, and control objects. Armed with this knowledge, you're ready to create serious, full-scale applications. However, you should know about two highly powerful Windows technologies that are fully implemented in dBASE for Windows: Object Linking and Embedding (OLE) and Dynamic Data Exchange (DDE). These technologies allow you to access other Windows applications and the data they work with. DDE and OLE are the subject of the next chapter.

Chapter 7

DDE and OLE

When two Windows applications perform similar tasks or access and alter the same data, it's often necessary to unite the two applications toward a single purpose. This is possible in the Windows environment, since Windows allows you to run more than one application at a time (a process known as *multitasking*). For example, a dBASE application could manipulate the data stored in a spreadsheet file by opening a session in the spreadsheet application and accessing the file, or a user could change a bitmap image in a dBASE table file with a graphics application like Paintbrush. For situations like these, there are standard Windows features known as dynamic data exchange (DDE) and Object Linking and Embedding (OLE). Both of these features are fully implemented in dBASE for Windows.

DDE is a method for exchanging data and instructions with another application. Properly designed, a DDE application written in the language of dBASE for Windows can integrate a dBASE session with a session in another Windows application, making the two sessions work together as if they are one and the same. Because of DDE, it is no longer necessary to tolerate the clumsiness and inefficiency of the standard import and export operations with which data were exchanged in the pre-Windows era.

OLE is a method for starting sessions in external applications, and using those sessions to use or alter items stored in a dBASE table. OLE is a method for connecting an item in dBASE with an external application, which is then accessible from the dBASE item. Because of OLE, it is no longer necessary to exit the current dBASE session before using the external application. As with DDE, OLE makes the two applications work together as if they are part of a single application.

The examples given in this chapter use Paintbrush, a Windows application usually stored in the Accessories group, and Quattro Pro for Windows, a spreadsheet application developed by Borland International. You almost certainly have Paintbrush in your Windows system, since it is installed automatically when you install Windows. Don't worry if you have some other spreadsheet application besides Quattro Pro; any Windows spreadsheet application with DDE and OLE capability (such as Microsoft Excel or Lotus 1-2-3) will do nicely. The chances are that you'll only have to make minor changes to the program code given in this chapter to accommodate the differences.

Dynamic Data Exchange

Data exchange with DDE is made possible by a channel of communication you establish between dBASE and the external application. This channel of communication is known as a *DDE link*. With a DDE link you can "marry" two applications together for a common purpose, even if the applications are dissimilar in form and function. In the exercises that follow, you use DDE to link dBASE for Windows with a spreadsheet application--two dissimilar applications.

Establishing a DDE Link

When a DDE link is established between two applications in the Windows environment, a *DDE conversation* is said to be initiated. Once this conversation is established, the two applications can almost literally talk to each other. Through a DDE conversation, you can send data to a server application, extract data from one of the server application's files, or tell the server application what to do by sending it instructions in its own language.

You create and control a DDE link with an object of the DDELink object class, and you establish the link with the Initiate() property, a member of the DDELink class.

Exercise 1

In this exercise you create a DDELINK object and initiate a DDE link with a spreadsheet application. Don't open a session in the spreadsheet application; in fact, if one is already open, close it. The Initiate() method opens a session for you automatically, so it isn't necessary to have an active session beforehand.

Before you perform this exercise, be sure that a blank spreadsheet file named NBOOK exists in the spreadsheet application's working directory. For example, if your spreadsheet application is Quattro Pro for Windows, an empty spreadsheet file named NBOOK.WB1 should exist in the working directory before you begin. If your spreadsheet application is Lotus 1-2-3, the file might be NBOOK.WK3.

1. First close all tables and clear all items from memory.

   ```
   CLEAR ALL
   ```

2. Start a program with the Text Editor.

   ```
   MODI COMM SPSHEET
   ```

3. Enter the following program code, then save and exit:

   ```
   GetIt = NEW DDELINK()
   GetIt.Initiate("QPW", "C:\QPW\SAMPLES\NBOOK.WB1")
   ```

   The second parameter in the last command assumes that the file NBOOK.WB1 exists in the SAMPLES subdirectory of the Quattro Pro installation directory. If the file is contained in a different directory, or if you installed Quattro Pro in a directory of a different name, adjust the parameter accordingly.

   Of course, if your spreadsheet application is other than Quattro Pro you'll need to change the parameters to accommodate the difference. For example, if your spreadsheet application is Lotus 1-2-3 and the spreadsheet file is in the SAMPLE subdirectory of the 1-2-3 installation directory, the command should look like this:

```
GetIt.Initiate("123W", "C:\123W\SAMPLE\NBOOK.WK3")
```

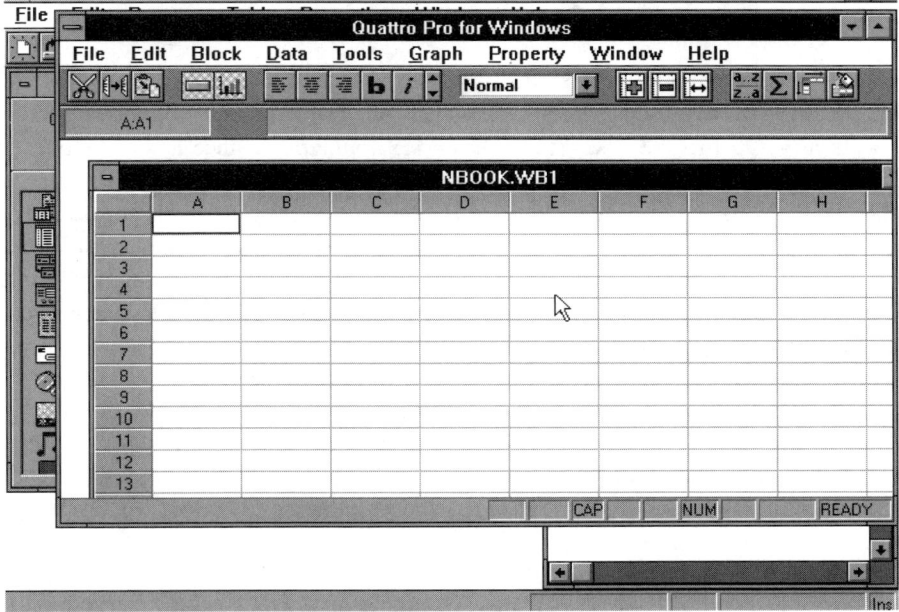

Figure 7.1 The spreadsheet session appears in the foreground

4. Run the program.

   ```
   DO SPSHEET
   ```

   In a few seconds, the spreadsheet's icon appears near the bottom of the screen, then disappears.

5. Press <Alt-Tab>.

   The spreadsheet session appears in the foreground, as shown in Figure 7.1.

6. Close the spreadsheet session by double-clicking its Control box at the upper left corner of the spreadsheet's application window.

   The dBASE session returns.

This small, two-line program accomplished quite a lot. Here's a step-by-step account of what it did:

1. Created a DDELINK object
2. Opened a session in Quattro Pro
3. Opened the spreadsheet file named NBOOK.WB1 (if your spreadsheet application was Quattro Pro)
4. Established a DDE link to the spreadsheet file

In Windows terminology, the spreadsheet file is known as a *server document*. A server document is any item in an external application to which dBASE for Windows establishes a DDE link. In turn, Quattro Pro is said to be the *server application*, since it is the application that was invoked by dBASE. dBASE, on the other hand, is the *client application*. Once dBASE establishes a DDE link, it can request information and send information or instructions to the server application in much the same way a human client does with an attorney or a contractor.

Once you closed the Quattro Pro session, the DDE link was severed automatically. (However, the DDELINK object class also has a property named Terminate() which removes the DDE link without closing the session in the client application.)

Note that the second command in Step 3 required two parameters:

```
GetIt.Initiate("QPW", "C:\QPW\SAMPLES\NBOOK.WB1")
```

The "QPW" parameter is the name of the spreadsheet application's main executable file, QPW.EXE. This file is usually contained in the installation directory of the spreadsheet application; if your spreadsheet application is Quattro Pro for Windows, the installation directory is probably C:\QPW. The second parameter identifies the document file with which you establish the DDE link. Note that the parameter includes the full path and file extension. This is absolutely necessary for most server applications (although not all). Unless you include path and extension, the DDE link might not be established properly. Most important: The installation directory of your spreadsheet application should be in your DOS path; otherwise, dBASE might not be able to find it.

Note that the DDELink object you created in this exercise was not contained by a form object in the same way as most of the other objects in previous chapters were. That is because a DDELink object is not a control object like a list box or a scroll bar. It has little to do with user interace at all, so it needn't be associated with a form.

Because there's always a possibility that the DDE link won't take (due to programming errors, path problems, or file problems), it's a good idea to provide for the possibility in your program, perhaps by delivering some message to the user in the event of a failure. Users usually appreciate this, since it keeps them informed of what's going on. The next exercise demonstrates this practice.

Exercise 2

In this exercise you alter the program to deliver one of two messages. When the DDE link is established correctly, the message is displayed in the Results pane of the Command window.

Chapter 7 DDE and OLE

When the DDE link fails, the message is displayed in a dialog box that allows the user to **Retry** or **Cancel**.

1. Open the program with the Text Editor.

   MODI COMM SPSHEET

2. Rewrite the program code as shown in Listing 7.1.

   Note that the file extension is removed from the second parameter in the Initiate() property. This is deliberate; it prevents the DDE link from being established, making the **Retry** or **Cancel** dialog box appear.

```
GetIt = NEW DDELINK()
IF GetIt.Initiate("QPW", "C:\QPW\SAMPLES\NBOOK")
   ? "Hooray! The DDE link works!"
ELSE
   Verdict = 4
   DO WHILE Verdict = 4
      Verdict =;
      MSGBOX("Sorry! The DDE link failed. "+;
             "Check file name and path.",;
      "OOPS! (No pun intended)", 21)
   ENDDO
ENDIF
```

Listing 7.1 Providing Confirmation or Error Messages

3. Save and exit.

4. Run the program.

   DO SPSHEET

   The **Retry** or **Cancel** dialog box appears, as shown in Figure 7.2.

5. Click the **Retry** pushbutton.

   The dialog box briefly disappears, then returns. This means that the second attempt to establish the DDE link failed.

6. Click the **Cancel** pushbutton.

   The dialog box disappears.

7. Go to the spreadsheet session by pressing <Alt-Tab>, then close the session.

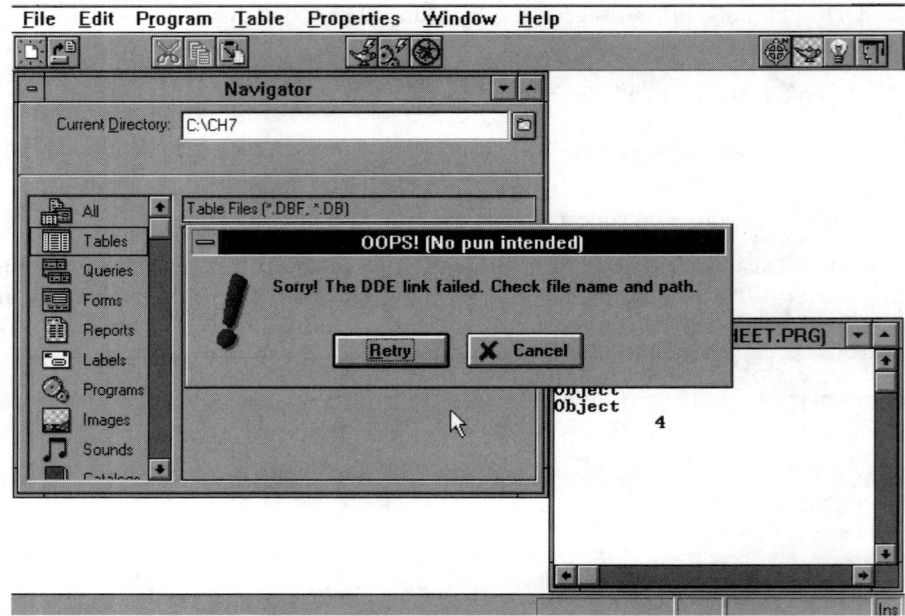

Figure 7.2 The Retry or Cancel dialog box appears

8. Now open the program again with the Text Editor.

   ```
   MODI COMM SPSHEET
   ```

9. Return the file extension to the second parameter of the Initiate() property.

   In its entirety, the line should now look like:

   ```
   IF GetIt.Initiate("QPW","C:\QPW\SAMPLES\NBOOK.WB1")
   ```

10. Save and exit, then run the program.

    ```
    DO SPSHEET
    ```

    This time, no dialog box appears; instead, the message **Hooray! The DDE link works!** is displayed in the Results pane.

11. Go to the spreadsheet session by pressing <Alt-Tab>, then close the session.

The Initiate() property does more than open a session in a server application and establish a DDE link with one of its document files. It also returns a logical value that indicates whether the DDE link was successfully established. You were therefore able to use it as an expression in an IF...ENDIF statement. This statement was designed such that an unsuccessful attempt would display a dialog box.

You created the dialog box with the MSGBOX() function, a highly useful tool for throwing up quick messages and evaluating the user's response. The authors urge you to investigate this function further. You can do this easily with the on-line help system by entering the following command in the Command window:

```
HELP MSGBOX()
```

Sending Data to a Server Document

Once a DDE link is established between dBASE and an external application, you can send data to a document in that application. You do this with an action known as a *poke request*. The next exercise shows how.

Exercise 3

In this exercise you add commands to the program that perform the following tasks:

- Open a QBE file
- Use the Poke() property to place a unit of information into a cell in the spreadsheet file NBOOK.WB1

The information you extract and send to the spreadsheet file is passed along the DDE link you establish with the Initiate() property of the DDE object class.

1. First close all tables and clear all items from memory.

   ```
   CLEAR ALL
   ```

2. Open the program file with the Text Editor.

   ```
   MODI COMM SPSHEET
   ```

3. Add the following line of program code at the top of the program:

   ```
   SET VIEW TO ACCOUNTS
   ```

4. Add the following line of program code:

   ```
   GetIt.Poke("A:A1", ADVERT->ACCOUNTNO)
   ```

   after the following line:

   ```
   ? "Hooray! The DDE link works!"
   ```

The program should now resemble the one in Listing 7.2.

The first parameter of the Poke() property determines the place in the server document (in this case, a spreadsheet) to which the data is written. The first character (**A**) identifies in which page in NBOOK.WB1 to place the data; this is necessary, since each Quattro Pro spreadsheet file contains multiple spreadsheet pages, much like a notebook. The other characters identify the column (**A**) and row (**1**) of the cell in which the data should be inserted.

If you use a spreadsheet application other than Quattro Pro, you may need to use a different specification for cells. For example, cells in Microsoft Excel version 4.0 are referenced by row and column only (for example, A1, B3, and C9).

The second parameter in the Poke() method specifies the data item to insert in the server document. In this case, you insert the value stored in the ACCOUNTNO field of ADVERT.DBF.

```
SET VIEW TO ACCOUNTS
GetIt = NEW DDELINK()
IF GetIt.Initiate("QPW", "C:\QPW\SAMPLES\NBOOK.WB1")
   ? "Hooray! The DDE link works!"
   GetIt.Poke("A:A1", ADVERT->ACCOUNTNO)
ELSE
   Verdict = 4
   DO WHILE Verdict = 4
      Verdict =;
      MSGBOX("Sorry! The DDE link failed. "+;
             "Check file name and path.",;
      "OOPS! (No pun intended)", 21)
   ENDDO
ENDIF
```

Listing 7.2 Sending dBASE Data to a Spreadsheet

5. Save and exit, then run the program.

   `DO SPSHEET`

7. Move to the spreadsheet session by pressing <Alt-Tab>.

   Note that the ACCOUNTNO value of the first record in ADVERT.DBF is inserted in Cell A:A1 of the spreadsheet (see Figure 7.3).

8. Close the spreadsheet session by double-clicking its Control box at the upper left corner of the application window. If a confirmation prompt asking if you want to keep changes is displayed, click on **No**; it isn't desirable to keep the changes made to the spreadsheet at this point.

   The dBASE session returns.

Chapter 7 DDE and OLE

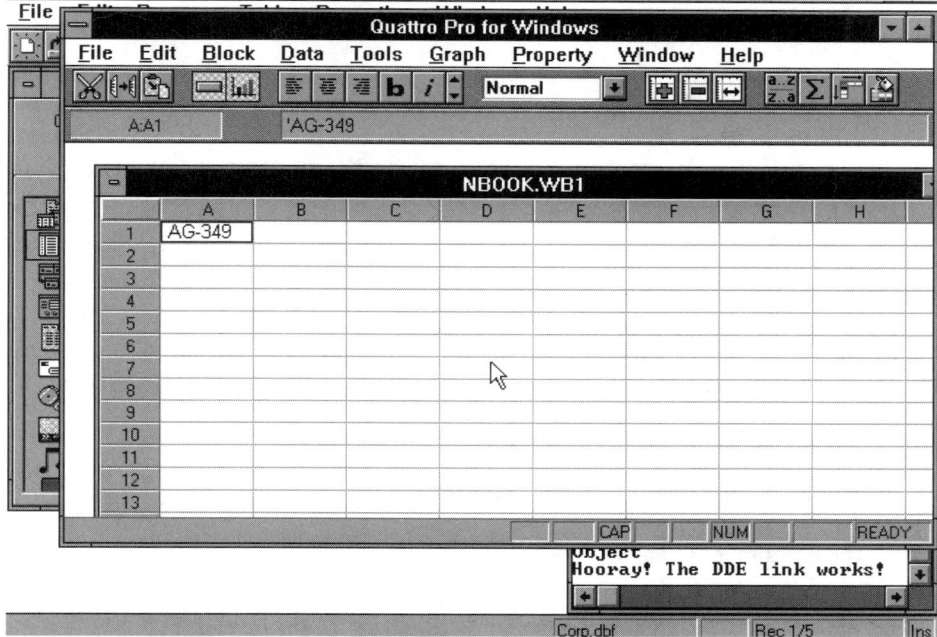

Figure 7.3 A data item is inserted in the cell A:A1

The Poke() property is the means by which you send data to a server document. As mentioned earlier, each attempt made by this property to send data is known as a poke request. In fact, most of the actions you attempt with a DDE link are requests of some kind; for example, each attempt to establish a DDE link is called an *initiate request*. We use this terminology for the remainder of this chapter.

Let's review what happened when you ran the program (see Listing 7.2).

1. The ACCOUNTS.QBE query was invoked, which opened CORP.DBF and ACCOUNTS.DBF, and joined them on a common field (ACCOUNTNO).

   ```
   SET VIEW TO ACCOUNTS
   ```

2. A DDELink object was created.

   ```
   GetIt = NEW DDELINK()
   ```

3. An attempt was made (in this case, a successful one) to start a server session in the spreadsheet application and establish a DDE link with one of its server documents; in other words, you made an initiate request.

   ```
   IF GetIt.Initiate("QPW", "C:\QPW\SAMPLES\NBOOK.WB1")
   ```

```
    * Commands
ELSE
    * Alternate commands
ENDIF
```

4. The attempt was successful, so the first sequence of commands was executed. The first command in this sequence sent a confirmation message to the Results pane of the Command window.

    ```
    ? "Hooray! The DDE link works!"
    ```

5. The next (and last) command in the sequence sent data to Cell A:A1 in the spreadsheet file (if your spreadsheet application is Quattro Pro for Windows).

    ```
    GetIt.Poke("A:A1", ADVERT->ACCOUNTNO)
    ```

    In other words, you made a poke request.

6. The program terminated.

Extracting Data From a Server Document

Just as you can send data items to a server document, you can also read data items from a server document. You do this with an action known as a *peek request*. The next exercise shows how.

Exercise 4

In this exercise you insert data items into the NBOOK spreadsheet manually. You then alter the dBASE program to establish a DDE link with the spreadsheet and read the data items.

1. First, make a copy of the original program from the previous exercises.

    ```
    COPY FILE SPSHEET.PRG TO SPSHEET2.PRG
    ```

2. Open the copy with the Text Editor.

    ```
    MODI COMM SPSHEET2
    ```

3. Replace the following line of program code:

    ```
    GetIt.Poke("A:A1", ADVERT->ACCOUNTNO)
    ```

    with the following lines:

    ```
    MSGBOX(GetIt.Peek("A:A1"),;
    ```

Chapter 7 DDE and OLE

```
"Here's the Data Item", 64)
```

Note that, although this code includes two lines, it is actually one command; recall that a semicolon at the end of a line means that the next line is a continuation of the original line.

The program should now look like the one in Listing 7.3.

Again, if your spreadsheet application is other than Quattro Pro for Windows, you may have to specify the cell location somewhat differently; for example, some spreadsheet applications don't have a page specification, so the proper command would be:

```
MSGBOX(GetIt.Peek("A1"),;
"Here's the Data Item", 64)
```

```
SET VIEW TO ACCOUNTS
GetIt = NEW DDELINK()
IF GetIt.Initiate("QPW", "C:\QPW\SAMPLES\NBOOK.WB1")
   ? "Hooray! The DDE link works!"
   MSGBOX(GetIt.Peek("A:A1"),;
   "Here's the Data Item", 64)
ELSE
   Verdict = 4
   DO WHILE Verdict = 4
      Verdict =;
      MSGBOX("Sorry! The DDE link failed. "+;
             "Check file name and path.",;
      "OOPS! (No pun intended)", 21)
   ENDDO
ENDIF
```

Listing 7.3 Program Modified to Read Data from the Spreadsheet

4. Save and exit, but don't run the program yet.

5. Start a session in your spreadsheet application from the Windows Program Manager and open the NBOOK spreadsheet file.

6. Click Cell A1, then enter the following string:

```
Hello! I'm a string of data in a spreadsheet file!
```

For example, if you're using Quattro Pro for Windows, the spreadsheet should resemble the one in Figure 7.4.

7. Save your changes and exit from the spreadsheet application.

8. Now run the program.

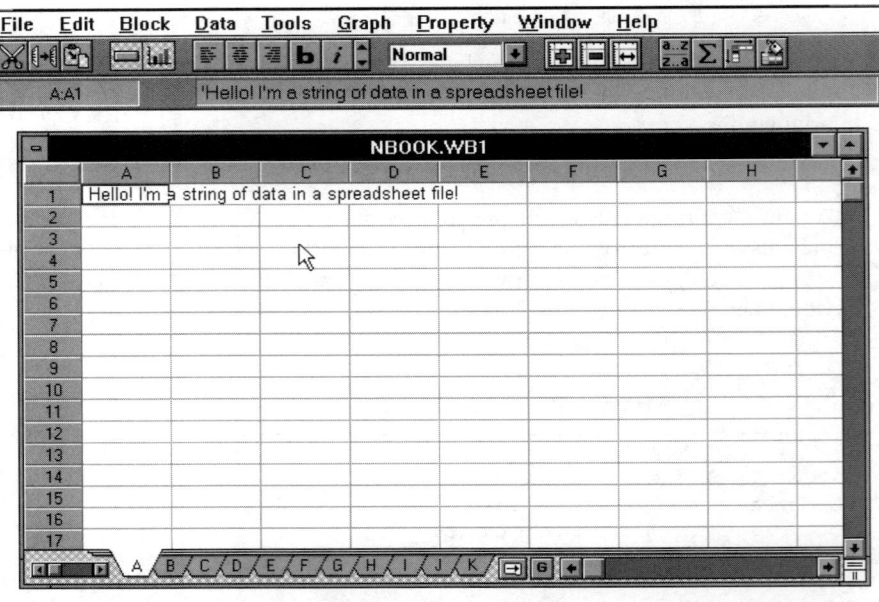

Figure 7.4 The spreadsheet with a string of data

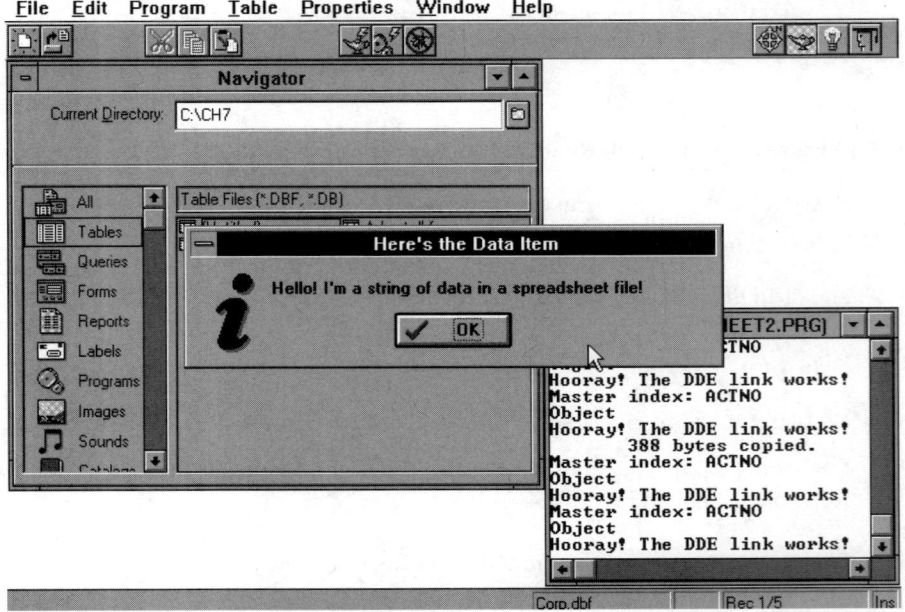

Figure 7.5 A dialog box appears containing the contents of cell A1

Chapter 7 DDE and OLE

```
DO SPSHEET2
```

In a few seconds, a dialog box appears containing the contents of Cell A1, as shown in Figure 7.5.

9. Click the **OK** button.

The dialog box disappears, and program execution is terminated.

Let's take a closer look at the command you inserted in Step 3:

```
MSGBOX(GetIt.Peek("A:A1"),;
"Here's the Data Item", 64)
```

Note that the first parameter of the MSGBOX() function is

```
GetIt.Peek("A:A1")
```

The Peek() property does the opposite of the Poke() property; instead of sending data to the server document, it receives data from the server document. Note that Peek() requires only one parameter, since only the source location in the server document is needed.

Sending Instructions To a Server Application

So far you've seen how to send and receive data from a server document. However, a DDE linkup gives you even more control than that; you can talk to the server application in its own language, making it perform tasks.

Exercise 5

In this exercise you send a command to the spreadsheet application. This command causes the application to close automatically, sparing you the chore of closing it manually. Commands that you send to server applications are usually referred to as *macros* or *macro commands*, and we use this terminology from here on.

Although most spreadsheet applications have a macro language, they do not have the same commands or capabilities and, consequently, the example given in this exercise may not be possible if your spreadhseet application is other than Quattro Pro for Windows. If this is the case, the authors encourage you to improvise by using a macro command of your own choosing.

1. First, make a copy of the original program file, SPSHEET.PRG.

   ```
   COPY FILE SPSHEET.PRG TO SPSHEET3.PRG
   ```

2. Open the copy with the Text Editor.

   ```
   MODI COMM SPSHEET3
   ```

3. If your spreadsheet application is Quattro Pro for Windows, add the following line of program code:

```
GetIt.Execute("{FileExit 0}")
```

after the following line:

```
GetIt.Poke("A:A1", ADVERT->ACCOUNTNO)
```

The program should now look like the one in listing 7.4.

If your spreadsheet application is other than Quattro Pro for Windows, it's unlikely that this macro will work for you. If this is so, try another macro command that your spreadsheet does support. For example, if you use Lotus 1-2-3, you might want to maximize the 1-2-3 application window automatically with the following macro directive:

```
GetIt.Execute("{APP-STATE 'Maximize'}")
```

```
SET VIEW TO ACCOUNTS
GetIt = NEW DDELINK()
IF GetIt.Initiate("QPW", "C:\QPW\SAMPLES\NBOOK.WB1")
   ? "Hooray! The DDE link works!"
   GetIt.Poke("A:A1", ADVERT->ACCOUNTNO)
   GetIt.Execute("{FileExit 0}")
ELSE
   Verdict = 4
   DO WHILE Verdict = 4
      Verdict =;
      MSGBOX("Sorry! The DDE link failed. "+;
             "Check file name and path.",;
      "OOPS! (No pun intended)", 21)
   ENDDO
ENDIF
```

Listing 7.4 Sending a Macro Command in the Server's Language

4. Save and exit, then run the program.

   ```
   DO SPSHEET3
   ```

5. Now press <Alt-Tab> until you are satisfied that the spreadsheet session is closed (or perhaps maximized, as with our suggestion in Step 3).

The {FileExit 0} directive of Step 3 is a Quattro Pro macro command that terminates the current Quattro Pro session. The parameter 0 tells Quattro Pro to shut down without displaying the **Save** prompt. You could have specified 1 as the parameter, which would have displayed the prompt before actually shutting the session down.

You're now acquainted with the three main tasks performed through a DDE link:

- Write data to a portion of a server document.

Chapter 7 DDE and OLE

- Read data from a server document.
- Send instructions to a server application in the server's own macro language.

So far, you've only read and written data from a single area of a server document (i.e., Cell A:A1 of the NBOOK spreadsheet file). However, most serious DDE applications must write data to multiple locations in a server document. For example, sending table data to a spreadsheet application usually requires that the contents of records be written to a spreadsheet field by field and cell by cell, a technique known as *region walking*.

Region Walking

Region walking is a process by which data items in the client and server applications are systematically selected and manipulated. Data items are specified by repeatedly constructing character strings that identify the elements. The routine that performs this task is known as a *region-walking algorithm*. In the next three exercises you create such an algorithm.

Moving from Field To Field, Cell to Cell

Because the dBASE language has functions that identify table fields through numeric values, you can create a region-walking algorithm that traverses the record structure of a table, reading data from or writing data to each field. The next exercise demonstrates this principle.

Exercise 6

In this exercise you write a routine that copies one record to a spreadsheet file. This record is written horizontally, starting at Cell A:A1 (or Cell A1, depending on which spreadsheet application you use). Each cell receives data from a single field in the source record.

1. First, be sure memory is clear of extraneous memory variables and close all open tables.

    ```
    CLEAR ALL
    ```

2. Start a new program file with the Text Editor.

    ```
    MODI COMM XDDE
    ```

3. Write the program shown in Listing 7.5, then save and exit.

```
SendData = NEW DDELINK()
SendData.Initiate("QPW", "C:\QPW\SAMPLES\NBOOK.WB1")
DataFile = "ADVERT"
SELECT 1
USE (DataFile)
ThisRow = 5
FieldNum = 1
CharNum = ASC("D")
```

```
DO WHILE FieldNum <= FLDCOUNT(DataFile)
   ThisField = FIELD(FieldNum)
   ThisCell = "A:"+CHR(CharNum)+LTRIM(STR(ThisRow))
   SendData.Poke(ThisCell, &ThisField)
   FieldNum = FieldNum + 1
   CharNum = CharNum + 1
ENDDO
```

Listing 7.5 Region Walking from Field to Field

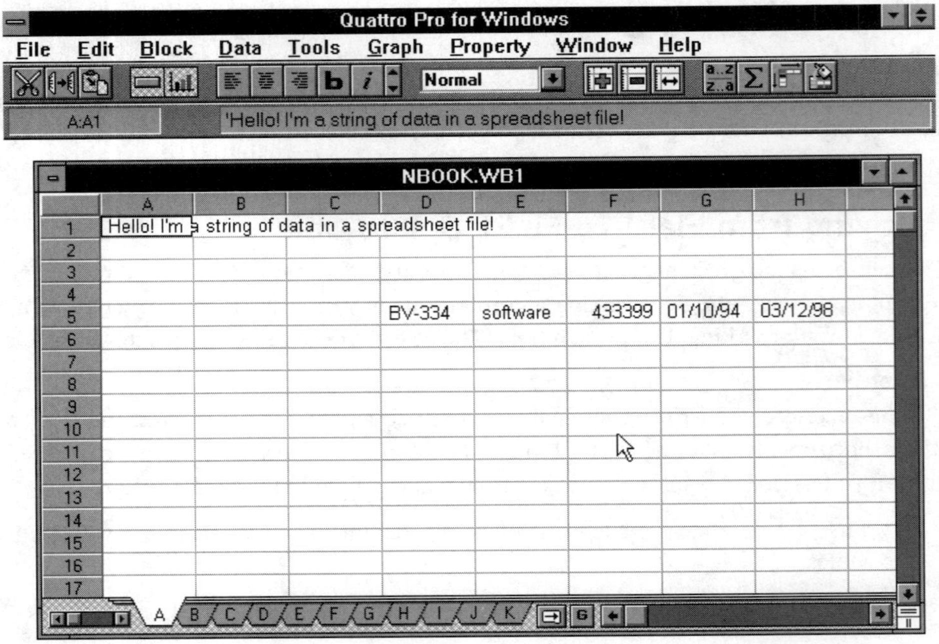

Figure 7.6 The contents of the first record are displayed in the spreadsheet

4. Run the program.

   ```
   DO XDDE
   ```

   In a few seconds, a session in your spreadsheet application is begun.

5. If necessary, bring the spreadsheet session to the foreground by pressing <Alt-Tab>.

   The contents of the first record in ADVERT.DBF are displayed in the spreadsheet, starting at Cell D5 (see Figure 7.6). The program *region-walked* from field to field in the first record of ADVERT.DBF and from cell to cell in the spreadsheet file, copying data from field to cell each time.

Note that the last two fields in the record structure, ART and SLOGANS, were not sent to the spreadsheet. This is because DDE wasn't designed to send memo and OLE fields; for this, you use OLE, a subject covered later in this chapter.

6. Terminate the spreadsheet session. Do not save changes to the spreadsheet file.

Let's examine the program you wrote (see Listing 7.5).

1. First, the program creates a DDELink object and uses it to establish a DDE link with the NBOOK server document.

   ```
   SendData = NEW DDELINK()
   SendData.Initiate("QPW", "C:\QPW\SAMPLES\NBOOK.WB1")
   ```

2. The program creates a memory variable named DataFile and uses it to open ADVERT.DBF.

   ```
   DataFile = "ADVERT"
   SELECT 1
   USE (DataFile)
   ```

   (The DataFile variable was used to provide flexibility, as you'll see in a later exercise.)

3. The program creates three memory variables.

   ```
   ThisRow = 5
   FieldNum = 1
   CharNum = ASC("D")
   ```

   ThisRow identifies the row of each spreadsheet cell into which data is written. The value contained in ThisRow is not changed in the program as of yet, since only one record is sent to the spreadsheet. In later versions of this program, you'll increment this value each time a new record is sent, causing each successive record to be written to a lower row of cells.

   FieldNum identifies the table field from which data is read. Each time the program reads a value from a field, this value is incremented by 1, selecting the next field from which to read data.

   CharNum is given a numeric value generated by the ASC() function. This numeric value represents the character "D." Each time the program writes a value to a spreadsheet cell, this value is incremented by 1, selecting the next cell to write data to.

4. The program begins a DO...WHILE...ENDDO loop that moves from field to field in the first record of ADVERT.DBF, and from cell to cell in the spreadsheet.

```
DO WHILE FieldNum <= FLDCOUNT(DataFile)
```

The FLDCOUNT() function returns the total number of fields in the record structure of ADVERT.DBF. The loop begins with the first field in the record structure, which happens to be ACCOUNTNO (see Figure 7.6). In the next execution of the loop, FieldNum is incremented by 1 (and is now set at 2), and the field written to the spreadsheet is PRODUCT. So it goes until the last field is reached--that is, until FieldNum exceeds the number returned by FLDCOUNT().

5. Each time the loop is executed, the program uses FieldNum and the FIELD() function to generate the name of the field.

```
ThisField = FIELD(FieldNum)
```

6. Each time the loop is executed, the program uses the CHR(), LTRIM(), and STR() functions to generate the identifying coordinates of a spreadsheet cell.

```
ThisCell = "A:"+CHR(CharNum)+LTRIM(STR(ThisRow))
```

Just as the ASC() function converts a character into a numeric value, the CHR() function converts a numeric value into a character. The first cell coordinates generated by this command are A:B1. The next time the loop is executed, CharNum is incremented by 1, so the cell coordinates are A:C1.

(If your spreadsheet application is other than Quattro Pro for Windows, you may need to omit the "A:" at the beginning of the concatenation, and perhaps make other changes as well.)

7. Each time the loop is executed, the program uses the Poke() method to send the contents of the designated field to the designated spreadsheet cell.

```
SendData.Poke(ThisCell, &ThisField)
```

(Note that it was necessary to use the macro substitution function (&) to treat the contents of ThisField as a field name instead of a mere character string.)

8. Each time the loop is executed, the program increments the FieldNum and CharNum variables, selecting the next field and the next cell, respectively.

```
FieldNum = FieldNum + 1
CharNum = CharNum + 1
```

9. The loop repeats.

Thus, region walking is essentially a process of incrementing or decrementing numeric values and converting them to character strings. These character strings identify items in the client and the server (in this case, cells and fields, respectively), allowing a systematic "walk" from item to item.

Moving From Record to Record, Row to Row

So far, you've sent the contents of a single record to the spreadsheet. In the next exercise, you copy the entire file to the spreadsheet by region walking from record to record in the table and from row to row in the spreadsheet.

Exercise 7

In this exercise you alter XDDE.PRG to move not only from field to field but from record to record in ADVERT.DBF. Similarly, the program moves from cell to cell and from row to row in the spreadsheet.

1. First, make a backup copy of the program.

    COPY FILE XDDE.PRG TO XDDE2.PRG

2. Open XDDE2.PRG in the Text Editor.

    MODI COMM XDDE2

3. Add the following line of program code:

    DO WHILE .NOT. EOF()

    after the following line:

    ThisRow = 1

4. Add the following lines of program code:

    ```
    SKIP
      ThisRow = ThisRow + 1
    ENDDO
    ```

    after the following lines:

    ```
        CharNum = CharNum + 1
    ENDDO
    ```

    The program should now look like the one in Listing 7.6.

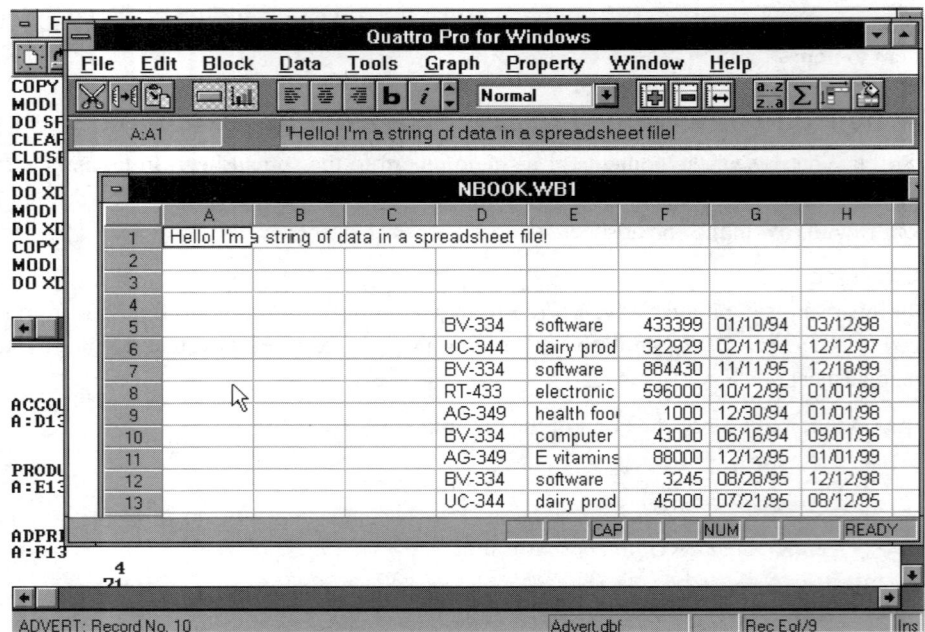

Figure 7.7 Field by field, record by record, data is placed in the cells

```
SendData = NEW DDELINK()
SendData.Initiate("QPW", "C:\QPW\SAMPLES\NBOOK.WB1")
DataFile = "ADVERT"
SELECT 1
USE (DataFile)
ThisRow = 5
DO WHILE .NOT. EOF()
   FieldNum = 1
   CharNum = ASC("D")

   DO WHILE FieldNum <= FLDCOUNT(DataFile)
      ThisField = FIELD(FieldNum)
      ThisCell = "A:"+CHR(CharNum)+LTRIM(STR(ThisRow))
      SendData.Poke(ThisCell, &ThisField)
      FieldNum = FieldNum + 1
      CharNum = CharNum + 1
   ENDDO

   SKIP
   ThisRow = ThisRow + 1
ENDDO
```

Listing 7.6 Region Walking from Field to Field and from Record to Record

Chapter 7 DDE and OLE

5. Save and exit, then run the program. (If you can, press <Alt-Tab> in time to see the region walk as it takes place.)

   ```
   DO XDDE
   ```

   When the region walk is finished, the spreadsheet should look like the one in Figure 7.7. Note that each record is displayed on a separate row.

6. Terminate the spreadsheet session. Do not save changes to the spreadsheet file.

The program now has an outer loop and an inner loop (see Listing 7.7). The outer loop moves from record to record and row to row, while the inner loop moves from field to field and cell to cell. Each time the inner loop completes its looping cycle, the following commands in the outer loop "walk" to the next record in ADVERT.DBF and to the next row of cells in the spreadsheet:

```
SKIP
ThisRow = ThisRow + 1
```

Now let's make the program more flexible. As is stands now, the program can access only one table file, ADVERT.DBF. Furthermore, you don't have a choice as to which row and column the first data item is inserted. The next exercise removes these limitations.

```
* Outer loop (for moving from record to record)
DO WHILE .NOT. EOF()
   FieldNum = 1
   CharNum = ASC("D")

   * Inner loop (for moving from field to field)
   DO WHILE FieldNum <= FLDCOUNT(DataFile)
   * Inner loop commands
   ENDDO

   SKIP
   ThisRow = ThisRow + 1
ENDDO
```

Listing 7.7 Schematic of Program Structure

Exercise 8

In this exercise you make major alterations to the program you created in the previous exercises. You create a custom class from the base class Form. The instances of this class serve as dialog boxes, which are windows that prompt the user for a response. A dialog box is always modal; consequently, it halts execution of the program that opened it until it is closed.

1. Open the XDDE2.PRG program file with the Text Editor.

   ```
   MODI COMM XDDE2
   ```

2. Insert the following line of program code at the beginning of the program:

   ```
   PUBLIC xVerdict
   ```

3. Change the following line of program code:

   ```
   DataFile = "ADVERT"
   ```

   to:

   ```
   DataFile = GETFILE("*.DBF")
   ```

4. Replace this line of program code:

   ```
   ThisRow = 1
   ```

   with:

   ```
   ThisCol = GETVAL("COL")
   ThisRow = GETVAL("ROW")
   ```

5. Change the following line of program code:

   ```
   CharNum = ASC("D")
   ```

   to:

   ```
   CharNum = ASC(ThisCol)
   ```

6. Change the following line of program code:

   ```
   DO WHILE FieldNum <= FLDCOUNT(DataFile)
   ```

   to:

   ```
   DO WHILE FieldNum <= FLDCOUNT(ALIAS())
   ```

   The program code should now look like Listing 7.8.

```
PUBLIC xVerdict
SendData = NEW DDELINK()
SendData.Initiate("QPW", "C:\QPW\SAMPLES\NBOOK.WB1")
DataFile = GETFILE("*.DBF")
SELECT 1
USE (DataFile)

ThisCol = GETVAL("COL")
ThisRow = GETVAL("ROW")
```

```
DO WHILE .NOT. EOF()
   FieldNum = 1
   CharNum = ASC(ThisCol)

   DO WHILE FieldNum <= FLDCOUNT(ALIAS())
      ThisField = FIELD(FieldNum)
      ThisCell = "A:"+CHR(CharNum)+LTRIM(STR(ThisRow))
      SendData.Poke(ThisCell, &ThisField)
      FieldNum = FieldNum + 1
      CharNum = CharNum + 1
   ENDDO

   SKIP
   ThisRow = ThisRow + 1
ENDDO
```

Listing 7.8 Changes in Original Program Code

7. Now create a custom class from which dialog boxes can be derived, as shown in Listing 7.9. (Add this code to the end of the program.)

   Note that the custom class has three procedure declarations. Recall that procedure declarations within a class are method properties of that class.

```
CLASS dBox OF FORM
   Set Procedure To C:\DBASEWIN\SAMPLES\BUTTONS.CC additive
   this.Height =  8
   this.Left   = 47
   this.Top    = 11
   this.Text   = ""
   this.Width  = 31
   this.OnSelection = CLASS::SHUTDOWN

   DEFINE ENTRYFIELD GETVAL OF THIS;
      PROPERTY;
        Height 1,;
        Left   14,;
        Border .T.,;
        Top    2,;
        Width  4,;
        Value  ""

   DEFINE PUSHBUTTON OKButn OF THIS;
      PROPERTY;
        Height      2,;
        Left        3,;
        OnClick CLASS::XOK,;
        Top         4,;
        Text        "OK",;
        Width       10,;
        ColorNormal "N/W",;
```

```
                   Default    .T.

   DEFINE PUSHBUTTON CancButn OF THIS;
      PROPERTY;
         Height  2,,;
         Left    19,,;
         OnClick CLASS::XCANCEL,,;
         Top     4,,;
         Text    "Cancel",,;
         Width   9

   PROCEDURE xOK
     IF LEN(TRIM(Form.GetVal.Value)) > 0
        xVerdict = Form.GetVal.Value
     ENDIF
   RETURN

   PROCEDURE xCancel
      CANCEL
   RETURN

   PROCEDURE ShutDown
     Form.Close()
   RETURN

ENDCLASS
```

Listing 7.9 Declaration of CLASS dBox

```
FUNCTION GETVAL (xType)
   xVerdict = "A"
   xBox = NEW dBox()
   DO CASE
      CASE xType = "ROW"
           xBox.Text = "Enter Row Number"
      CASE xType = "COL"
           xBox.Text = "Enter Column Letter"
   ENDCASE
   xBox.MDI = .F.
   xBox.ReadModal()
   xBox.Close()
   xBox.Release()
   IF xType = "ROW"
      IF LEN(TRIM(xVerdict)) = 0
         xVerdict = 1
      ELSE
         xVerdict = VAL(xVerdict)
      ENDIF
   ELSE
      IF LEN(TRIM(xVerdict)) = 0
         xVerdict = "A"
      ELSE
```

Chapter 7 DDE and OLE

```
            xVerdict = UPPER(xVerdict)
        ENDIF
    ENDIF
RETURN xVerdict
```

Listing 7.10 Procedure that Opens a Dialog Box and Returns the User's Response

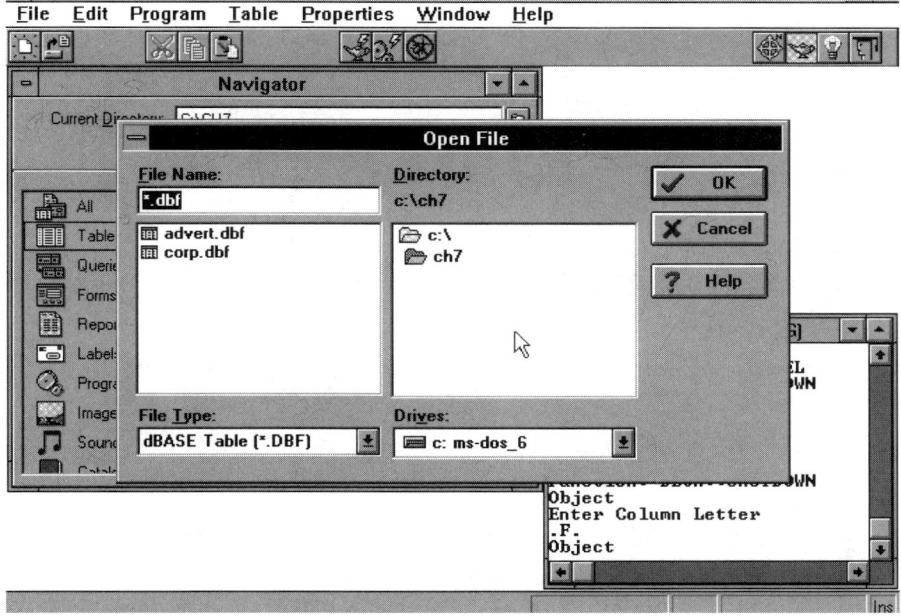

Figure 7.8 The Open File dialog box appears

8. Add FUNCTION GETVAL (Listing 7.10) to the end of the program (that is, after the dBox class declaration).

9. Save and exit, then run the program.

   DO XDDE

   The Open File dialog box appears, as shown in Figure 7.8.

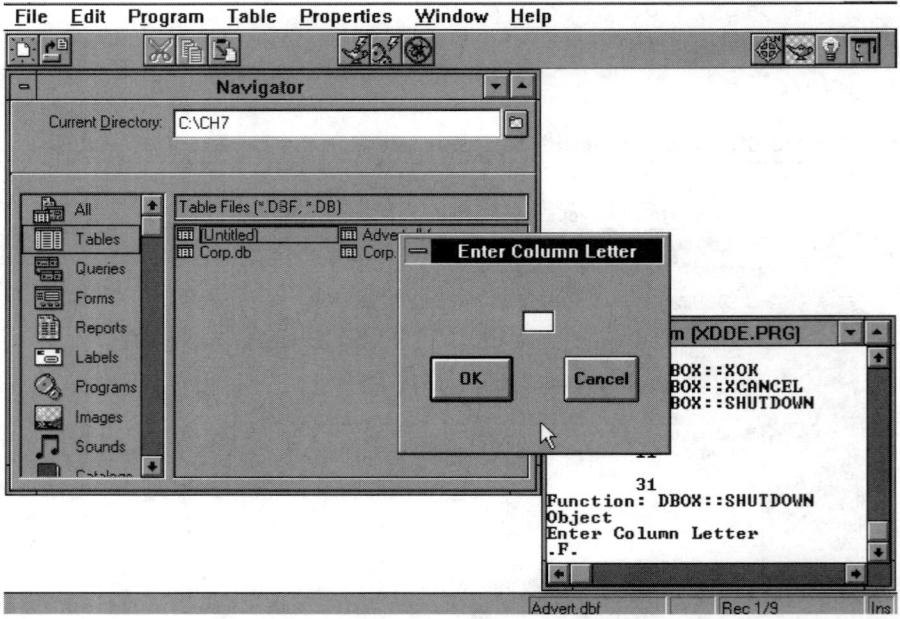

Figure 7.9 A prompt to enter a column letter appears

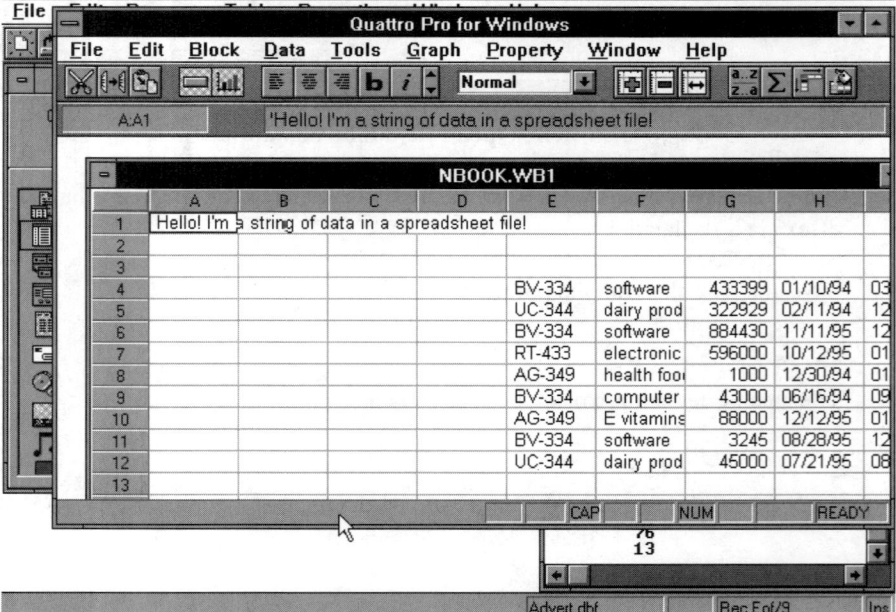

Figure 7.10 Data appears in user specified location

Chapter 7 DDE and OLE

10. Select **advert.dbf**, then click the **OK** button.

    The Open File dialog box disappears. In a few seconds, a dialog box appears, as shown in Figure 7.9. Note that the caption bar of the dialog box displays the prompt **Enter Column Letter**.

11. Enter **E**, then click the **OK** pushbutton.

    The dialog box disappears very briefly, then returns, this time with the prompt **Enter Row Number**.

12. Enter 4, then click the **OK** pushbutton.

    The dialog box disappears.

13. Go to the spreadsheet session by pressing <Alt-Tab>.

    When the region walk is over, the spreadsheet should resemble the one in Figure 7.10.

14. Terminate the spreadsheet session. Do not save changes to the spreadsheet file.

The advantages of DDE over standard import and export operations are obvious. In this example you were not only able to send table data to a spreadsheet, but you were able to send it to a specific location in the spreadsheet. Thus, the major advantage that DDE has over traditional data transfer methods is flexibility--the ability to fine-tune the data transfer to suit your needs exactly.

As powerful as DDE is for transferring data of the basic type (that is, character, numeric, float, date, and logical) it isn't much help in transferring graphic or other binary data. For this, use Object Linking and Embedding.

Object Linking and Embedding

Many Windows applications create files that contain graphic images, sounds, or other items not suitable for transfer with DDE (or even Import or Export). To use, alter, and share these files from a session in dBASE for Windows, use object linking and embedding (OLE).

Binary files that are used in an OLE application are called *OLE documents*. With OLE, you link an OLE document to a field in a dBASE table or embed the OLE document in the OLE field directly. Once an OLE document is linked or embedded in an OLE field, you can start a session in the external application that created it by double-clicking on the field. (Another way is to execute the DoVerb() method, which is a property of control objects of the OLE Object class.)

When you *link* an OLE document to an OLE field, the document itself is stored in an external file--*and* in the OLE field. For example, if you create a bitmap image in the Windows Paintbrush accessory program and save it in a .BMP file, you can link this file to an OLE field.

Later, you can start a session in Paintbrush by double-clicking the document in a dBASE session. When the Paintbrush application window is displayed, the OLE document file is opened automatically, and is ready to be viewed or edited within the Paintbrush session. Once edited, all changes are written to the copies of the document that are stored in the file and the OLE field.

When you *embed* an OLE document in an OLE field, the document is actually stored in the field. For example, if you create a bitmap image in Paintbrush and embed it in an OLE field, no file need be created. As with linked documents, you can start a session in Paintbrush by double-clicking the embedded document in a dBASE session. When the Paintbrush application window is displayed, the embedded OLE document is displayed, and you can view or edit it.

The external application that you use to create and modify OLE documents is called the *OLE server application*, or *OLE server* for short. In the examples that follow we use Windows Paintbrush as the OLE server, since it comes with all Windows installations and is easy to use. However, most Windows applications that have OLE capability work in similar ways; the authors suggest experimentation with whatever other OLE-capable applications you may have.

Linking To OLE Document Files

Use linking when you want to keep and maintain an external copy of an OLE document, while still accessing it from a dBASE session. One of the greatest advantages of linking is that you can deliver copies of the document to other computers via a network or by disk-swapping, without having to deliver an entire table file.

Exercise 9

In this exercise you create an OLE server document file in Paintbrush, then link it to an OLE field (LOGO in CORP.DBF). You terminate the Paintbrush session, then start a new Paintbrush session from the dBASE session.

1. First, be sure your environment is clean.

   ```
   CLEAR ALL
   ```

2. Open CORP.DBF, then open a browse window.

   ```
   USE CORP
   BROWSE
   ```

3. Press <Alt-Tab> until you reach the Program Manager, then start a session in Paintbrush.

   (In most systems, Paintbrush is located in the Accessories Group.)

4. Create any image you wish with the Paintbrush tools. (The image shown in Figure 7.11 is typical.)

Chapter 7 DDE and OLE

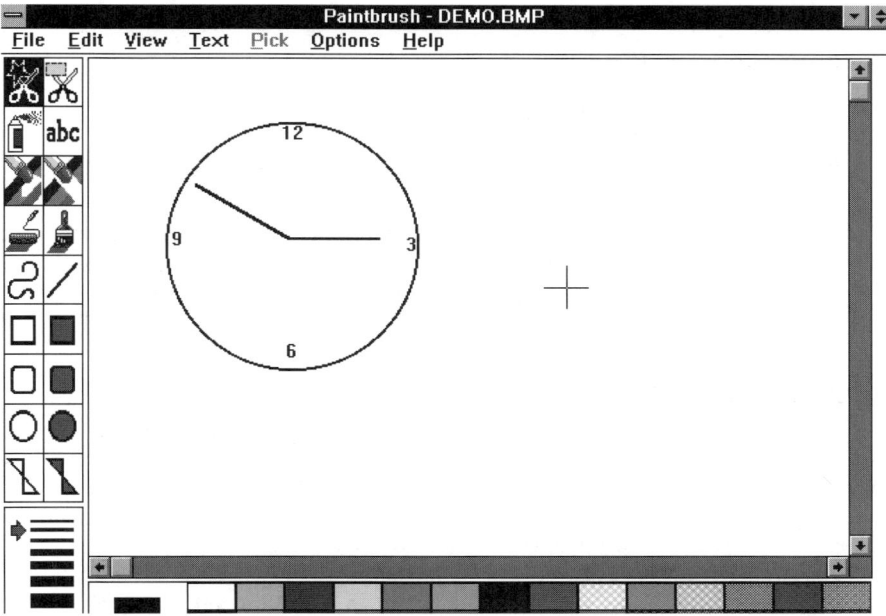

Figure 7.11   Image created with the Paintbrush tools

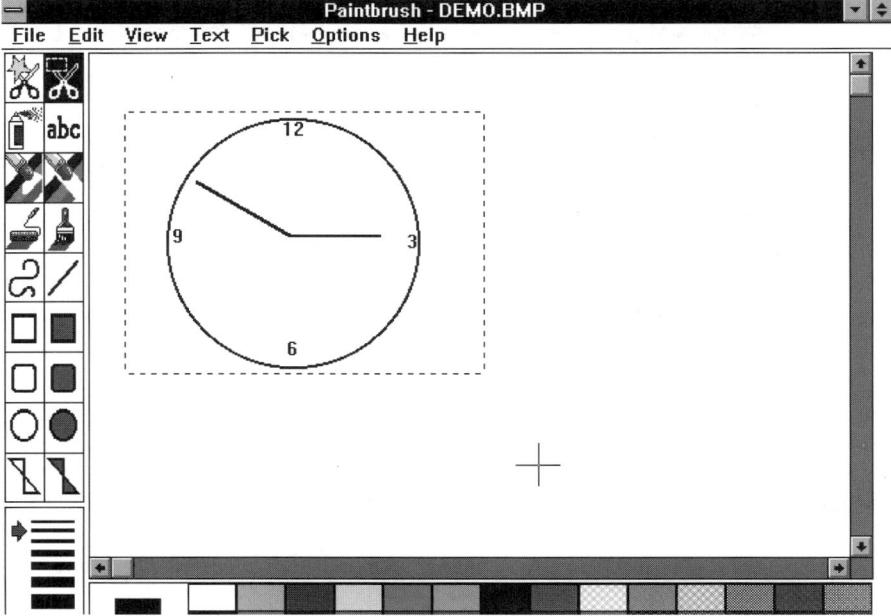

Figure 7.12   The image is surrounded by a faint line

5. Select **File | Save**.

    The Paintbrush Save As dialog box appears.

6. Enter the file name DEMO.BMP, then click the **OK** button.

    The Save As dialog box disappears, and the new file is created.

7. Click on the Cut icon at the top right of the tool bar, then place the cursor at the upper left portion of the image. Hold down the left mouse key, then drag the cursor to the lower right portion of the image. Release the mouse key.

    The image should now be surrounded by a faint line (see Figure 7.12).

8. Select **Edit | Copy**.

    This action temporarily saves the image in the Windows Clipboard, a region in memory that serves as a buffer for data you want to transfer somewhere else.

9. Press <Alt-Tab> until you reach the dBASE session.

10. Maximize the browse window, then scroll to the right until you reach the LOGO field.

11. Double-click the LOGO field in the first record.

    The OLE viewer window is displayed, as shown in Figure 7.13.

12. Select **Edit | Paste Link**.

    The image appears in the OLE viewer window, as shown in Figure 7.14.

13. Press <Alt-Tab> until you reach the Paintbrush session, then terminate the session.

    The dBASE session returns.

14. Double-click the OLE viewer window.

    In a few seconds, a new Paintbrush session is begun.

15. Select **File | Open**, and note that **demo.bmp** is currently open.

    This demonstrates that when an OLE document file is linked to a dBASE OLE field, launching the OLE server application opens the file automatically.

16. Make a change to the image (any change you wish), then select **File | Save**.

17. Terminate the Paintbrush session.

Chapter 7 DDE and OLE

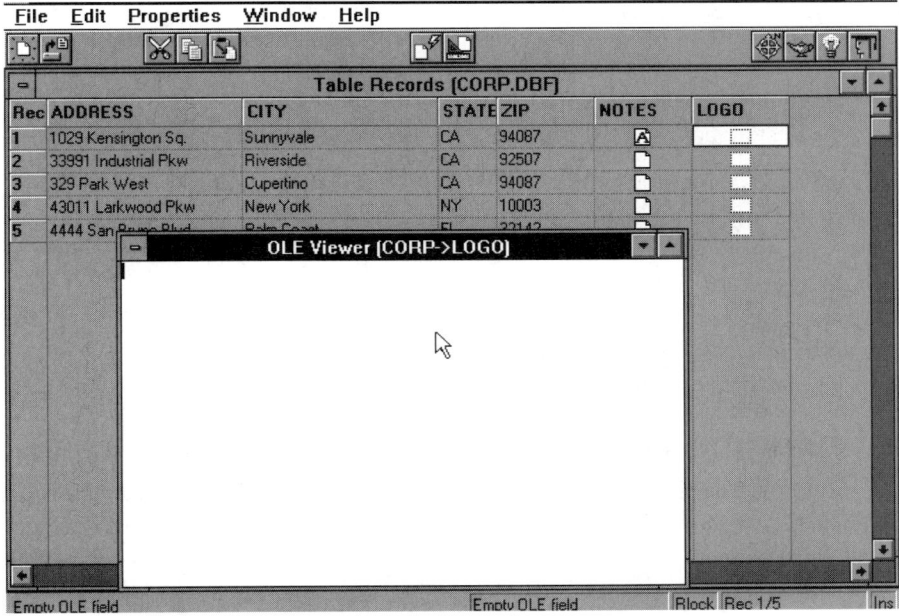

Figure 7.13 The OLE Viewer window is displayed

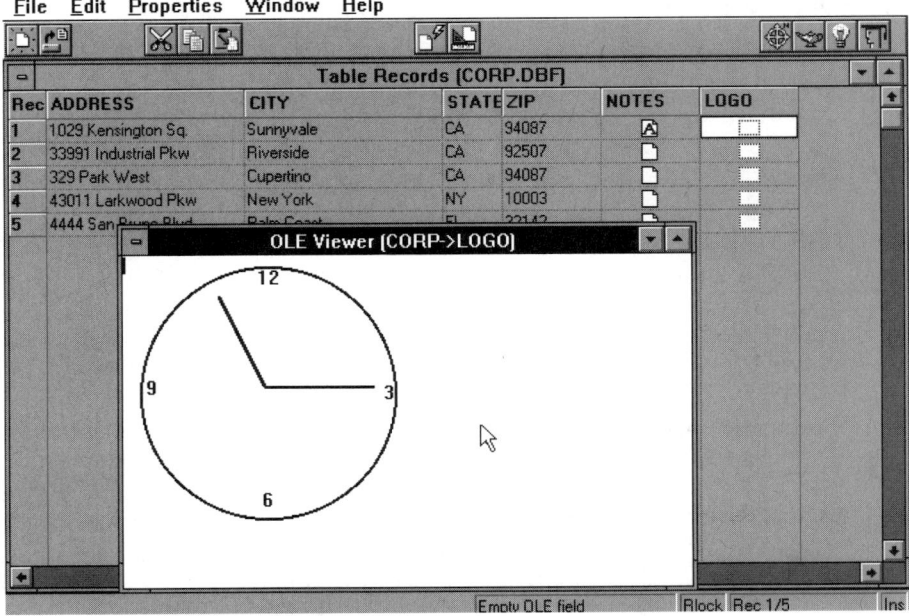

Figure 7.14 The image appears in the OLE Viewer window

The dBASE session returns. Note that the change is reflected in the OLE server window.

18. Close the OLE viewer window, restore the browse window to its original size (with the Restore button at the upper right corner), then close the browse window.

This exercise demonstrates that OLE is a powerful data-sharing tool for uniting two or more applications toward a common purpose. For example, you were able to invoke sessions in Paintbrush from a dBASE session with a simple double-click event. You were able to effect changes in the OLE document file from a Paintbrush session and immediately see the changes reflected in the OLE field. In this way, OLE increases the power of your dBASE applications by making external resources available to your users.

Now let's look at an example of embedding.

Embedding OLE Documents

Use embedding when you want to store binary information without needing auxiliary files (like DEMO.BMP in the previous exercise). The major advantage of embedding is simplicity; you needn't worry about any files except the table file (.DBF) and its own auxiliary files (.DBT and .MDX).

Exercise 10

In this exercise you create a graphic image, embed it in an OLE field, then modify it through an OLE server session.

1. First, be sure your environment is clean.

    ```
    CLEAR ALL
    ```

2. Open CORP.DBF, then open a browse window.

    ```
    USE CORP
    BROWSE
    ```

3. Press <Alt-Tab> until you reach the Program Manager, then start a session in Paintbrush.

4. Create any image you wish with the Paintbrush tools. (The image shown in Figure 7.15 is typical.)

5. Click on the Cut icon at the top right of the tool bar, then place the cursor at the upper left portion of the image. Hold down the left mouse key, then drag the cursor to the lower right portion of the image. Release the mouse key.

    As before, the image should now be surrounded by a faint line.

Chapter 7 DDE and OLE

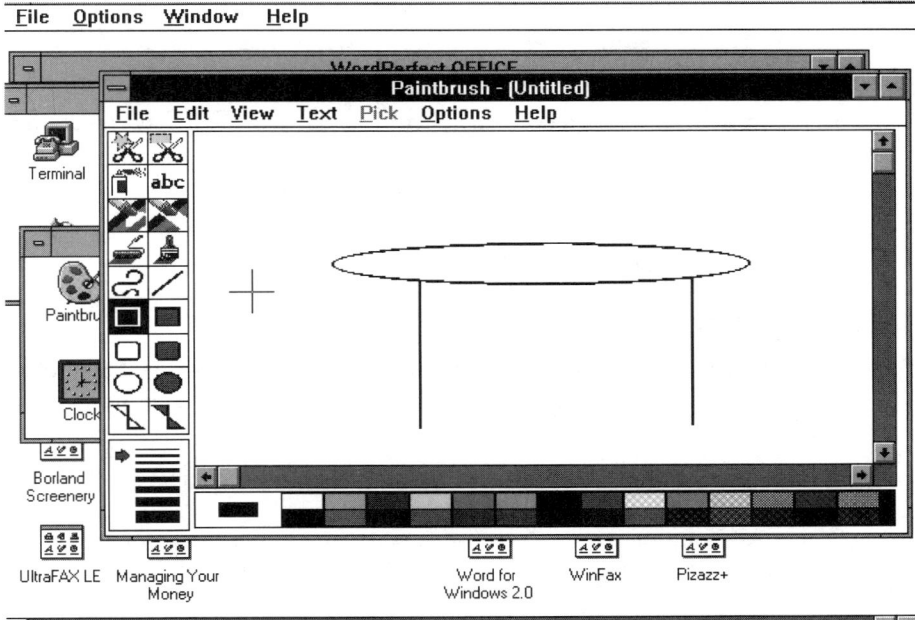

Figure 7.15 An Image created with the Paintbrush tools

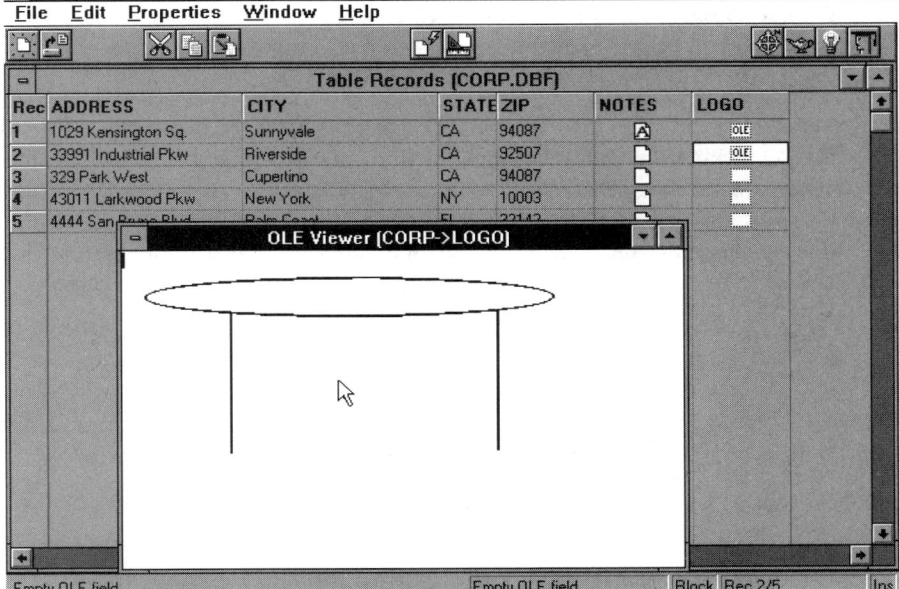

Figure 7.16 The image appears in the OLE Viewer window

6. Select **Edit | Copy**.

7. Press <Alt-Tab> until you reach the dBASE session.

8. Maximize the browse window, then scroll to the right until you reach the LOGO field.

9. Double-click the LOGO field in the second record.

    The OLE viewer window is displayed.

10. Select **Edit | Paste**.

    (*Do not* select **Paste Link**, which isn't available now anyway. The **Paste Link** option is unavailable because you didn't save the image to a file as you did in the previous exercise.).

    The image appears in the OLE viewer window, as shown in Figure 7.16.

11. Press <Alt-Tab> until you reach the Paintbrush session, then terminate the session. When the confirmation prompt appears, select the **Yes** pushbutton.

    The dBASE session returns.

12. Double-click the OLE viewer window.

    In a few seconds, a new Paintbrush session is begun.

13. Select **File | Open**, and note that no bitmap file is open.

    This demonstrates that when an OLE document file is embedded in a dBASE OLE field, launching the OLE server application does not open a file, and that the binary data is stored in the dBASE table only.

14. Make a change to the image (any change you wish), then terminate the Paintbrush session. When the confirmation prompt appears, select the **Yes** pushbutton.

    The dBASE session returns. Note that the change is reflected in the OLE server window.

15. Close the OLE viewer window, restore the browse window to its original size (with the Restore button at the upper-right corner), then close the browse window.

Now let's look at another way to access OLE server applications.

Using OLE objects

As might be expected, dBASE for Windows has a special control object that serves the same purpose as the OLE viewer window. Known as an *OLE object*, it lets the user launch a server session from a form. Since it's an object, it has all of the capabilities of an OLE viewer window and much more. It has a complete set of properties that give you, the programmer, much flexibility. Let's create one now.

Exercise 11

In this exercise you create an OLE object that starts a session in Paintbrush.

1. First, be sure your environment is clean.

   CLEAR ALL

2. Open CORP.DBF, then open a browse window.

   USE CORP
   BROWSE

3. Press <Tab> until the highlight reaches the LOGO field of the first record, then double-click the field.

   The OLE viewer window is displayed.

4. Press <Alt-Tab> until you reach the Program Manager, start a session in Paintbrush, then create any image you wish.

5. Click **File | Save**.

   The Save As dialog box appears.

6. Save the image as DEMO2.BMP, then click the **OK** pushbutton.

   The dialog box disappears.

7. Click on the Cut icon at the top right of the tool bar, then place the cursor at the upper left portion of the image. Hold down the left mouse key, then drag the cursor to the lower right portion of the image. Release the mouse key.

   As before, the image should now be surrounded by a faint line.

8. Select **Edit | Copy**.

   As before, the image is now stored in the Windows Clipboard.

234   Easy dBASE for Windows Object-Oriented Programming

9. Press <Alt-Tab> until you reach the dBASE session, then click once on the OLE viewer window to be sure it has focus.

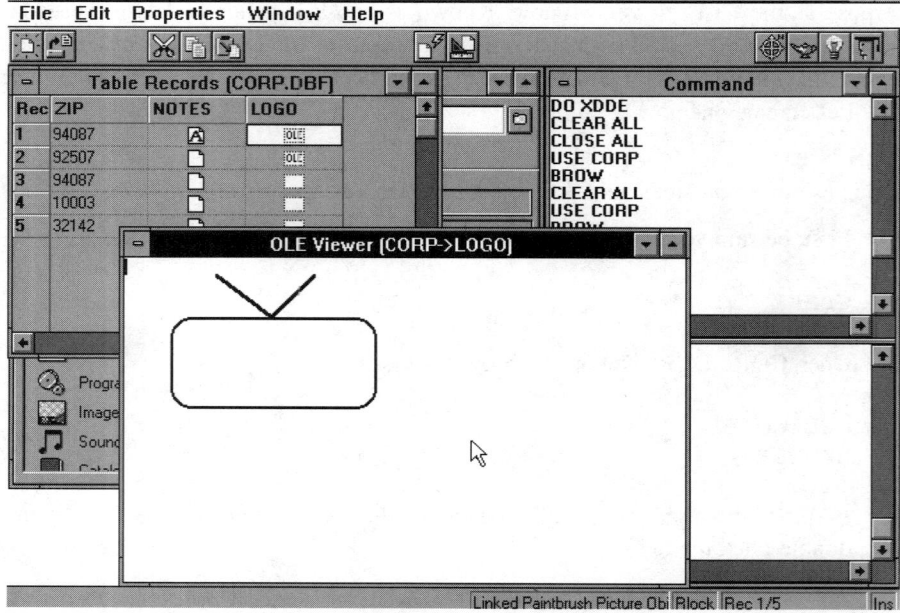

Figure 7.17   The bitmap image appears in the OLE Viewer window

10. Click **Edit | Paste Link**.

    The bitmap image appears in the OLE viewer window (see Figure 7.17). You just linked DEMO2.BMP to the OLE field.

11. Close CORP.DBF.

    CLOSE DATABASE

12. Press <Alt-Tab> until you reach the Paintbrush session, then close the session.

    The dBASE session reappears.

13. Now start a session in the Form Designer.

    CREATE FORM XOLE

    The design surface, the Object Inspector, and the Control Palette are displayed.

14. Click the View item in the Object Inspector, then click the Tool button at the right.

Chapter 7 DDE and OLE 235

The Choose View dialog box appears.

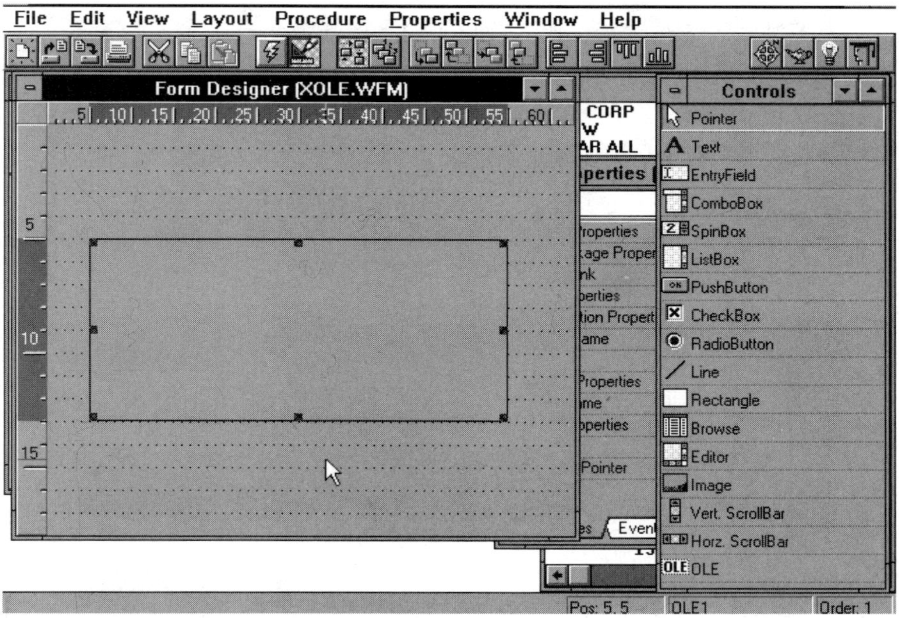

Figure 7.18 Creating an OLE object

15. Double-click **corp.dbf** in the pick list at the left.

    The dialog box disappears, and **CORP.DBF** is displayed in the View item.

16. If the OLE item in the Control Palette is not visible (it's at the bottom), click the vertical scroll bar on the right edge of the Control Palette. Then click the OLE item.

17. Place the mouse pointer at Row 5, Column 5, hold the left mouse key down, and drag the mouse pointer to Row 13, Column 55. Then release the mouse key.

    The OLE object you just created should look like the one in Figure 7.18.

    Now let's assign an OLE field to the OLE object.

18. If necessary, double-click the Data Linkage Properties item in the Object Inspector to display the DataLink item. Click the DataLink item, then click the Tool button that appears on the right.

    The Choose Field dialog box appears.

19. Double-click the LOGO field.

The dialog box disappears, and **CORP->LOGO** is displayed in the DataLink item.

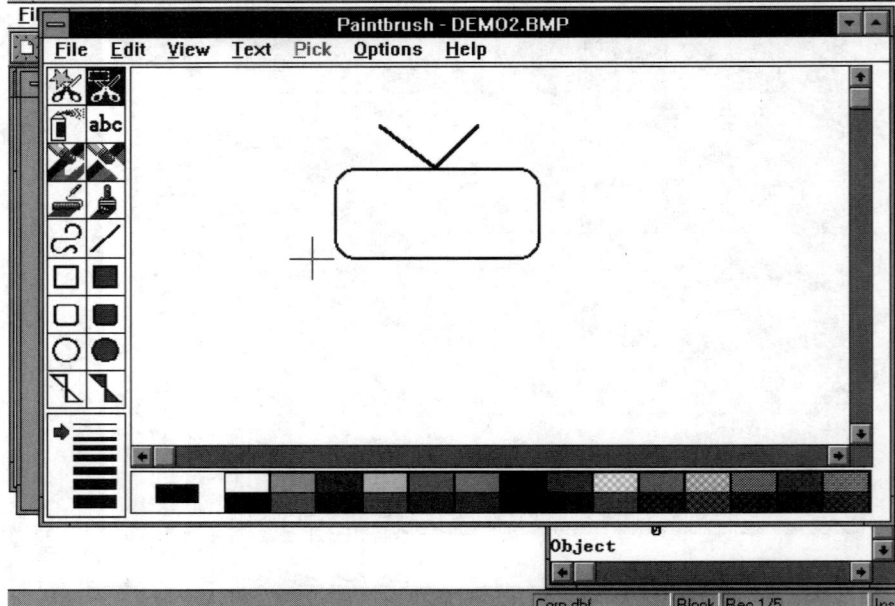

Figure 7.19 Paintbrush is activated and DEMO2.BMP is displayed

20. Click the Run pushbutton (the one with the lightning bolt).

    The form goes into Run mode.

21. Double-click the OLE object.

    In a few seconds, Paintbrush is activated, displaying DEMO2.BMP (see Figure 7.19).

22. Terminate the Paintbrush session.

23. Close the form.

Now let's look at another way to start an OLE server session. So far you've used the method of double-clicking the OLE document (in either an OLE object or an OLE viewer window) for starting such a session. Although these techniques are easy and intuitive for users, there may be times when clicking some other object might be preferable. For situations like these, OLE objects have a powerful property called DoVerb().

Using the DoVerb Property

The DoVerb() property is a member of the OLE object class. It explicitly launches an OLE server session, bypassing the requirement of double-clicking an OLE server document.

Exercise 12

In this exercise you use DoVerb() to start an OLE server session by clicking a pushbutton.

1. First, be sure your environment is clean.

    CLEAR ALL

2. Open the form in the Form Designer.

    MODI FORM XOLE

3. Click the **PushButton** item in the Control Palette, then create a pushbutton just below the OLE object.

4. Click the OLE object once.

5. If necessary, double-click the **Identification Properties** item in the Object inspector to display that set of properties. Note that the Name property contains the character string OLE1.

    You'll use this knowledge in a moment.

6. Click the pushbutton once to give it focus.

7. Click the **Events** tab of the Object Inspector, click the **OnClick** item, then click the Tool button that appears at the right.

    The Procedure Editor appears.

8. Enter the following line of program code:

    Form.OLE1.DoVerb(0, "a dBASE session.")

9. Click the Run pushbutton.

    In a few seconds, the form goes into Run mode.

10. Click the pushbutton.

    In a few seconds, a Paintbrush session is started (see Figure 7.20).

11. Close the Paintbrush session.

12. Close the form.

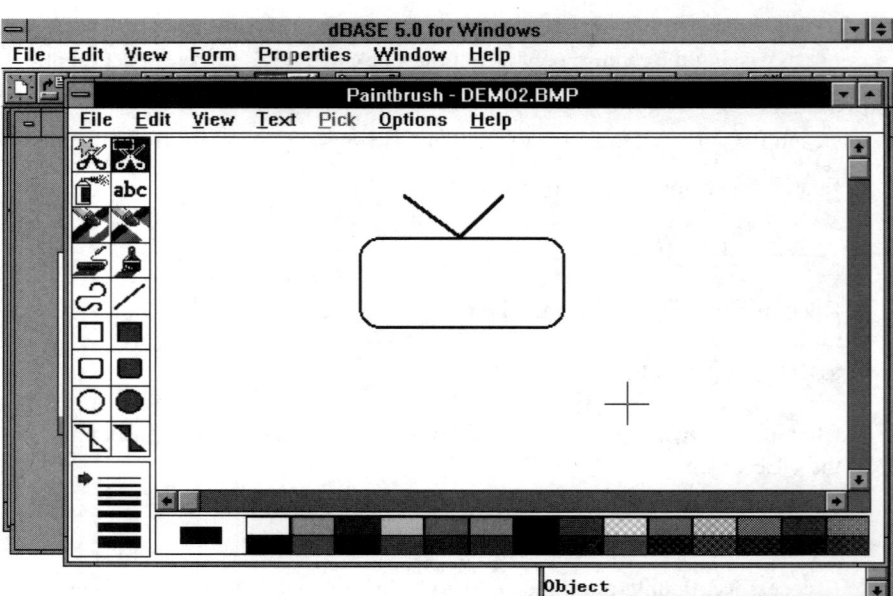

Figure 7.20 A Paintbrush session appears

The first parameter of the DoVerb() property is known as the *OLE verb*, and it determines what kind of server session is started. Most Windows applications (including Paintbrush) have only one run mode, which is denoted by the number zero. Even so, some Windows applications have more than one run mode. For example, most sound applications (which create binary files that generate sounds) run in two modes, Play (which usually requires a verb of 0) or Edit (which usually requires a verb of 1). If you have any doubts about which OLE verbs to use in a Windows application, consult the documentation that comes with the application.

What Now?

The exercises in this book have provided you with the fundamental skills, concepts, and terminology to become a professional OOP programmer in the dBASE language. The final stage in the learning process is to tackle a real-world problem--something only a client or an employer can give you. If neither is available at this time, you might start by serving as your own client; that is, create an application that is useful in your own daily affairs or in your current job.

Whatever your first programming task is, don't be intimidated. The OOP language of dBASE for Windows was specifically designed to be easy and intuitive. That, plus powerful two-way tools like the Form Designer and the Menu Designer, can see you through even the most daunting challenges.

We wish you the best in your programming endeavors.

Index

—A—

Access Properties, 71, 72
actions, 1, 13, 14, 17, 24, 65, 67, 73, 86, 94, 98, 113, 116, 179, 189, 192, 207
application window, 39, 60, 62, 169, 170, 201, 206, 212, 226
array object, 18, 24
Array objects, 15
attribute, 1, 12, 24, 27, 64, 65, 67, 69, 72, 96, 98, 99
attribute properties, 64, 65, 69, 72, 98, 99

—B—

base class, 99, 219
Binary type, 8, 9, 225
bitmap icons, 164, 165
browse, 3, 18, 23, 39, 40, 41, 43, 44, 45, 57, 62, 63, 75, 76, 77, 78, 79, 80, 81, 86, 87, 89, 90, 102, 103, 104, 105, 106, 107, 115, 118, 119, 120, 121, 126, 136, 137, 140, 142, 143, 144, 149, 176, 177, 179, 180, 226, 228, 230, 232, 233
browse object, 3, 18, 23, 43, 45, 76, 77, 78, 79, 80, 81, 86, 87, 89, 90, 102, 103, 104, 105, 106, 107, 115, 118, 119, 120, 121, 126, 136, 137, 140, 142, 143, 144, 149, 176, 177, 179, 180
browse window, 39, 40, 41, 43, 44, 45, 57, 62, 63, 76, 77, 79, 226, 228, 230, 232, 233

—C—

cascading menu, 189, 192, 193, 194, 195, 196
character, 2, 4, 5, 15, 16, 22, 29, 30, 32, 33, 34, 50, 68, 76, 82, 100, 119, 142, 149, 190, 191, 197, 213, 215, 216, 225, 237
Character Type, 4
child object, 107, 111, 174
codeblock, 12, 13, 14, 15, 16, 17, 23, 68, 83, 84, 116, 119, 148, 175, 178, 180, 186, 188
Codeblock Type, 13
combo box, 5, 30, 31, 32
Command window, 29, 35, 63, 66, 67, 97, 106, 123, 202, 205, 208
compound index, 19, 46, 50, 52
concatenation, 4, 22, 50, 216
contained, 8, 17, 18, 27, 29, 46, 58, 63, 66, 67, 76, 94, 98, 102, 103, 105, 106, 107, 110, 111, 112, 113, 116, 121, 136, 137, 143, 154, 160, 172, 174, 196, 200, 202, 215
containership, 66, 76, 102, 107, 112, 174
control, 2, 9, 12, 17, 18, 34, 38, 43, 50, 63, 64, 79, 96, 102, 107, 112, 121, 136, 140, 143, 149, 164, 165, 167, 198, 200, 202, 211, 225, 232
control objects, 2, 12, 17, 79, 102, 112, 149, 165, 167, 198, 225
controls, 2, 5, 7, 132
custom classes, 95, 96, 119, 131
Custom Properties, 84

—D—

Data Linkage Properties, 155, 235
Data types, 2, 4, 5, 7, 15, 16, 18, 20, 22, 27, 29, 30, 32, 33, 34, 50, 68, 76, 82, 100, 118, 119, 142, 149, 190, 191, 197, 213, 215, 216, 225, 237
database management system, 1, 191
databases, 27
date, 2, 7, 15, 16, 18, 20, 27, 118, 119, 225
date type, 7, 16
DDE, 198, 199, 200, 202, 203, 204, 205, 206, 207, 208, 209, 211, 212, 213, 214, 215, 225
DDE conversation, 200
DDE Link, 200
DECLARE, 18
DEFINE object syntax, 25, 90, 94
Dot Operator, 24, 174
DoVerb Property, 236
dropdown list, 5, 30, 32, 53, 71, 72, 177
Dynamic Data Exchange, 198, 199

—E—

editor object, 9, 10
Embedding OLE Documents, 230
entry field, 5, 7, 16, 18, 23, 56, 149, 150, 151, 152, 153
event handler, 24, 68, 73, 113
event properties, 65, 68, 70, 86, 133, 143, 188
event property, 68, 81, 87, 116, 119, 143, 149, 178, 197
events, 1, 12, 24, 64, 67, 68, 73, 86, 90, 98
Expression Builder, 53, 55

—F—

field, 5, 8, 9, 11, 17, 18, 20, 22, 28, 30, 32, 34, 35, 38, 39, 41, 43, 44, 46, 47, 48, 49, 50, 51, 52, 53, 56, 58, 61, 62, 63, 79, 82, 89, 146, 149, 150, 151, 152, 153, 156, 191, 192, 206, 207, 213, 214, 215, 216, 217, 218, 219, 225, 226, 228, 230, 232, 233, 234, 235
Field names, 15
File Viewer, 33, 34
float, 2, 5, 6, 7, 15, 16, 32, 225
float type, 5
Float Types, 5
form, 24, 25, 63, 66, 68, 70, 72, 74, 96, 97, 98, 99, 100, 109, 111, 115, 119, 120, 124, 125, 128, 129, 130, 131, 132, 133, 136, 137, 138, 140, 141, 142, 143, 145, 147, 148, 149, 153, 155, 157, 158, 160, 161, 162, 163, 164, 165, 166, 167, 169, 175, 178, 179, 182, 187, 188, 219, 222, 234, 237, 239
Form Designer, 63, 70, 131, 132, 133, 136, 137, 138, 140, 141, 142, 143, 145, 147, 149, 153, 155, 157, 158, 160, 161, 162, 163, 164, 165, 166, 167, 182, 188, 234, 237, 239
Form object, 24, 25, 66, 68, 98, 99, 111, 119, 128
Form object class, 24, 25, 66, 68, 98, 99, 111, 119, 128
forms, 2, 18, 66, 67, 83, 84, 90, 99, 112, 113, 126, 131, 132, 160, 168, 172, 198
function, 11, 12, 13, 14, 15, 16, 18, 19, 22, 23, 33, 49, 50, 55, 68, 81, 82, 86, 102, 116, 148, 177, 178, 197, 200, 205, 211, 215, 216
Function Call Operators, 22
function pointer, 12, 14, 15, 16, 102, 197
Function Pointer Type, 14

—I—

Identification Properties, 111, 237
IF...ENDIF, 204
image object, 9
index, 27, 43, 46, 48, 50, 53, 54, 56, 57
Index Operator, 24
index tag, 44, 45, 46, 47, 50, 52, 53, 56
indexing, 4, 35, 44, 47, 48, 50, 51
inheritance, 96, 98, 111, 112, 116
Initiate(), 200, 203, 204, 205
input pane, 29, 33, 34, 36, 38, 39, 43, 46, 48, 50, 53, 66, 67, 68, 70, 123
instance, 23, 24, 25, 66, 96, 99, 128, 141, 143

—K—

key field, 32, 34, 44, 46, 47, 48, 50, 58, 63

—L—

Language Elements, 1
Linking To OLE Document Files, 226
list box, 5, 18, 102, 103, 154, 155, 156, 157, 158, 202
literals, 15, 16, 17, 19
logical, 2, 7, 8, 15, 16, 19, 27, 44, 45, 48, 49, 58, 204, 225
Logical Operators, 19
Logical Type, 7
logical values, 7

—M—

macro commands, 211
macros, 211
Mathematical Operators, 20
MDI property, 148, 168, 170, 171, 172, 177
member access operator, 24
member functions, 101, 102, 143, 147
memo field, 8, 9
Memo type, 8, 9
menu bar, 106, 169, 170, 171, 172, 173, 177, 185, 188, 190, 192, 195
Menu Designer, 137, 168, 182, 183, 185, 186, 187, 188, 189, 190, 192, 195, 197, 239
Menu object class, 168, 170, 178
menus, 167, 168, 169, 170, 171, 172, 173, 180, 182, 183, 190, 192, 196, 198
methods, 14, 24, 65, 102, 116, 225
modified index, 46, 47, 48, 53, 82, 84, 137
MODIFY COMMAND, 73, 77, 80, 81, 82, 84, 86, 90, 97, 132, 137
mouse, 31, 34, 41, 55, 60, 68, 72, 73, 100, 133, 135, 136, 143, 151, 154, 166, 167, 178, 180, 181, 228, 233, 235
mouse event, 143

—N—

Navigator, 29, 43
NEW Operator, 23
NEW operator syntax, 25, 90
numeric, 2, 5, 6, 7, 15, 16, 30, 32, 149, 153, 213, 215, 216, 225

Index

Numeric types, 5, 6, 17, 30

—O—

object class, 65
Object Grouping, 154
Object Inspector, 69, 70, 72, 106, 107, 109, 110, 111, 112, 113, 116, 118, 135, 137, 138, 143, 145, 151, 152, 153, 155, 183, 188, 189, 234, 235, 237
Object Linking and Embedding, 11, 198, 199, 225
Object Operators, 23
object oriented programming, 1, 2, 16, 25, 63, 64, 65, 66, 68, 69, 73, 74, 76, 77, 95, 96, 99, 101, 238
Object Pallette, 135, 151, 164, 165, 166, 167
object properties, 106, 132
object reference, 12, 13, 15, 16, 23, 24, 25, 66, 68, 75, 76, 94, 99, 102, 103, 109, 110, 111, 112, 113, 116, 141, 143, 148, 172, 196
Object Reference Type, 12
objects, 1, 2, 3, 12, 15, 16, 17, 18, 23, 25, 64, 65, 66, 67, 68, 69, 73, 75, 76, 79, 84, 86, 90, 94, 99, 102, 103, 111, 112, 119, 121, 136, 143, 148, 149, 151, 153, 154, 158, 160, 162, 163, 165, 167, 172, 178, 190, 198, 202, 225, 232, 236
OLE, 8, 9, 11, 12, 17, 65, 198, 199, 214, 225, 226, 228, 229, 230, 231, 232, 233, 234, 235, 236, 237, 238
OLE document, 9, 11, 225, 226, 228, 230, 232, 236
OLE field, 9, 11, 214, 225, 226, 228, 230, 232, 234, 235
OLE server, 11, 226, 228, 230, 232, 236
OLE Types, 8
OLE Viewer window, 11, 229, 231, 234
OnNavigate, 73, 80, 81, 82, 83, 85, 86, 87, 92
operator, 15, 18, 19, 20, 21, 22, 23, 24, 25, 75, 76, 90, 91, 99, 102, 111, 116

—P—

Paintbrush, 9, 11, 199, 225, 226, 227, 228, 230, 231, 232, 233, 234, 236, 238
parameter, 23, 121, 168, 172, 175, 177, 185, 200, 202, 203, 204, 205, 206, 211, 212, 238
parent object, 107, 111, 112, 121
peek, 208
poke, 205, 207, 208
primary key, 51
Procedure Editor, 133, 143, 144, 145, 183, 193, 194, 195, 197, 237
properties, 16, 24, 64, 65, 66, 67, 68, 69, 70, 71, 72, 76, 79, 82, 84, 86, 94, 95, 96, 98, 99, 100, 101, 102, 106, 107, 109, 110, 111, 112, 113, 118, 119, 132, 133, 135, 142, 143, 155, 160, 161, 162, 163, 164, 165, 166, 167, 169, 188, 197, 221, 235, 237
pushbutton, 66, 67, 68, 69, 70, 71, 72, 74, 75, 76, 86, 87, 89, 90, 94, 107, 109, 110, 111, 113, 115, 121, 123, 126, 127, 147, 148, 154, 155, 156, 157, 158, 162, 163, 165, 167, 177, 178, 203, 225, 232, 233, 236, 237

—Q—

query by example, 27, 38, 57, 58, 61, 62, 73, 74, 75, 76, 77, 79, 80, 83, 85, 87, 90, 91, 92, 104, 108, 114, 117, 120, 122, 124, 125, 129, 136, 137, 138, 139, 140, 141, 142, 147, 151, 155, 175, 177, 178, 179, 180, 181, 182, 187, 189, 195, 197, 205, 207
Query Designer, 27, 58, 59, 60, 122, 123, 137, 179, 180

—R—

radio button, 5, 16, 163, 165
record, 3, 8, 27, 28, 29, 34, 37, 38, 39, 41, 43, 44, 46, 48, 60, 63, 73, 77, 79, 80, 81, 84, 86, 89, 90, 126, 127, 144, 146, 148, 191, 192, 206, 213, 214, 215, 217, 218, 219, 228, 232, 233
refreshing, 149, 153
region walking, 213, 216, 217, 218, 219, 225
region-walking, 213, 214, 218
relational model, 27, 57
Relational Operators, 20, 21, 22
Results pane, 33, 35, 68, 76, 97, 202, 204, 208
RETURN, 14, 15, 74, 81, 83, 85, 86, 88, 92, 93, 94, 100, 101, 104, 109, 115, 117, 118, 124, 126, 130, 144, 194, 195, 197, 222
Run SpeedButton, 145, 153, 158

—S—

scroll bar, 6, 7, 41, 55, 56, 102, 103, 149, 151, 152, 153, 154, 202, 235
SDF, 191, 192, 194, 195, 196, 197

secondary key, 51
server application, 11, 200, 202, 204, 211, 212, 213, 226, 228, 232
simple index, 13, 46, 50, 53, 68, 73, 168, 230
slider button, 6, 41, 42, 153
Snap To Grid, 160, 162, 163
spin box, 6, 7, 31, 149, 151, 152, 153, 154, 157, 158, 163
SpinBox, 151, 152
stock classes, 65, 96, 119
String Operators, 22
strings, 4, 5, 15, 22, 213, 216
structure, 27, 32, 34, 35, 38, 213, 214, 215
sub class, 99
superclass, 99

—T—

tabbing order, 154, 156, 157, 158

table, 3, 8, 13, 17, 26, 27, 28, 29, 32, 33, 34, 35, 36, 38, 43, 44, 45, 46, 47, 57, 58, 61, 62, 73, 90, 146, 155, 195, 197, 199, 213, 215, 217, 219, 225, 226, 230, 232
table design window, 28, 29, 30, 32, 33, 34, 38
Table Designer, 28, 29, 30, 34
Table Edit window, 36, 37
text box, 30, 31
Text Editor, 80, 100, 103, 105, 112, 113, 116, 123, 128, 147, 158, 168, 169, 175, 176, 179, 181, 182, 185, 186, 188, 190, 192, 200, 204, 205, 208, 211, 213, 217, 219
tool button, 53, 71, 72, 110, 113, 138

—V—

Variables, 15, 16
Vertical ScrollBar, 151
View table data icon, 62
Visual Properties, 72